THE SMITHS
The Singles Collection

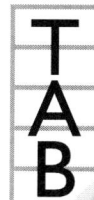

ISBN 978-1-84609-102-0

HAL•LEONARD®

For all works contained herein:
Unauthorized copying, arranging, adapting, recording, internet posting, public performance,
or other distribution of the music in this publication is an infringement of copyright.
Infringers are liable under the law.

Visit Hal Leonard Online at
www.halleonard.com

World headquarters, contact:
Hal Leonard
7777 West Bluemound Road
Milwaukee, WI 53213
Email: info@halleonard.com

In Europe, contact:
Hal Leonard Europe Limited
42 Wigmore Street
Marylebone, London, W1U 2RY
Email: info@halleonardeurope.com

In Australia, contact:
Hal Leonard Australia Pty. Ltd.
4 Lentara Court
Cheltenham, Victoria, 3192 Australia
Email: info@halleonard.com.au

Order No. AM983092

Unauthorised reproduction of any part of this publication by
any means including photocopying is an infringement of copyright.
Singles Collection logo designed by Michael Bell Design.

Cover photograph courtesy of LFI.
Music arrangements by Arthur Dick, Matt Cowe & Martin Shellard.
Music processed by Paul Ewers Music Design.

Printed in EU.

Ask · 4
Bigmouth Strikes Again · 14
The Boy With The Thorn In His Side · 20
Girlfriend In A Coma · 24
Hand In Glove · 32
Heaven Knows I'm Miserable Now · 28
How Soon Is Now? · 39
I Started Something I Couldn't Finish · 56
Last Night I Dreamt That Somebody Loved Me · 64
Panic · 70
Shakespeare's Sister · 74
Sheila Take A Bow · 92
Shoplifters Of The World Unite · 100
Stop Me If You Think You've Heard This One Before · 83
That Joke Isn't Funny Anymore · 106
There Is A Light That Never Goes Out · 115
This Charming Man · 122
What Difference Does It Make? · 127
William, It Was Really Nothing · 132

Guitar Tablature Explained · 142

Ask

Words & Music by
Morrissey & Johnny Marr

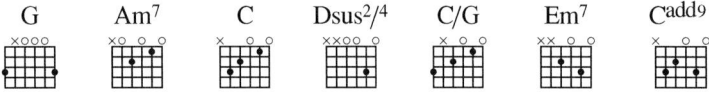

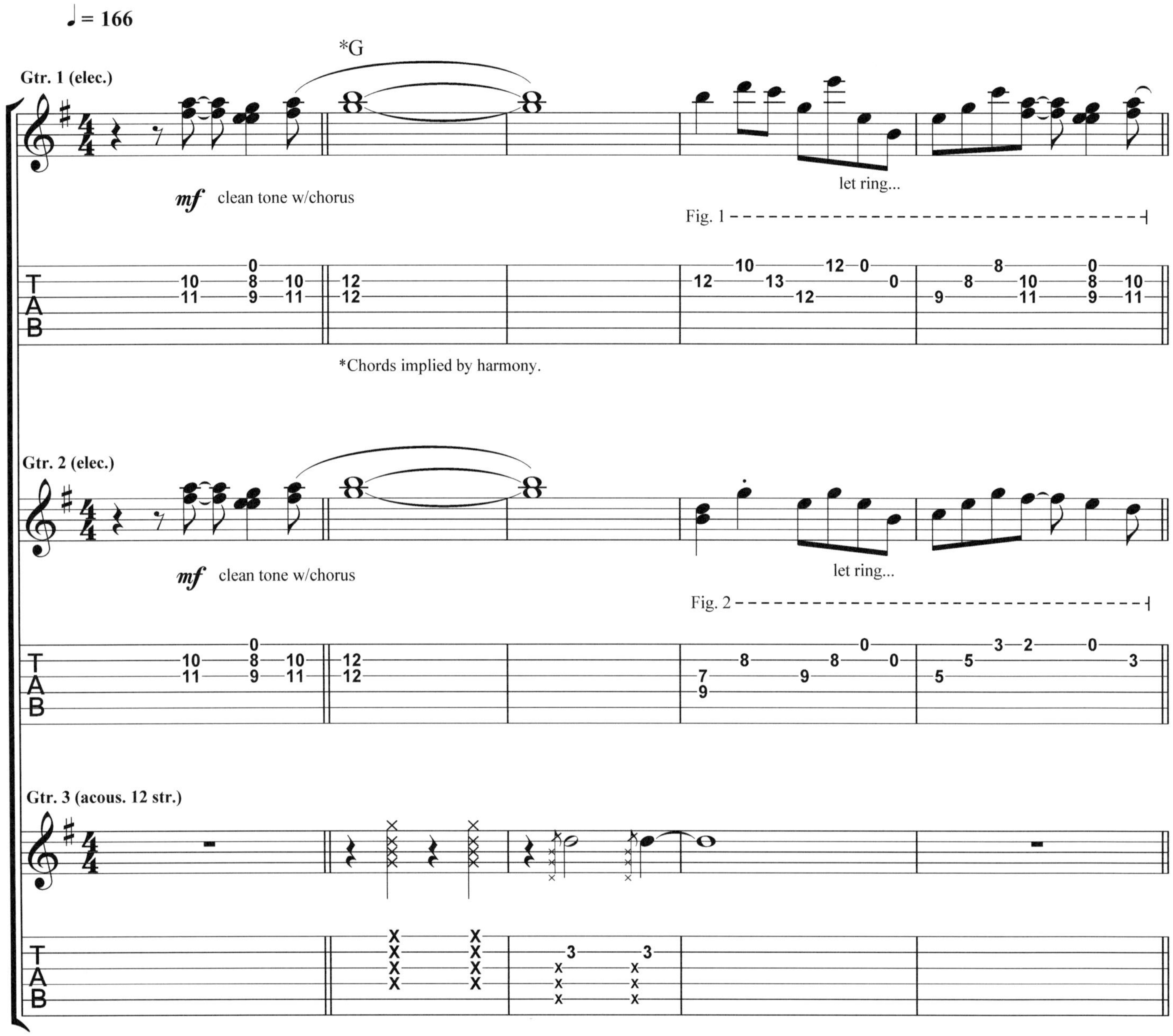

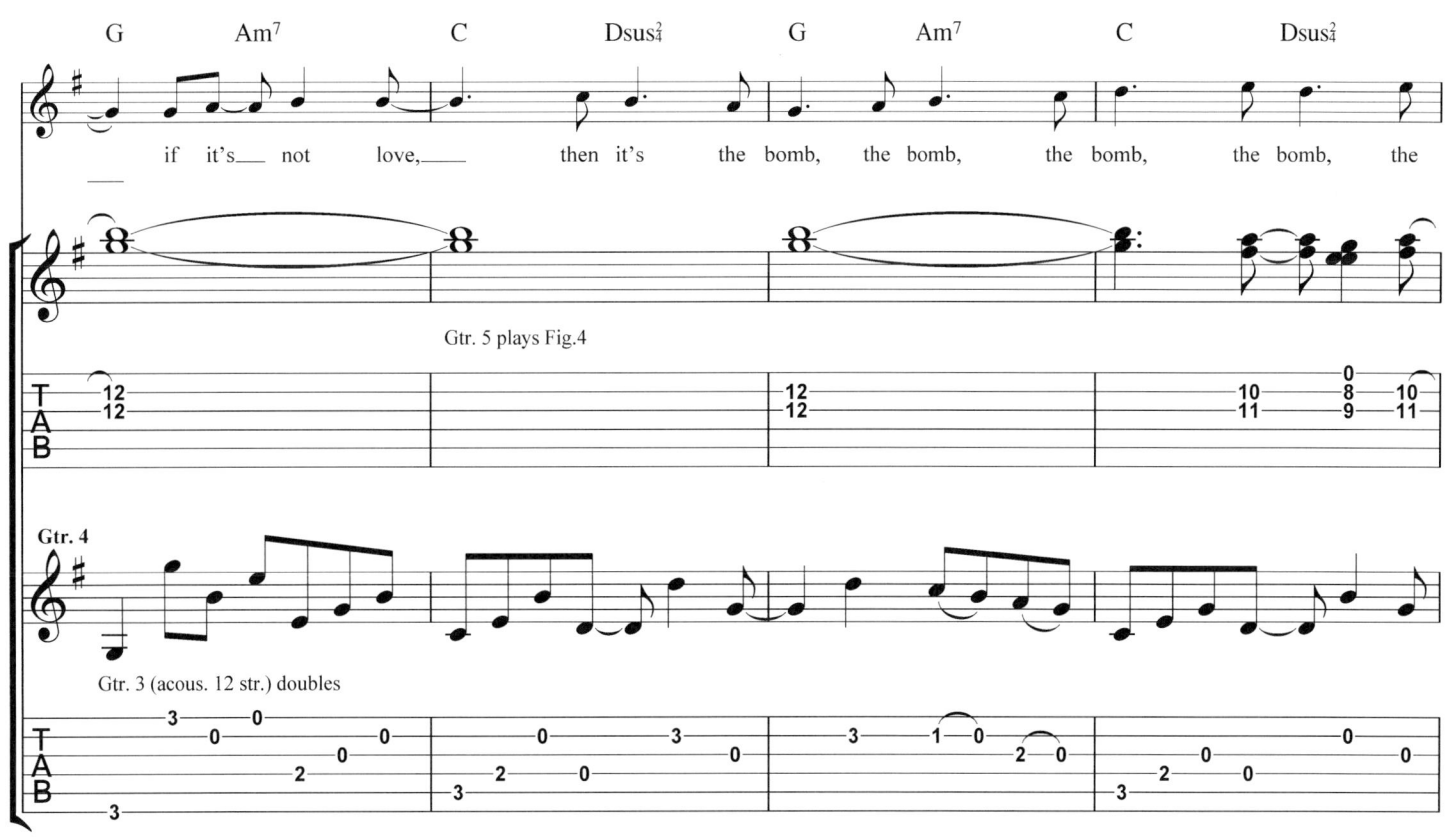

1.
Interlude
G
Am7
C
Dsus2/4
Em7
Dsus2/4
bomb, the bomb, the bomb that will bring us to - geth - er.
8va
Gtr. 6
Gtr. 7
Gtrs. 1+2 tacet
mp w/slide + clean tone
Cadd9
Em7
Dsus2/4
Gtr. 6
Gtr. 7
8va
mp w/slide + clean tone

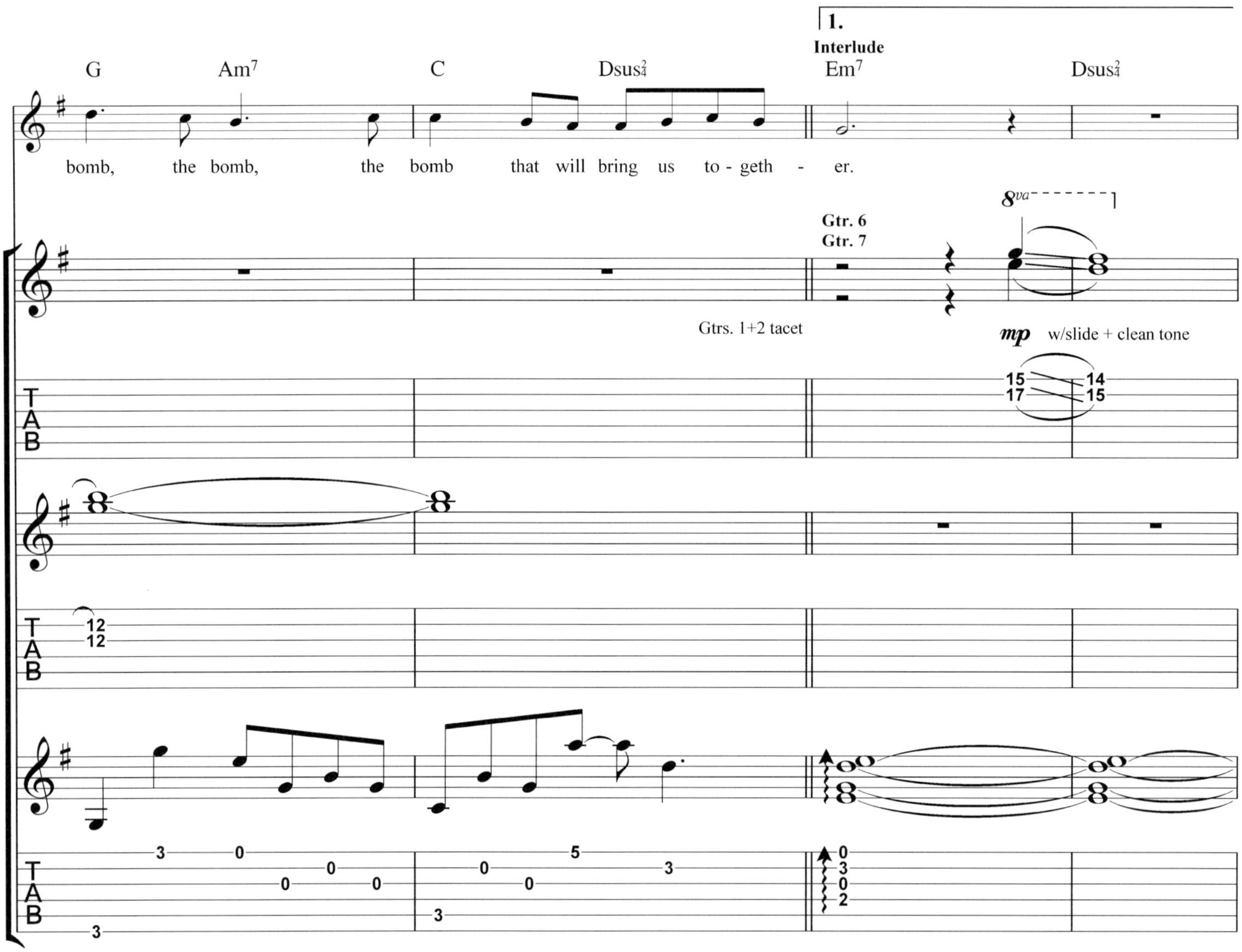

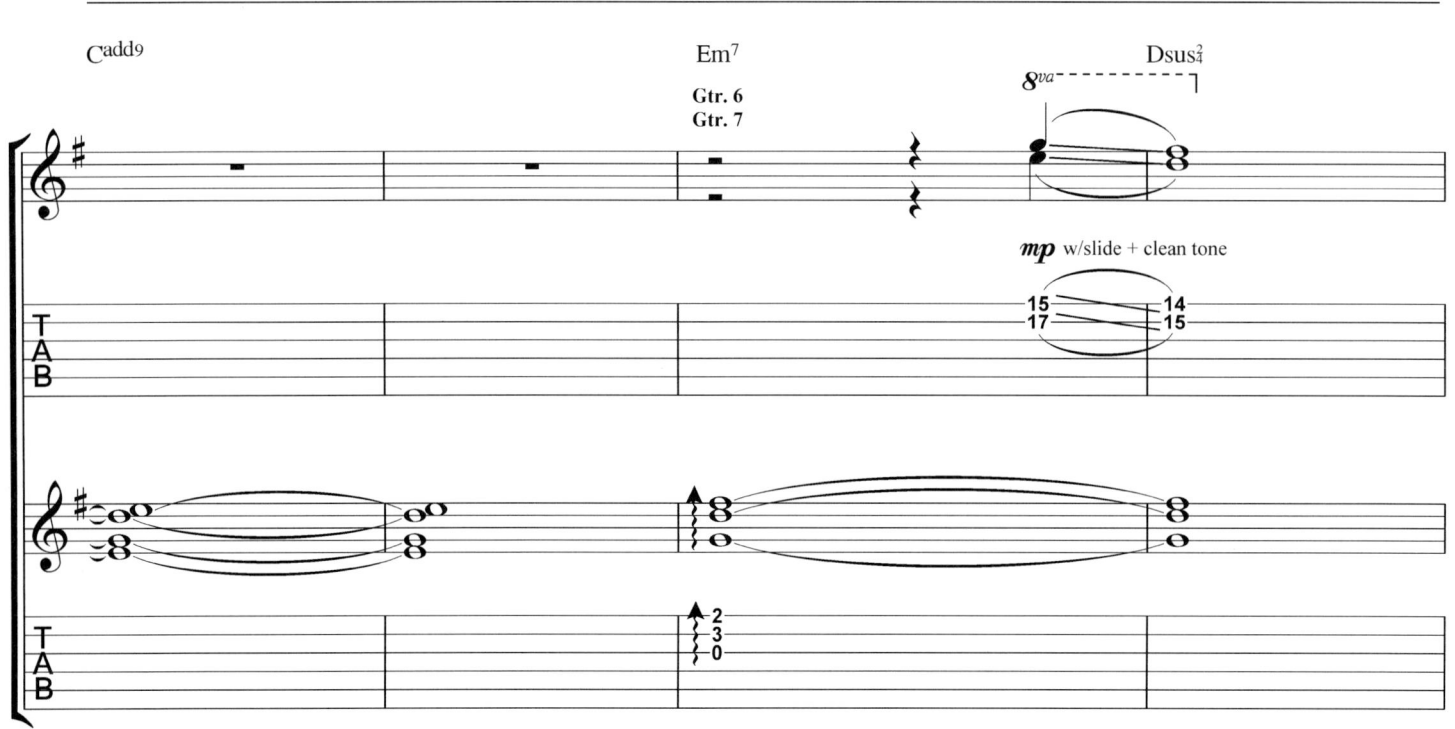

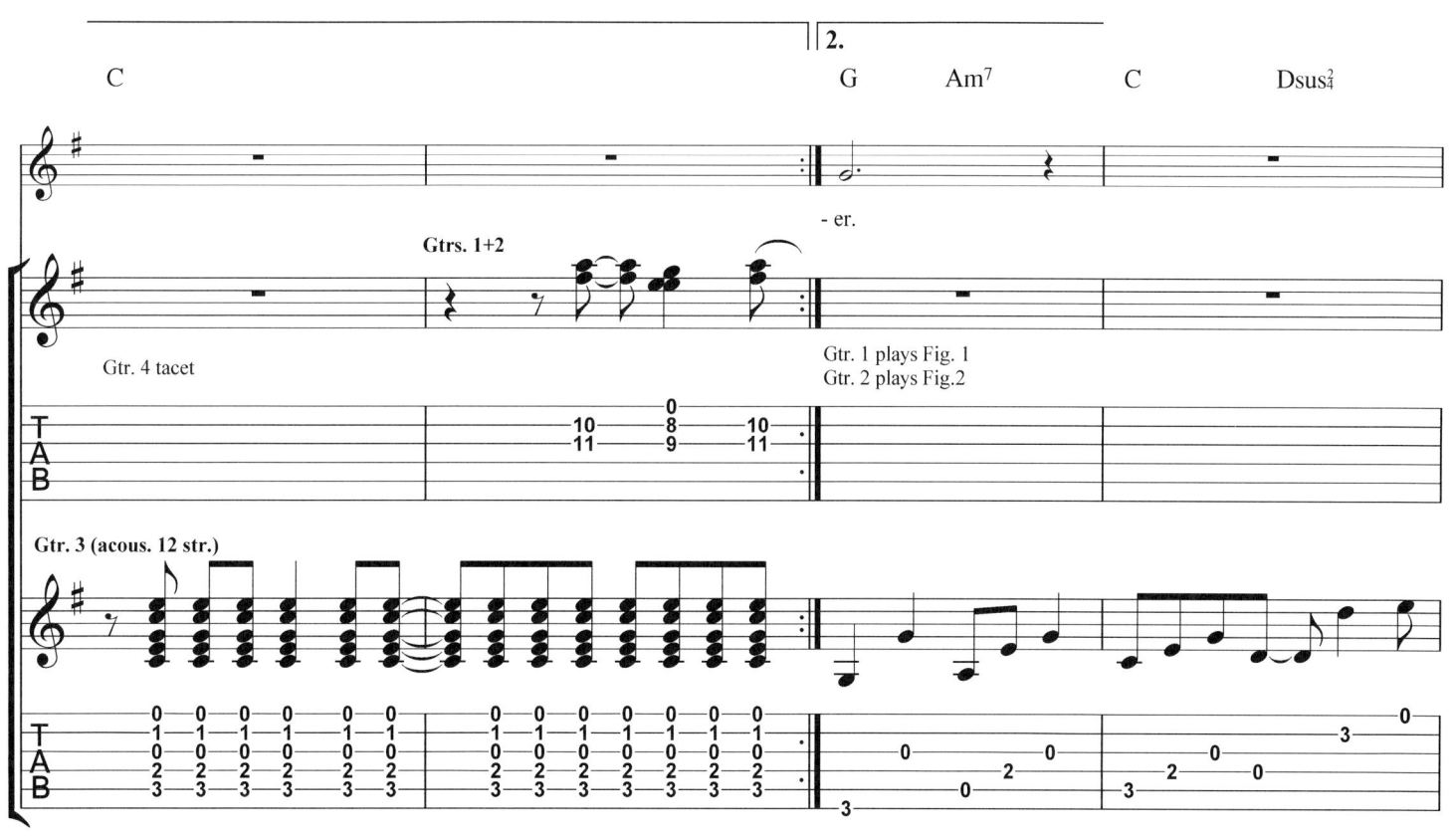

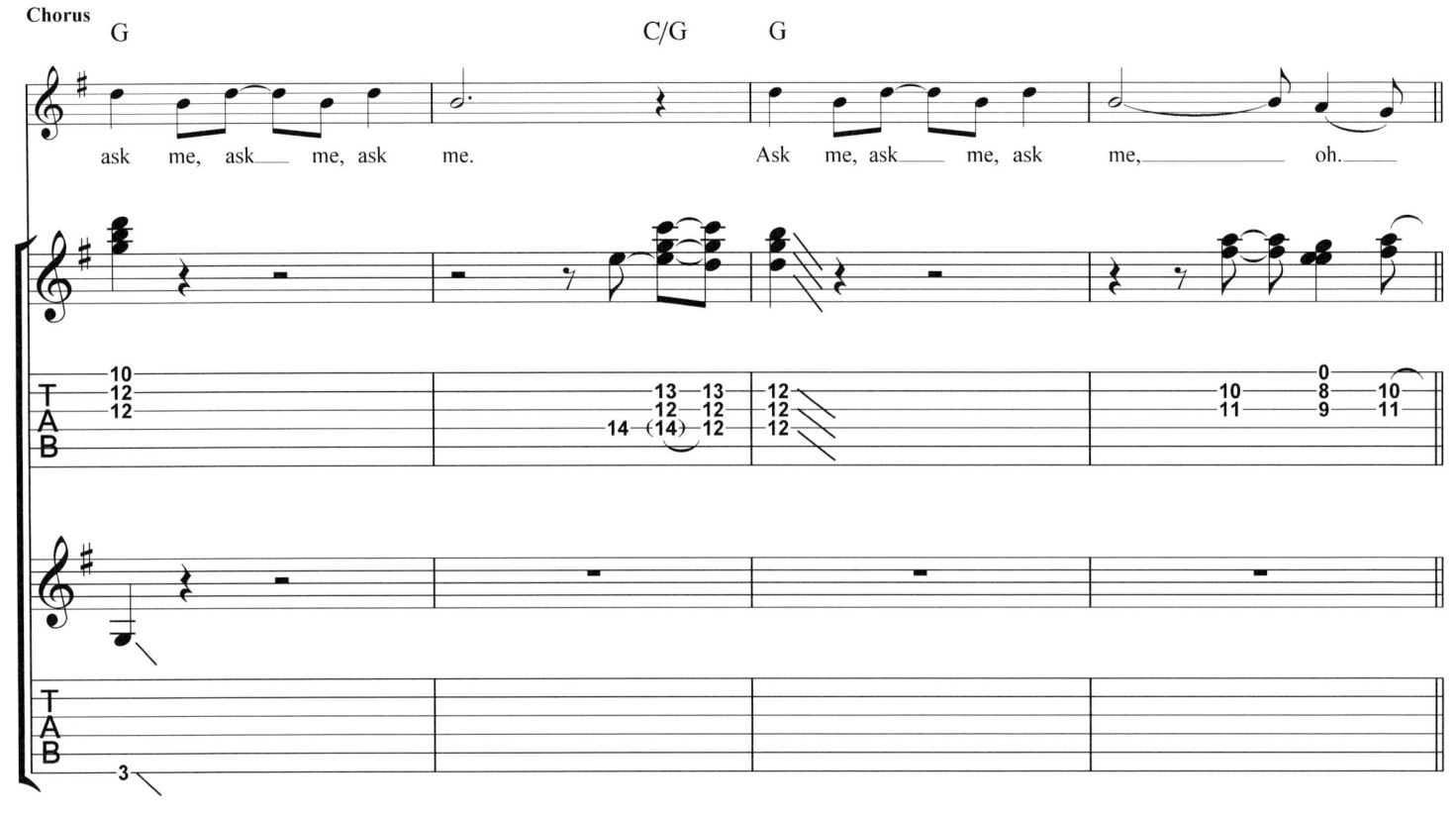
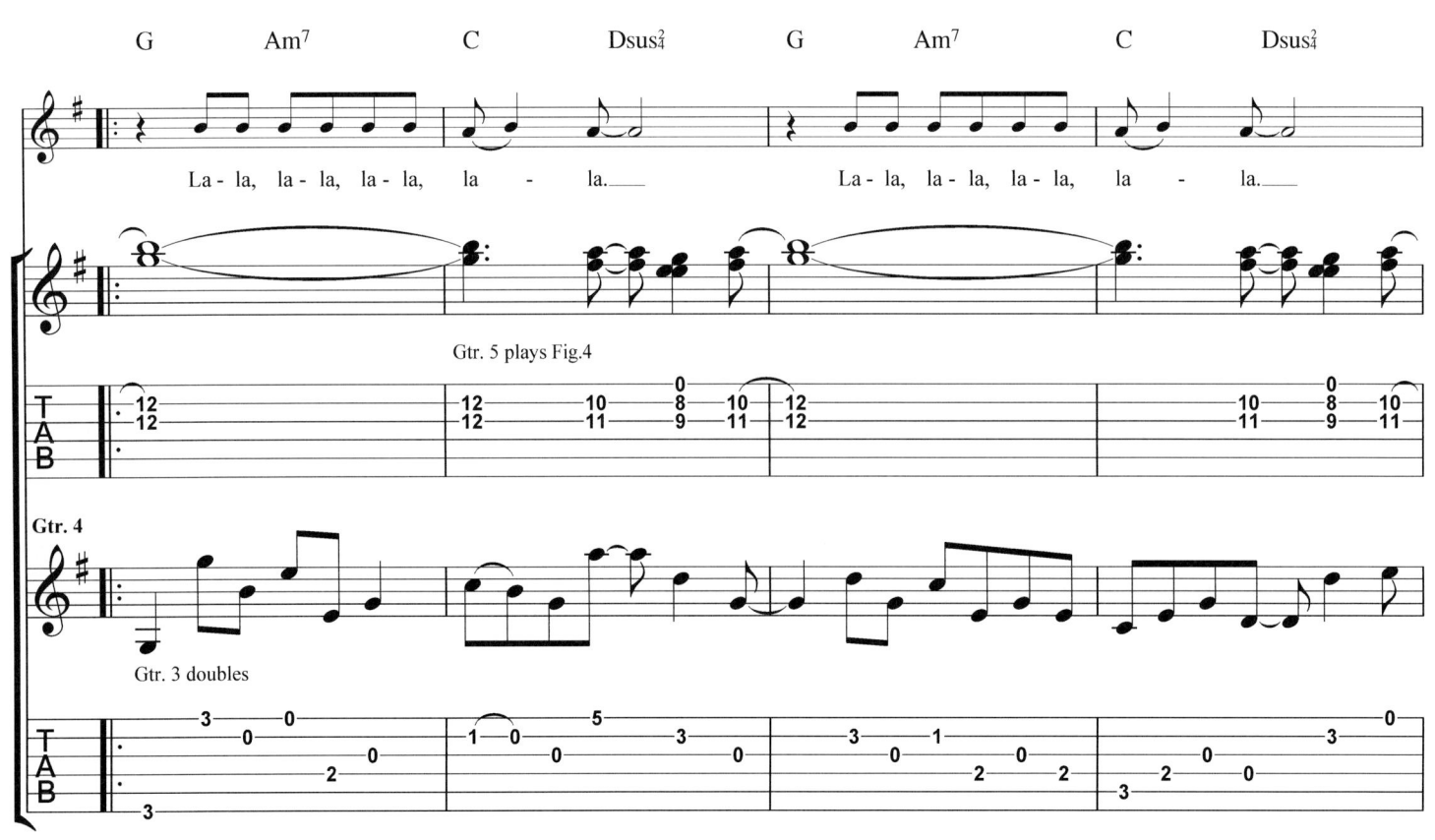

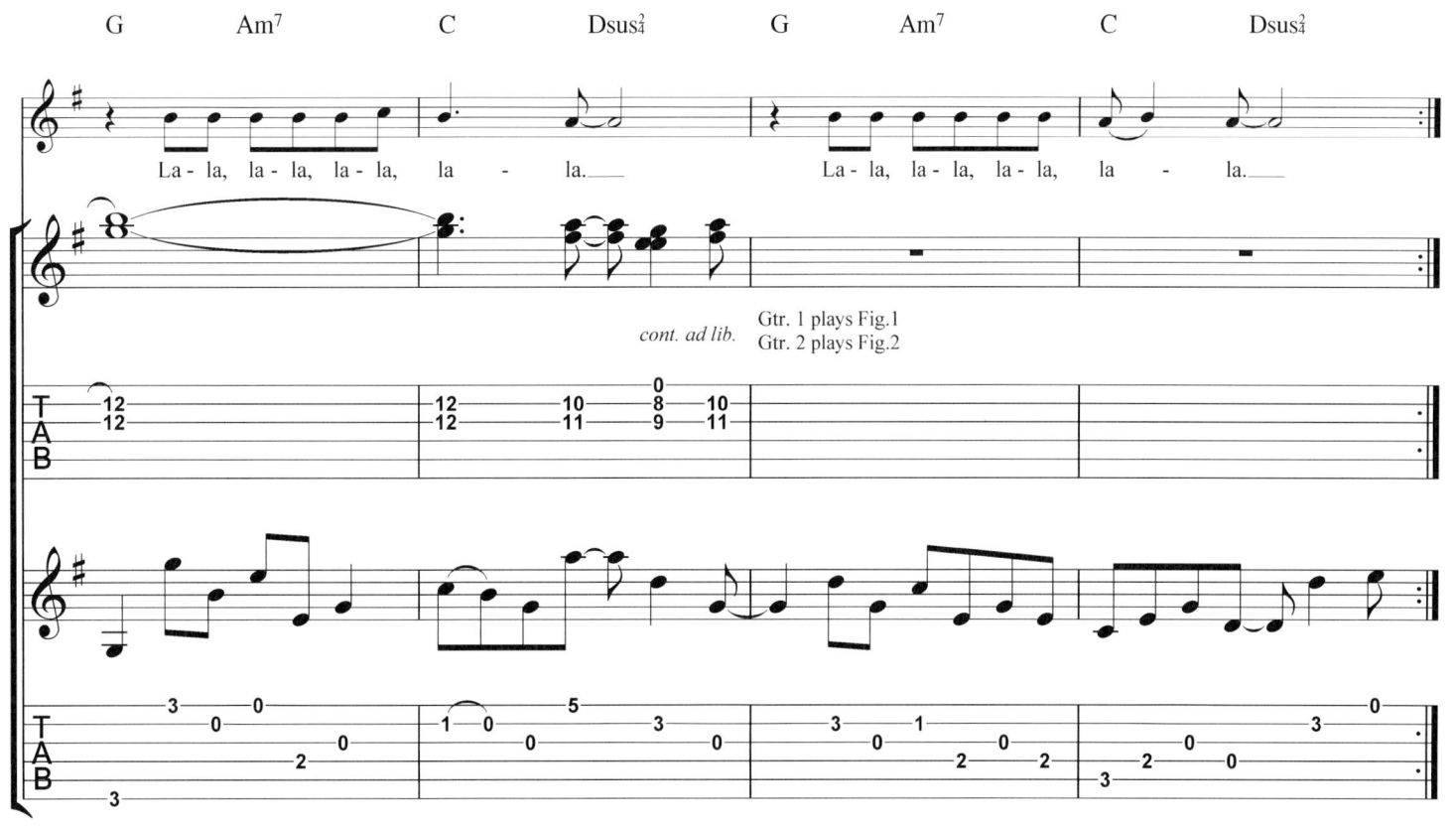

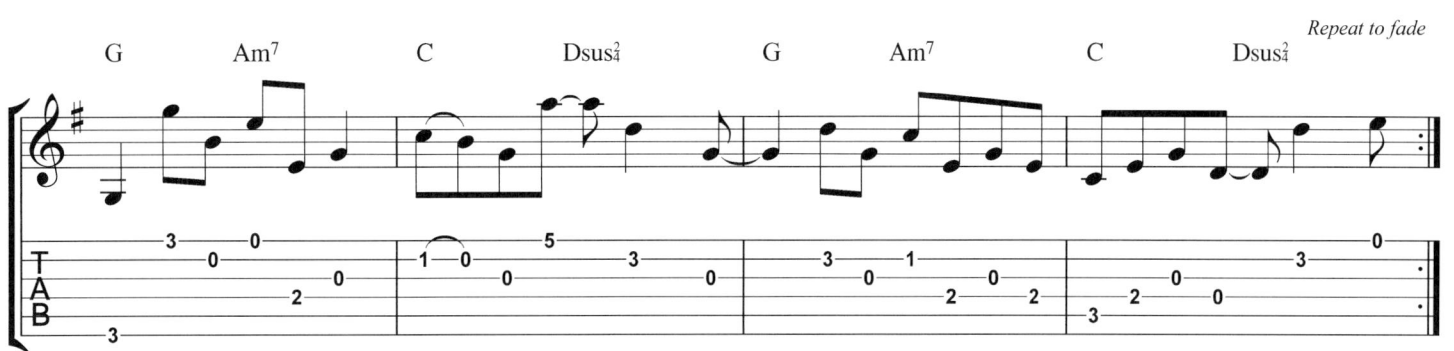

Bigmouth Strikes Again

Words & Music by
Morrissey & Johnny Marr

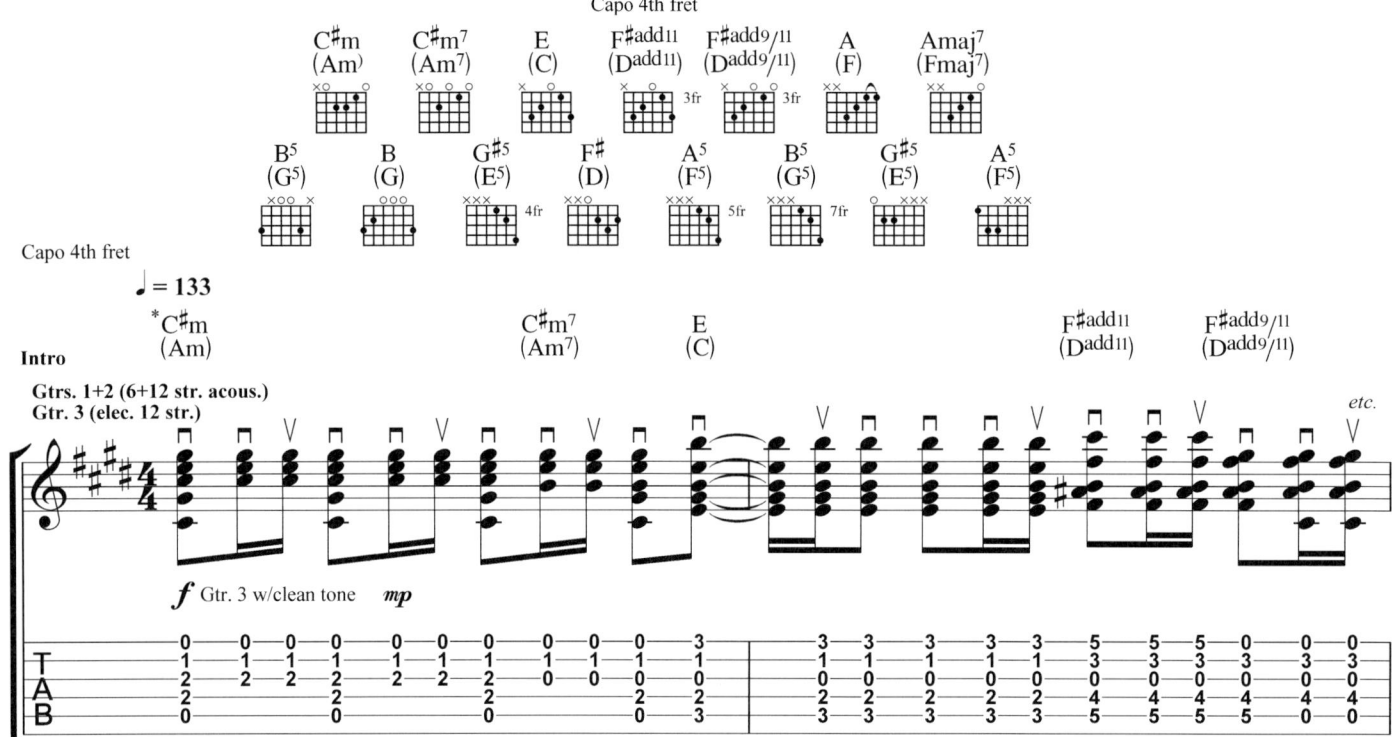

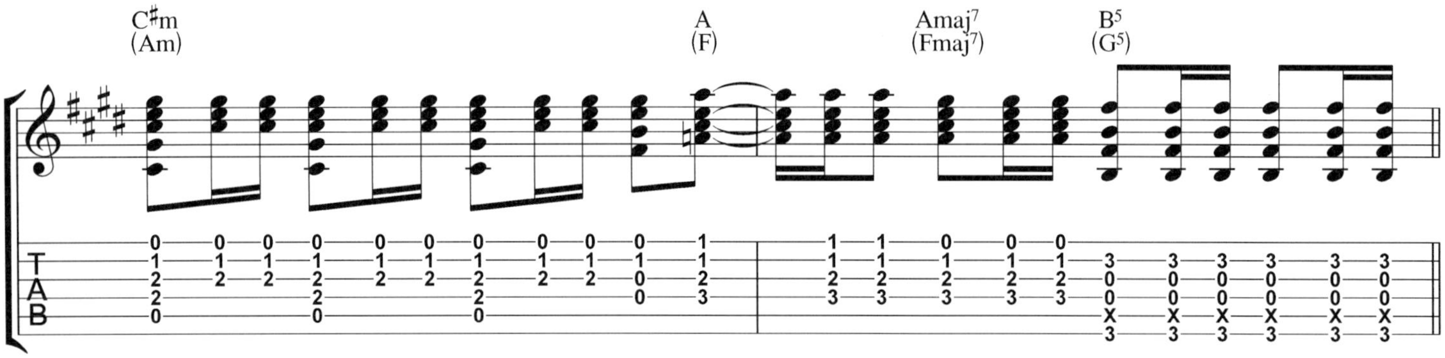

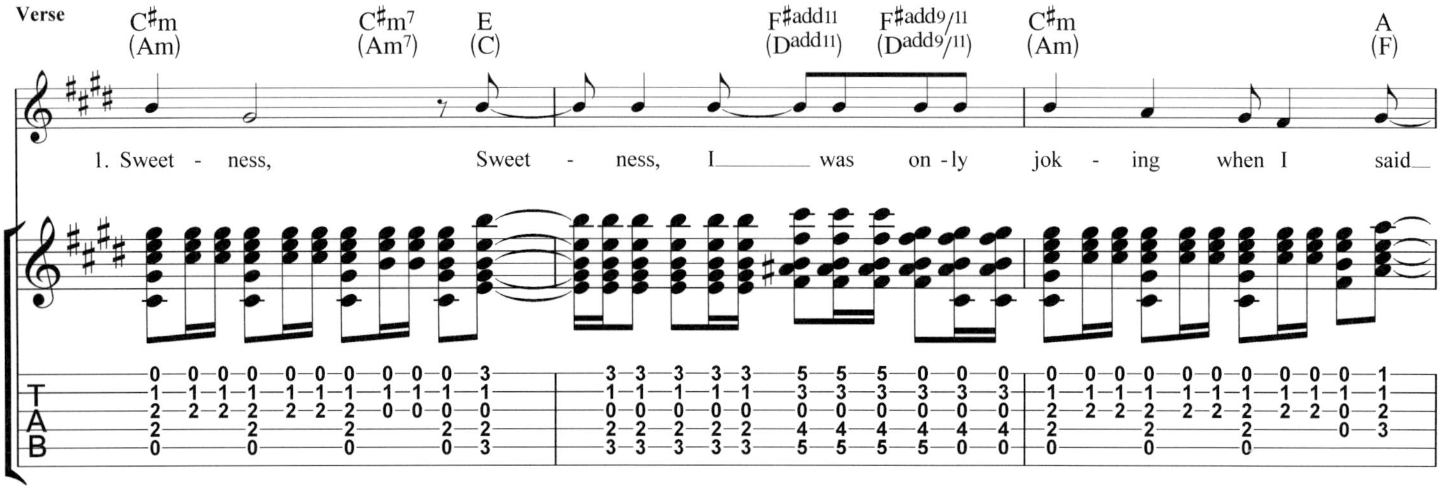

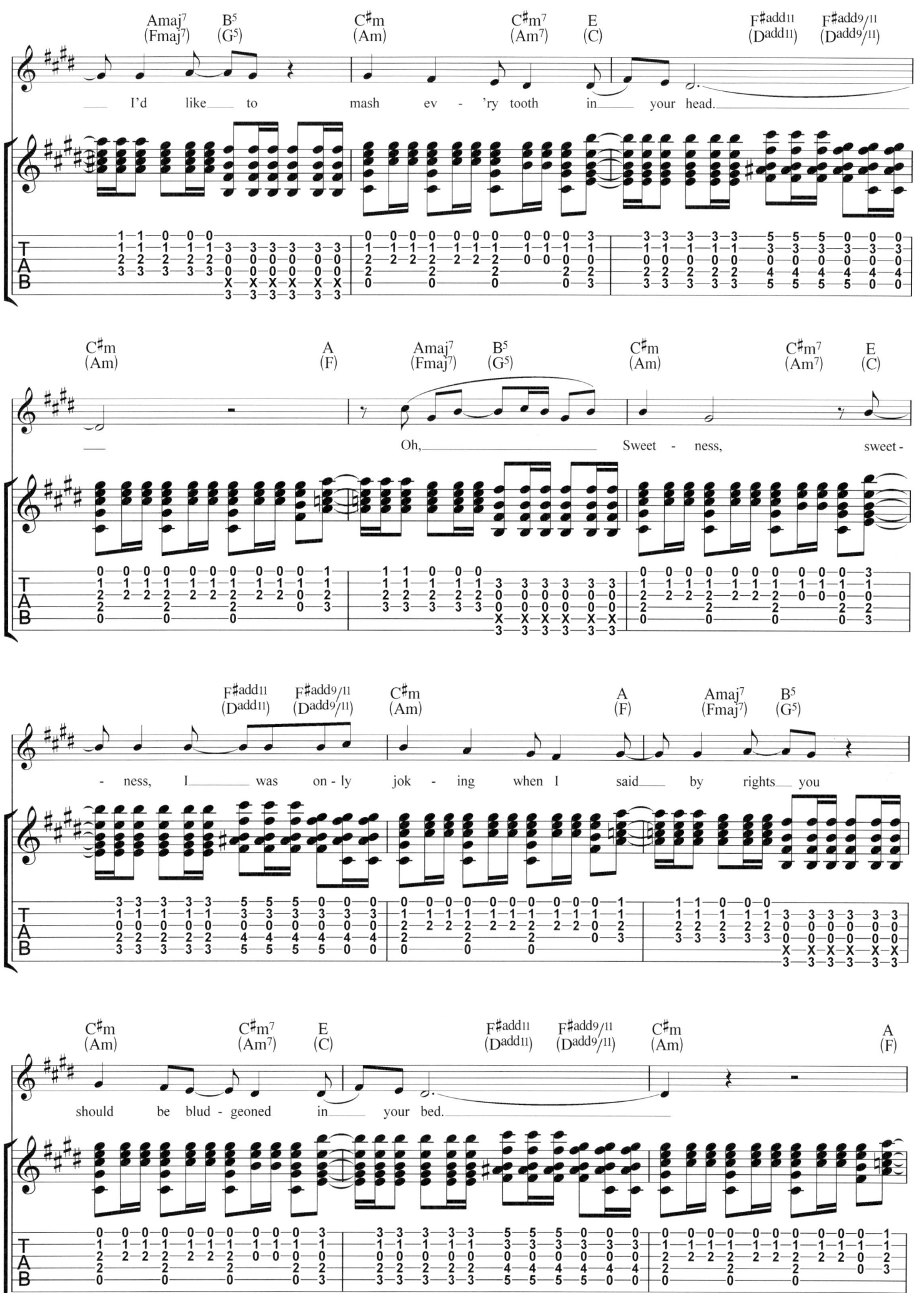

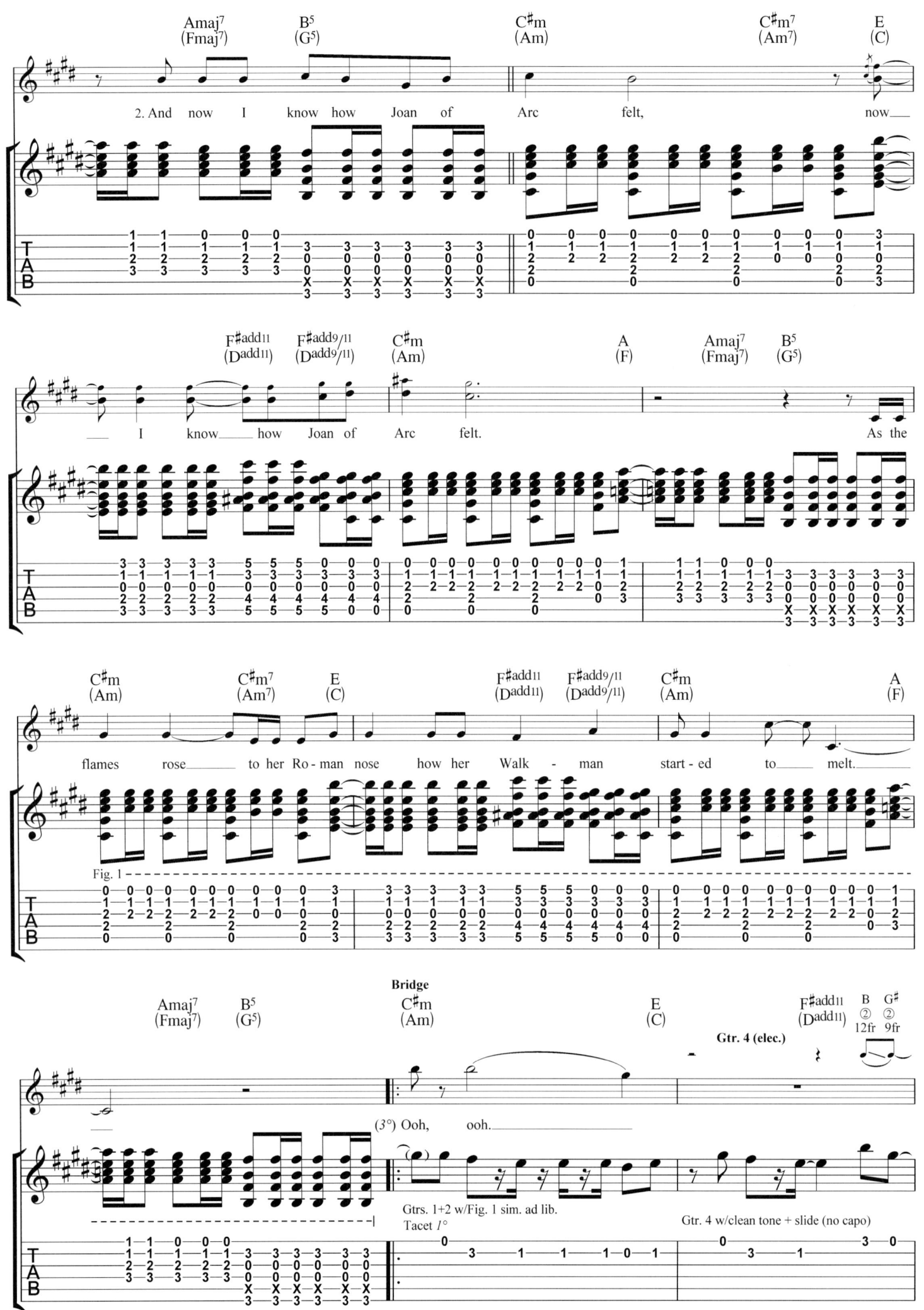

The Boy With The Thorn In His Side

Words & Music by
Morrissey & Johnny Marr

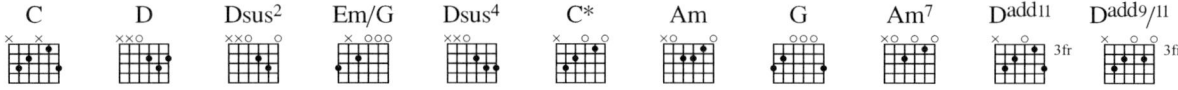

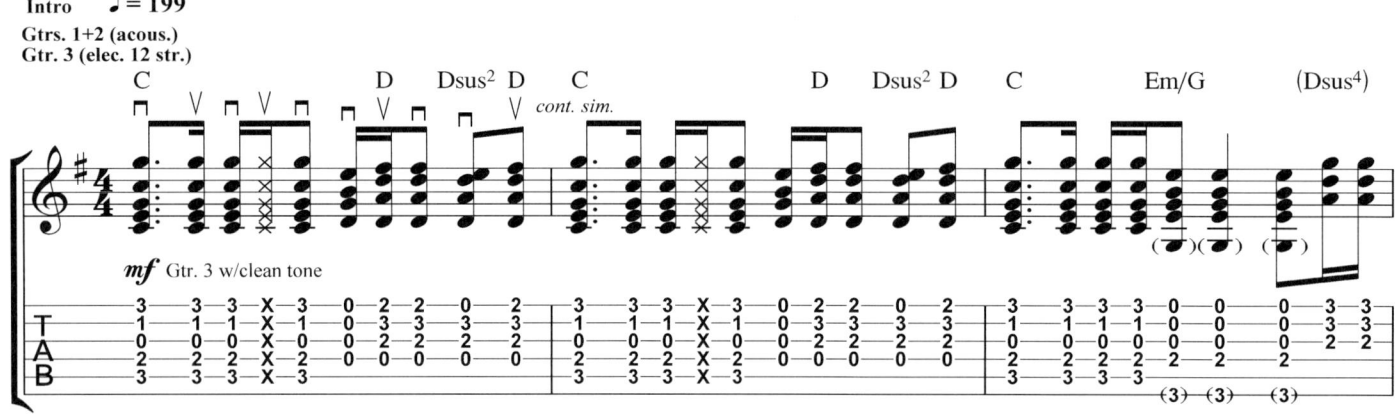

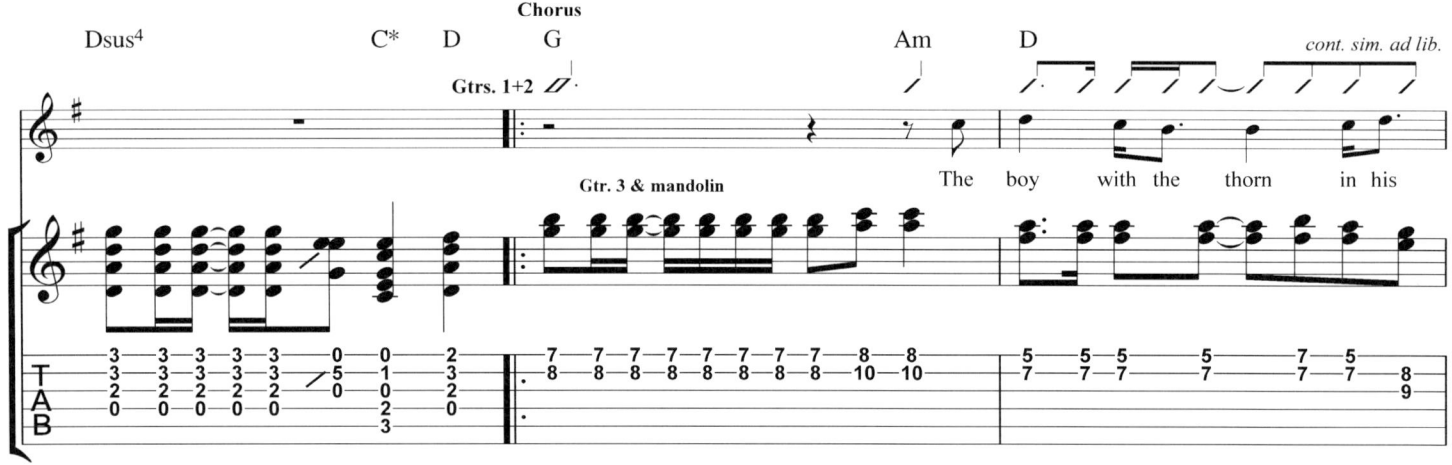

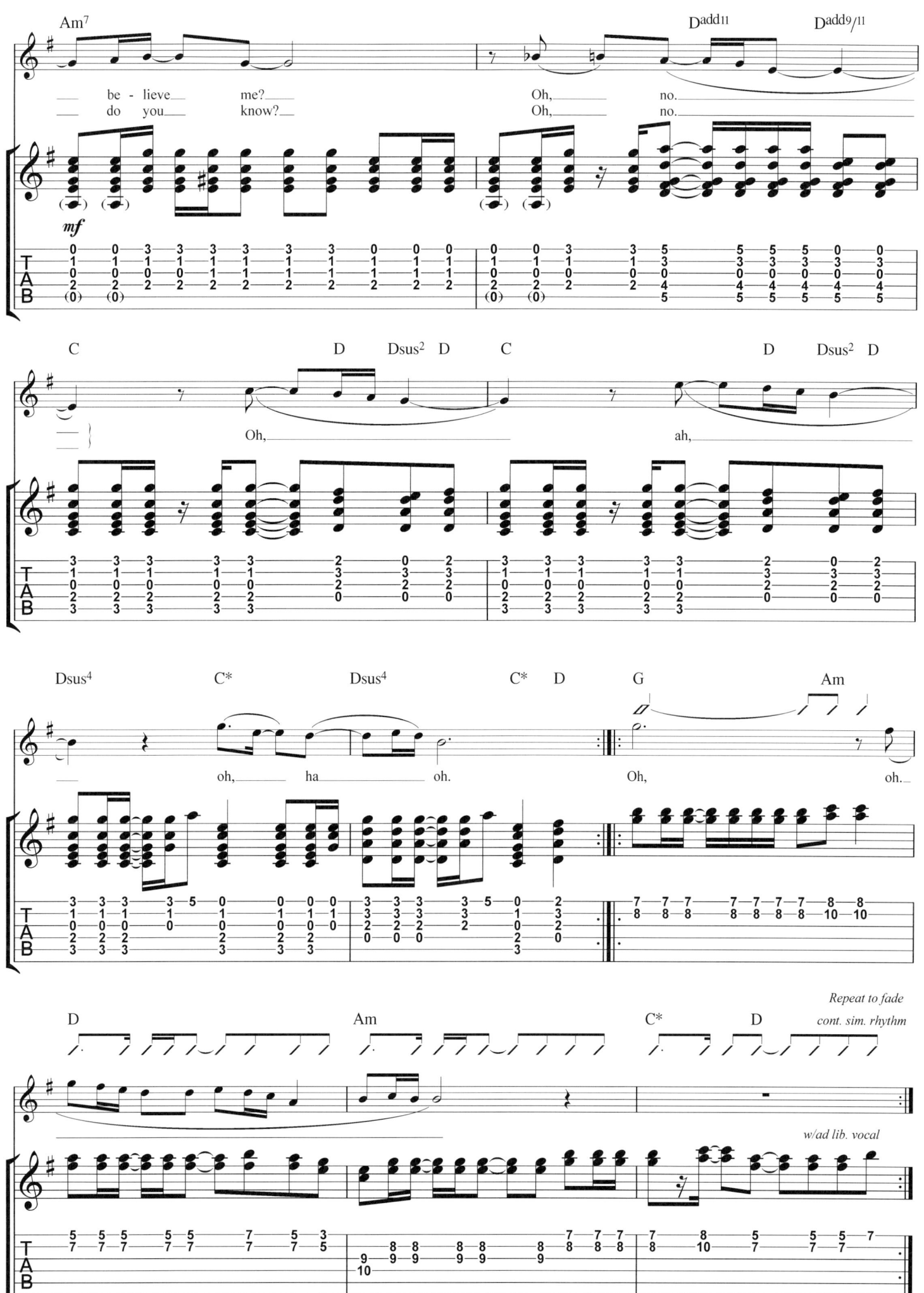

Girlfriend In A Coma

Words & Music by
Morrissey & Johnny Marr

Heaven Knows I'm Miserable Now

Words & Music by
Morrissey & Johnny Marr

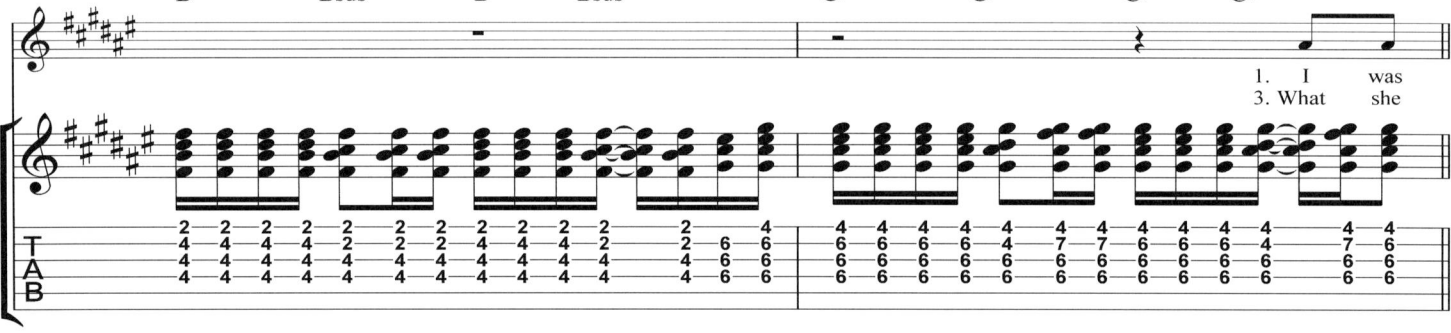

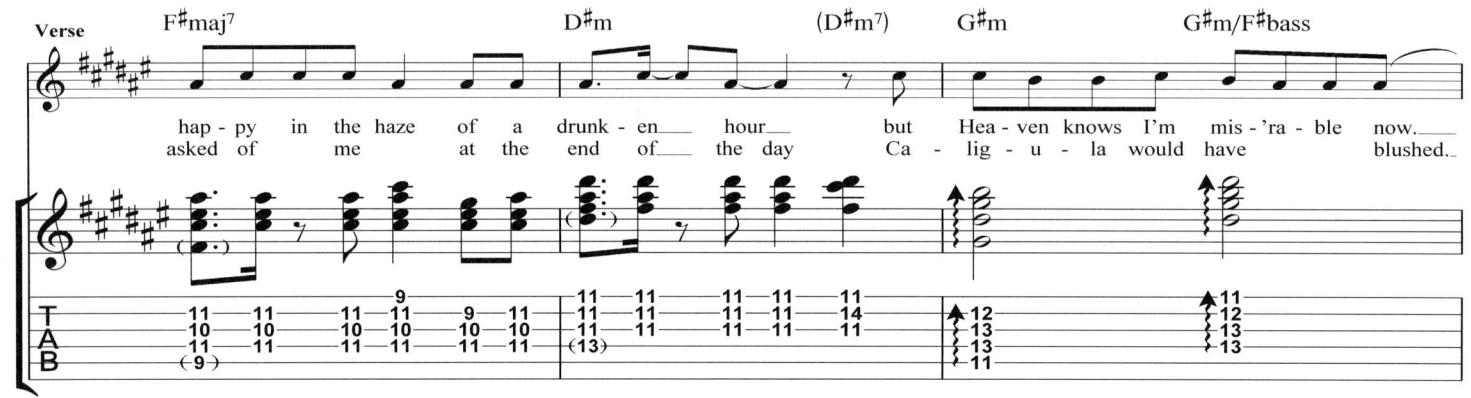

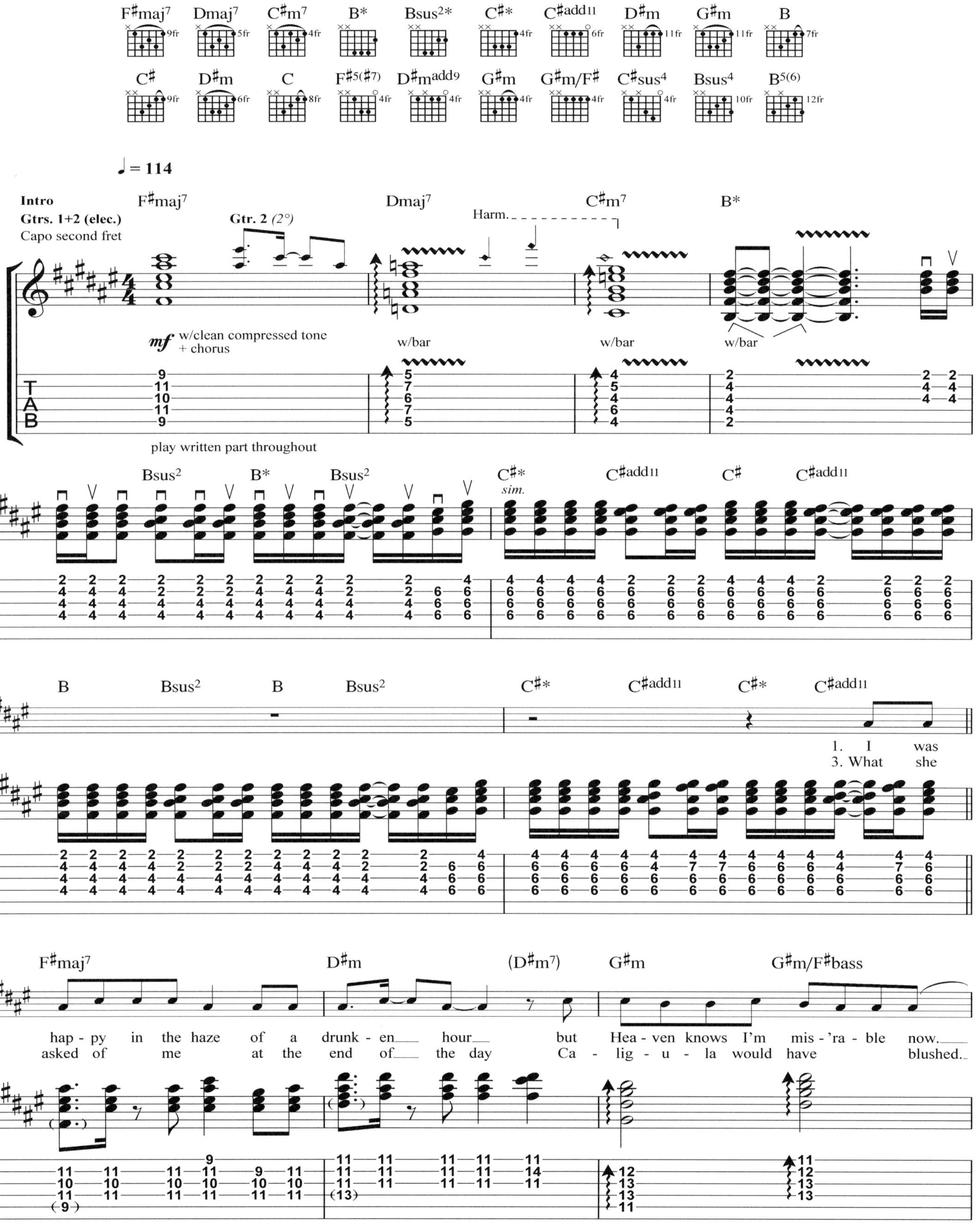

© Copyright 1984 Marr Songs Limited/Artane Music Incorporated.
Chrysalis Music Limited (50%)/Universal Music Publishing Limited (50%).
All Rights Reserved. International Copyright Secured.

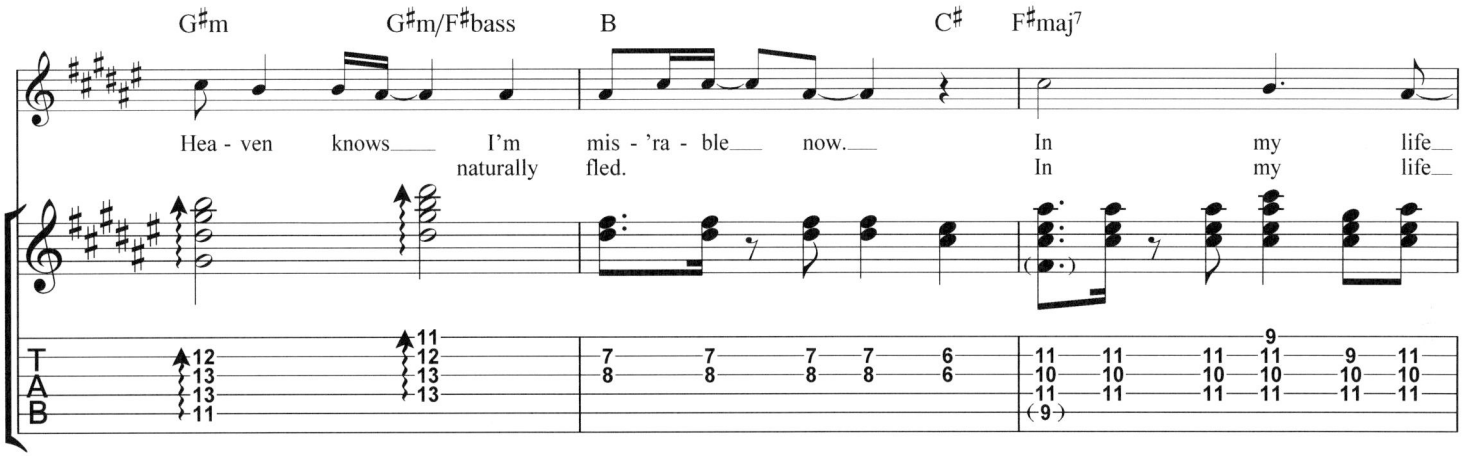
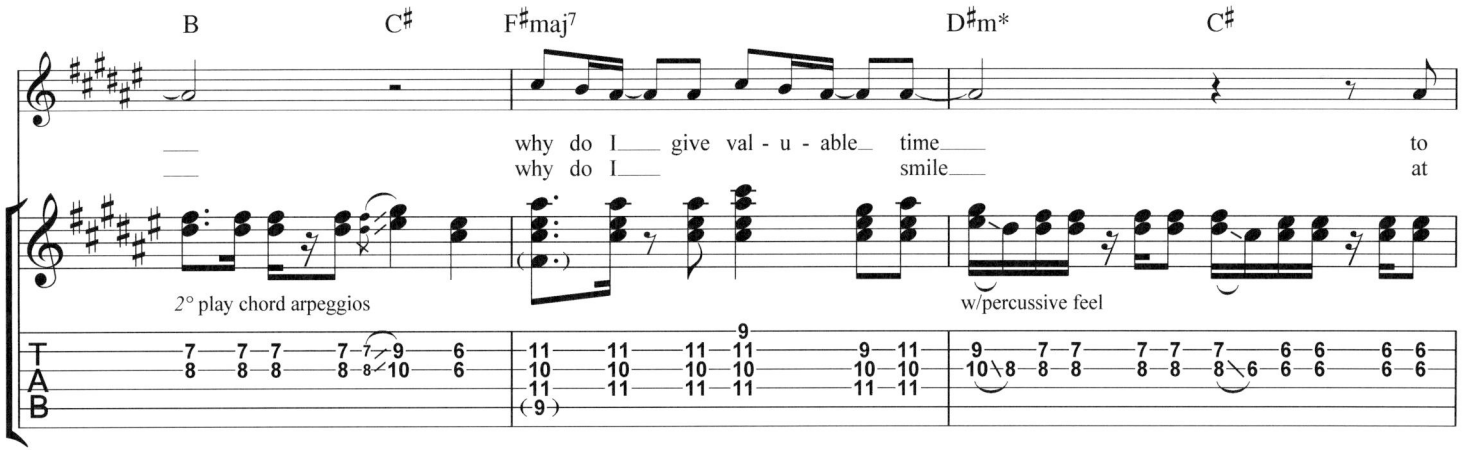
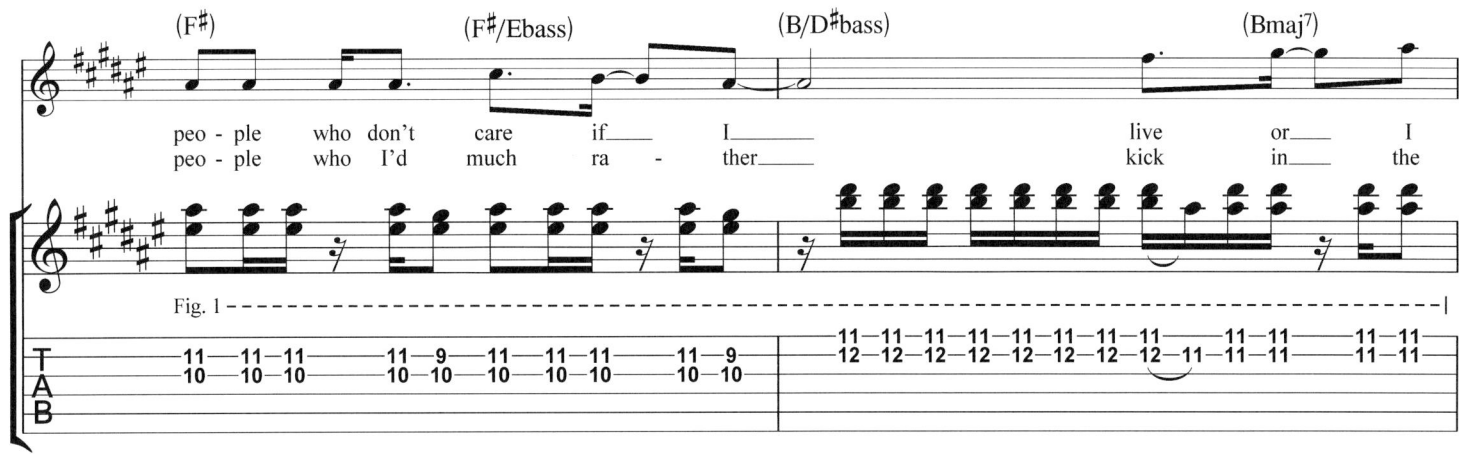

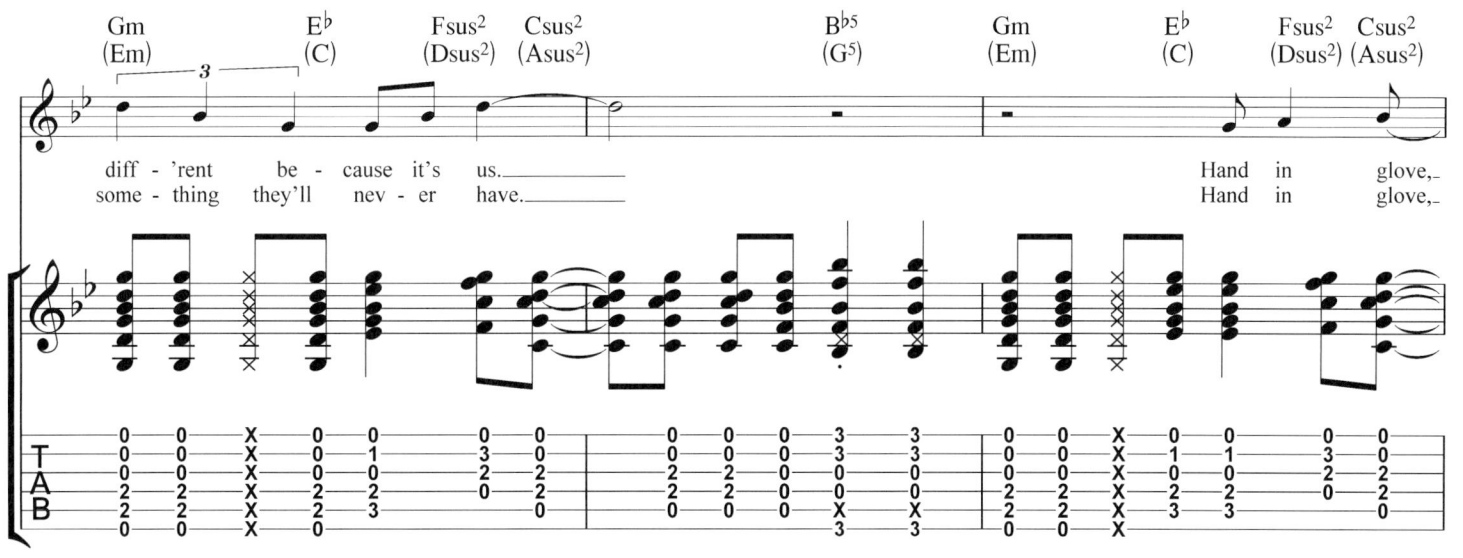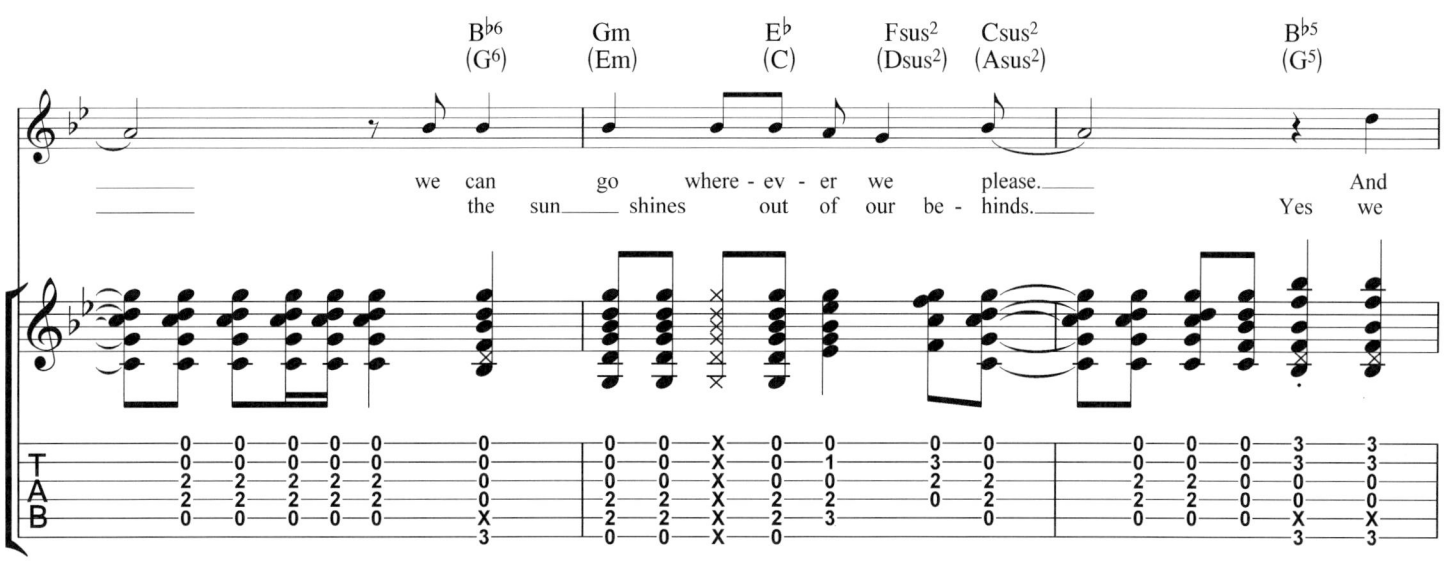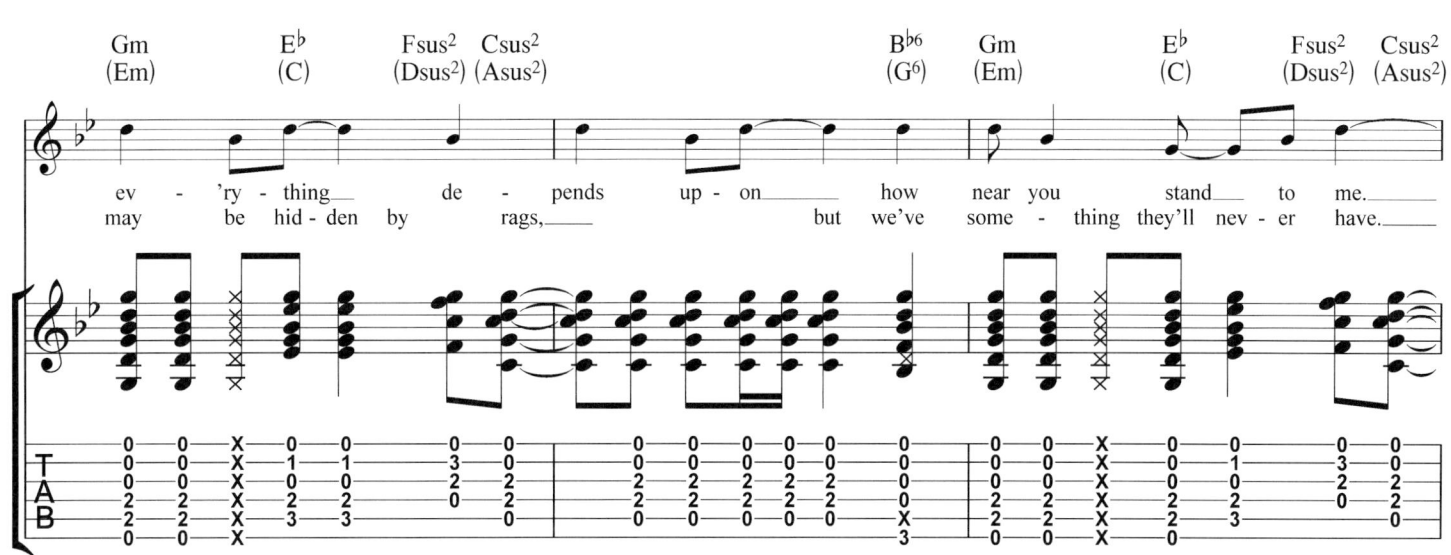

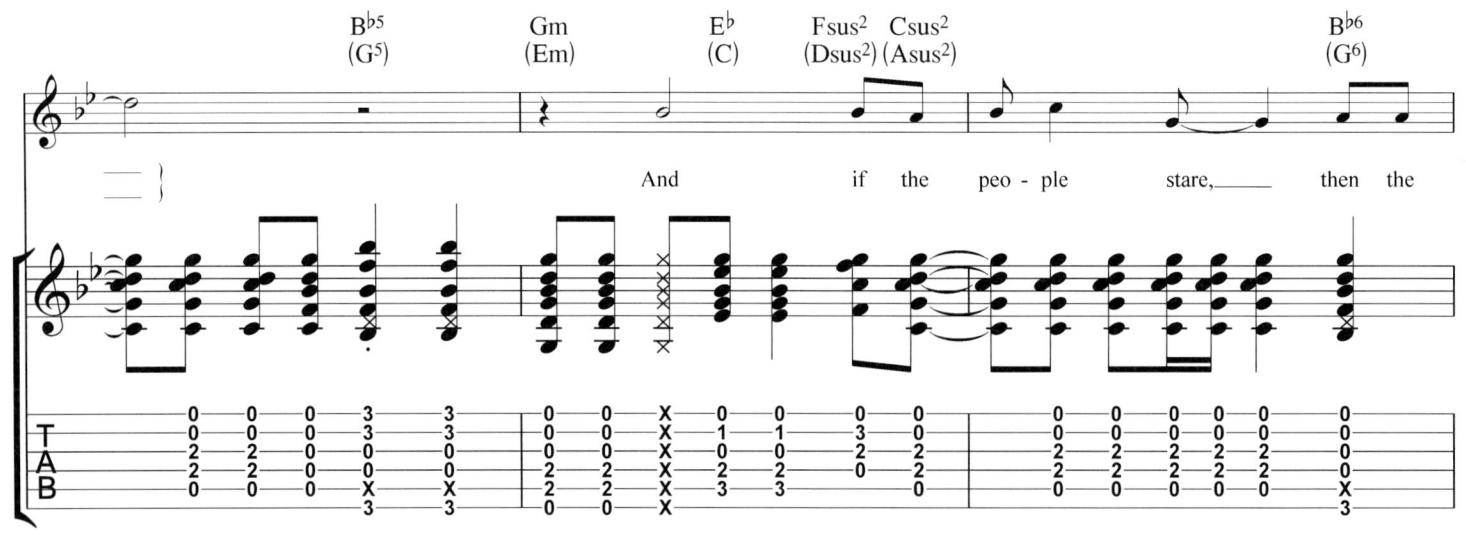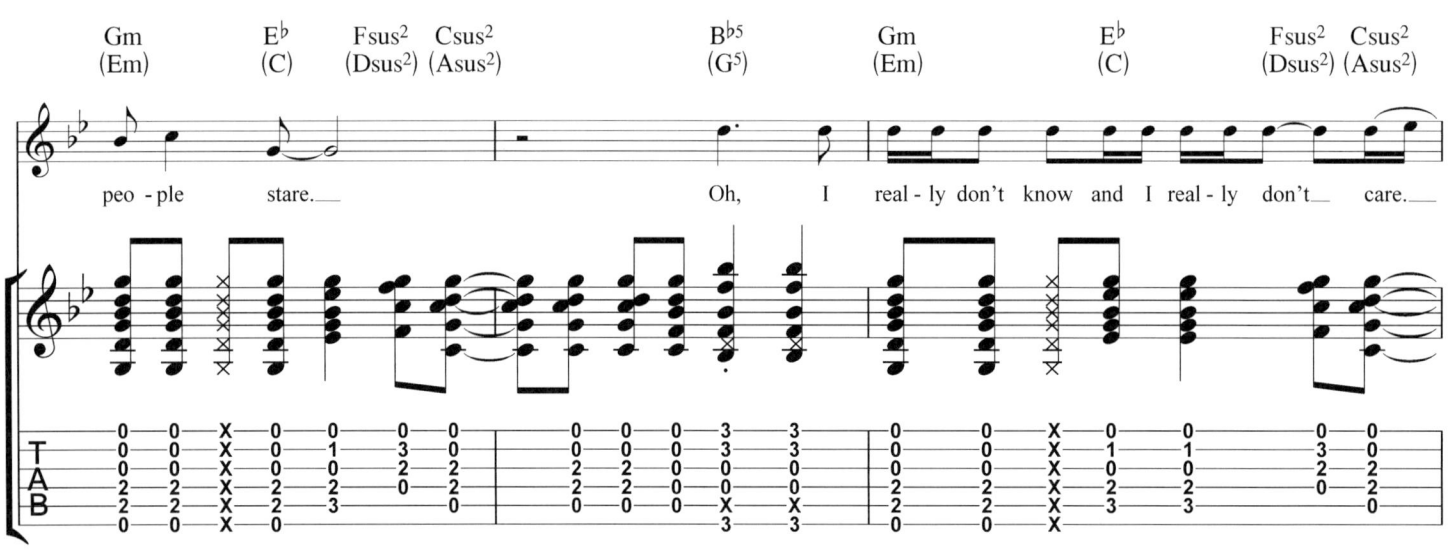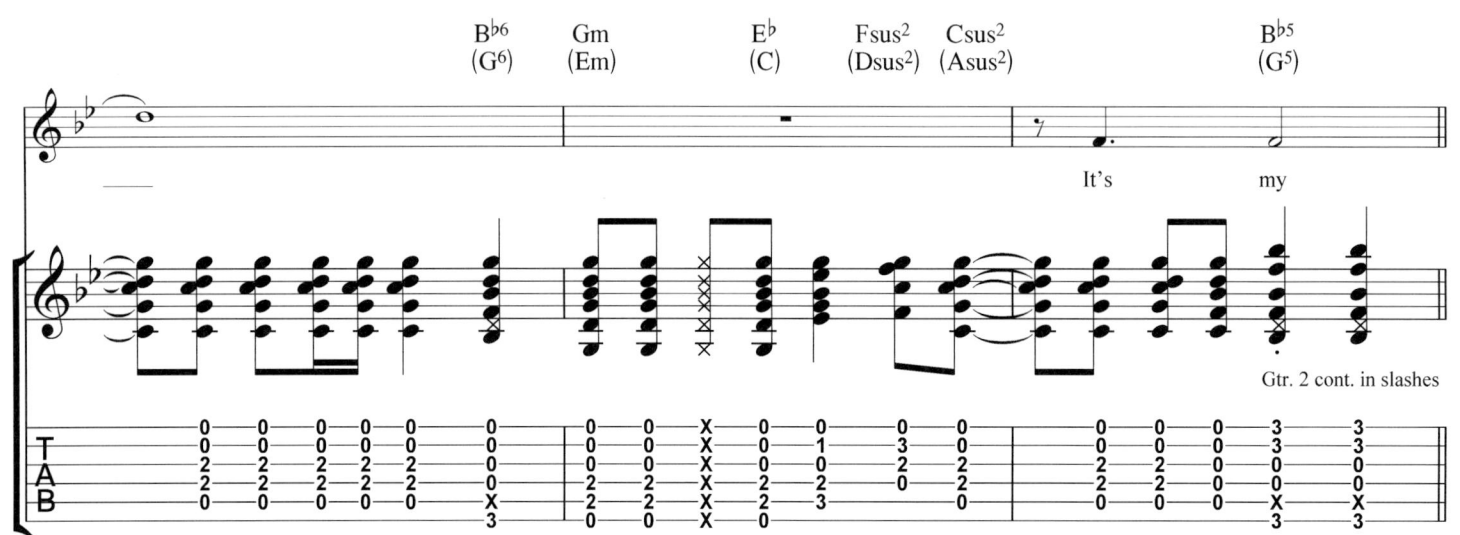

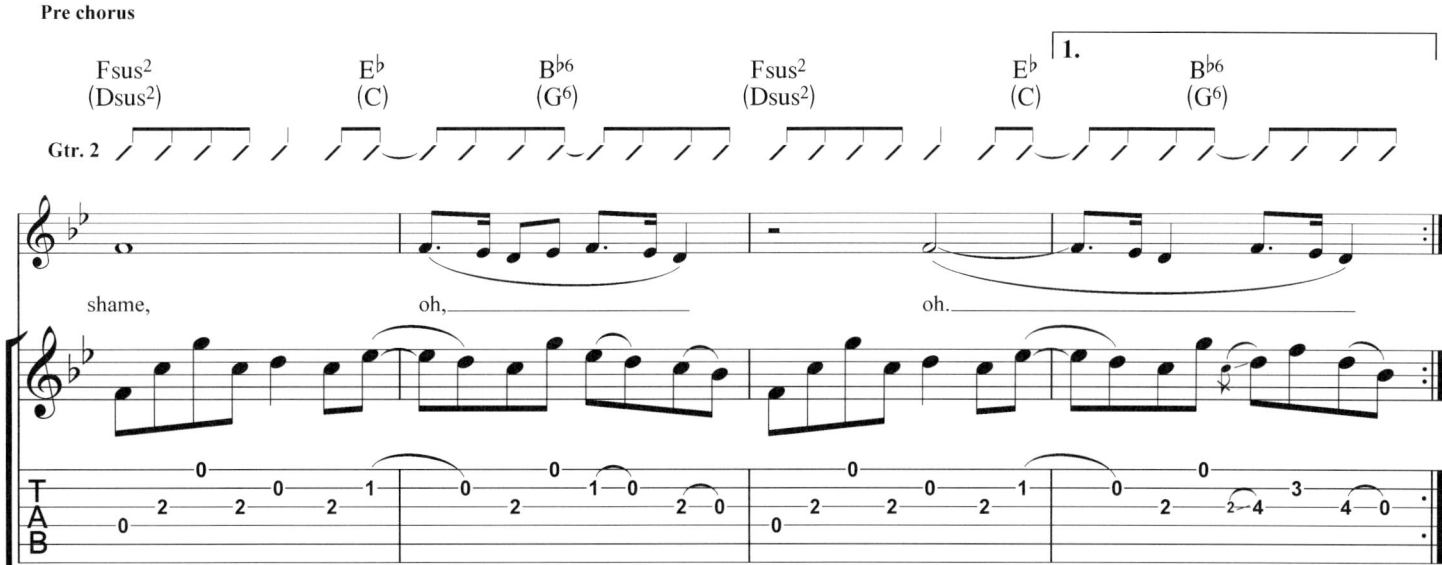
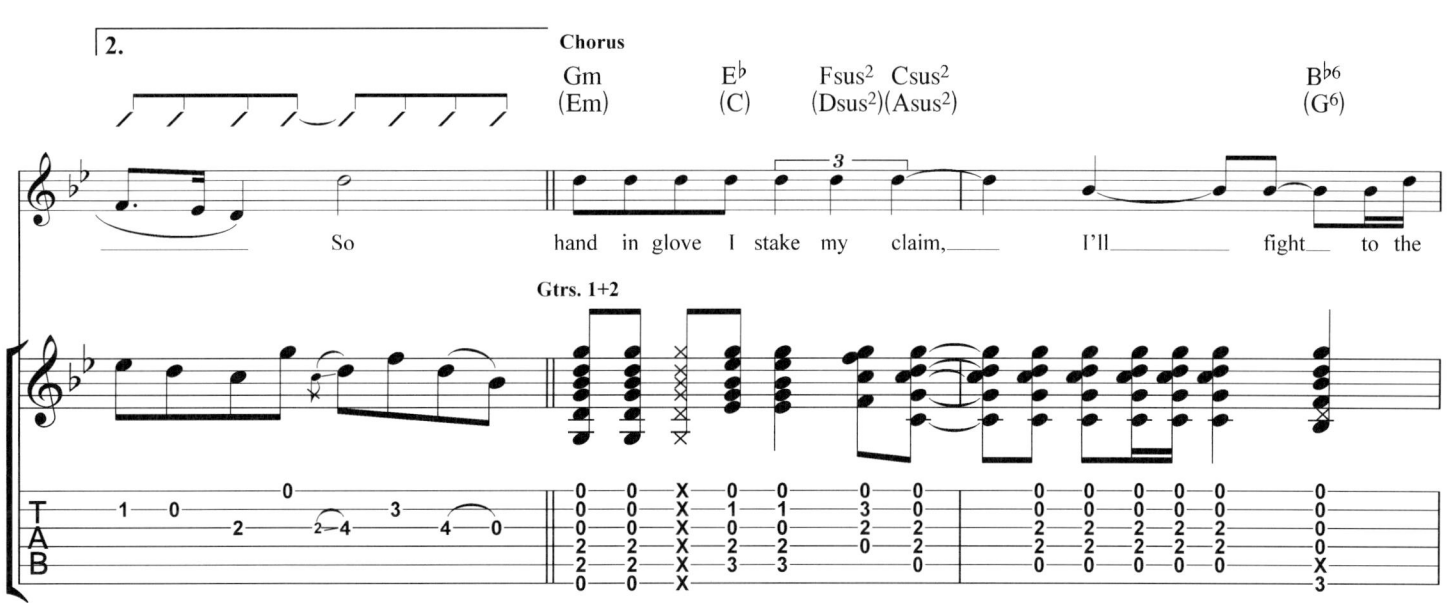
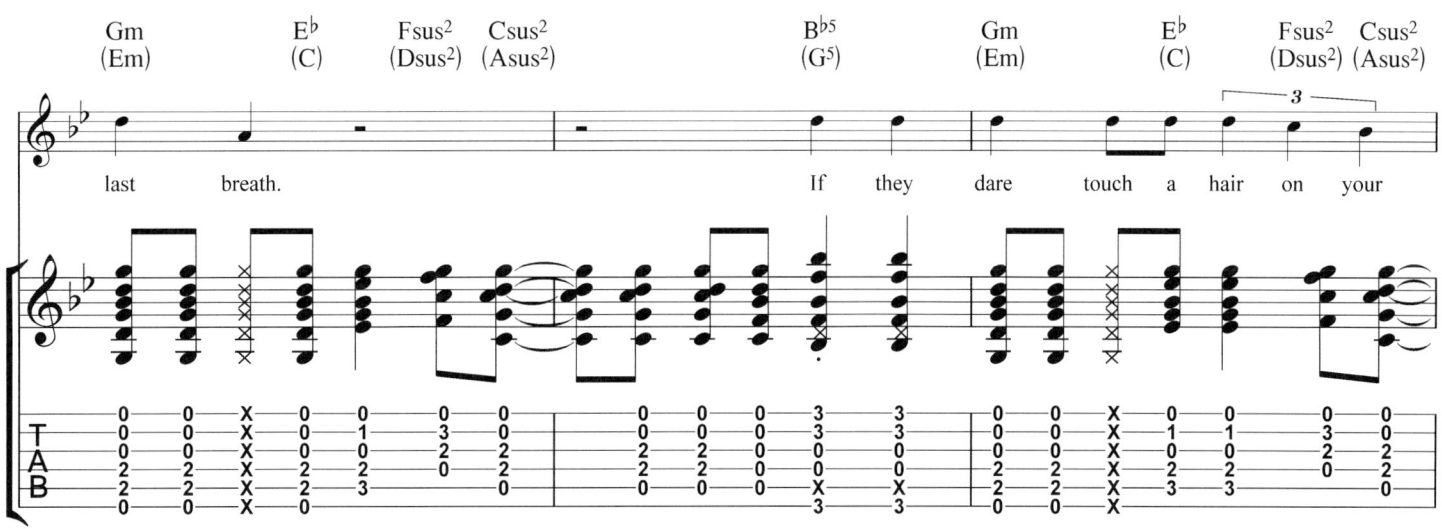

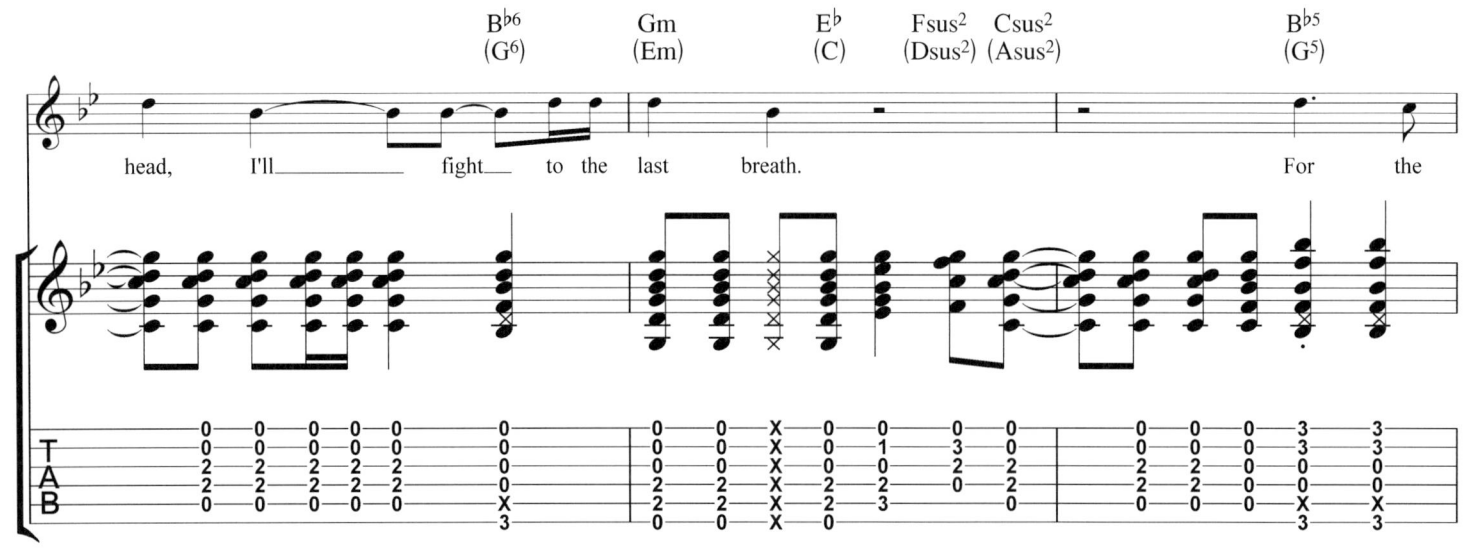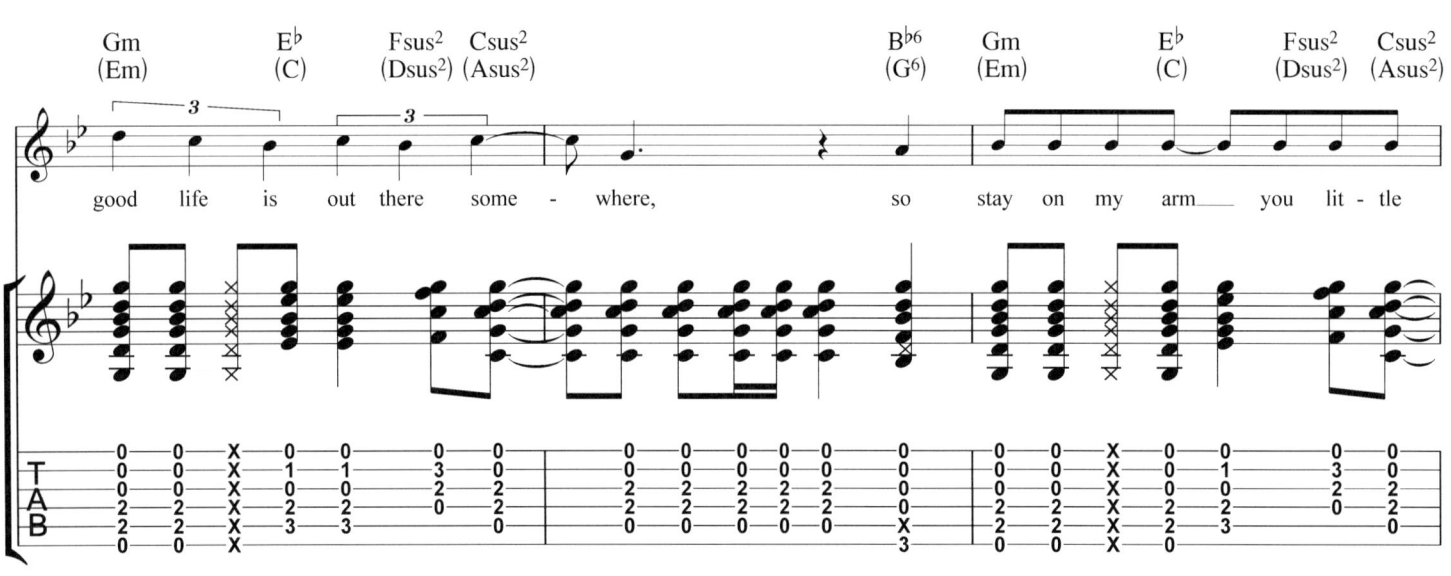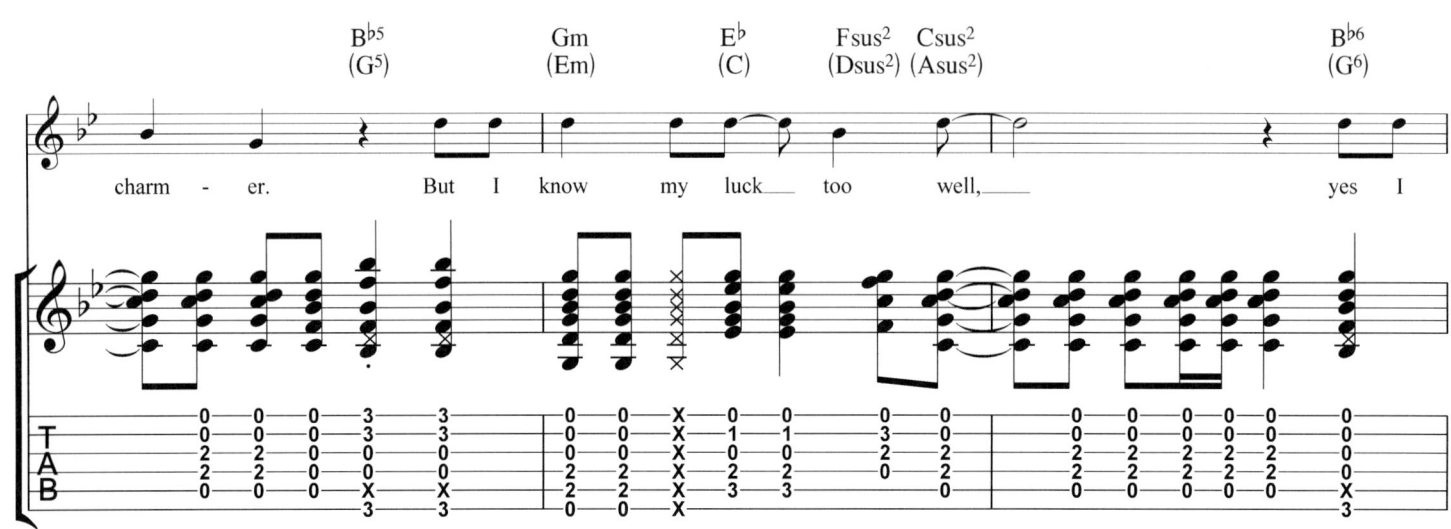

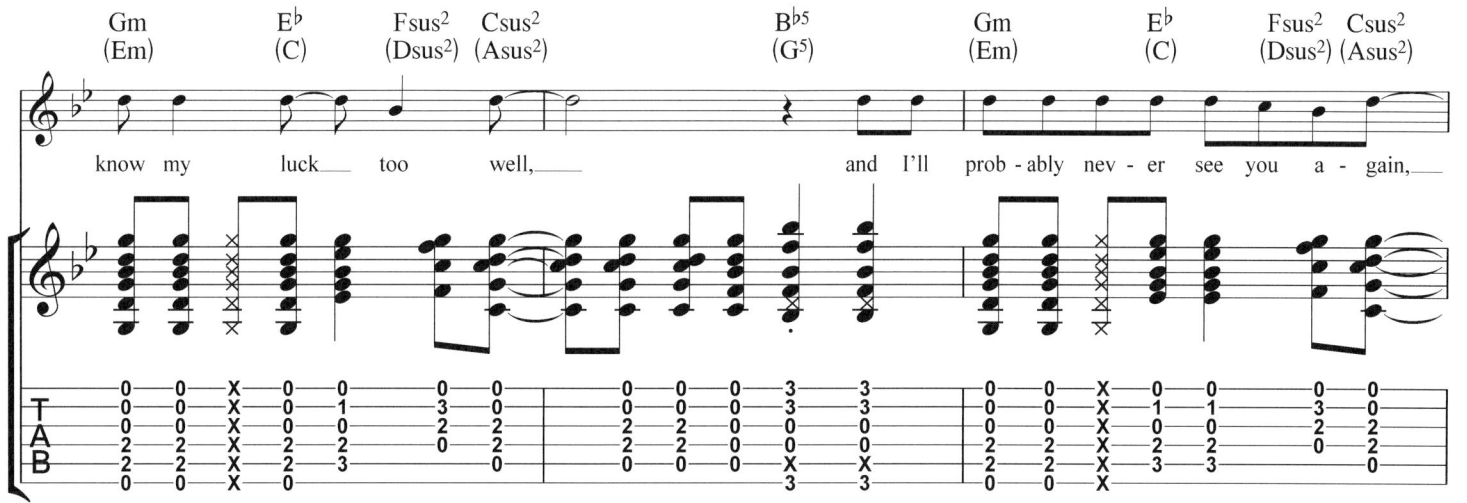
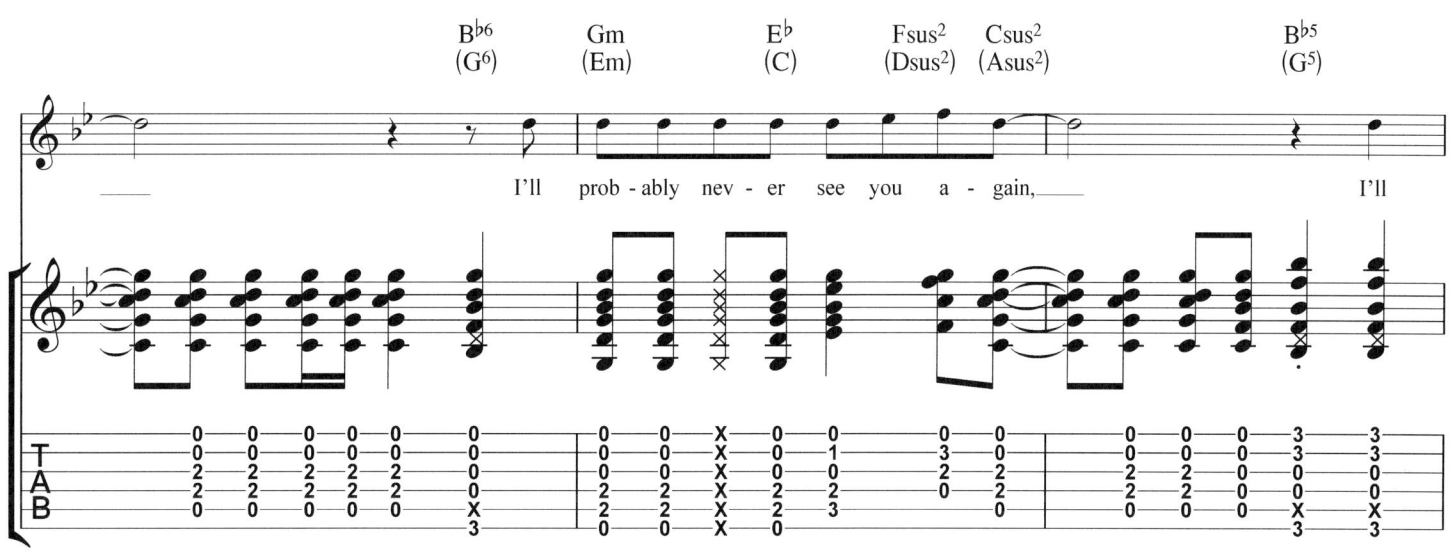
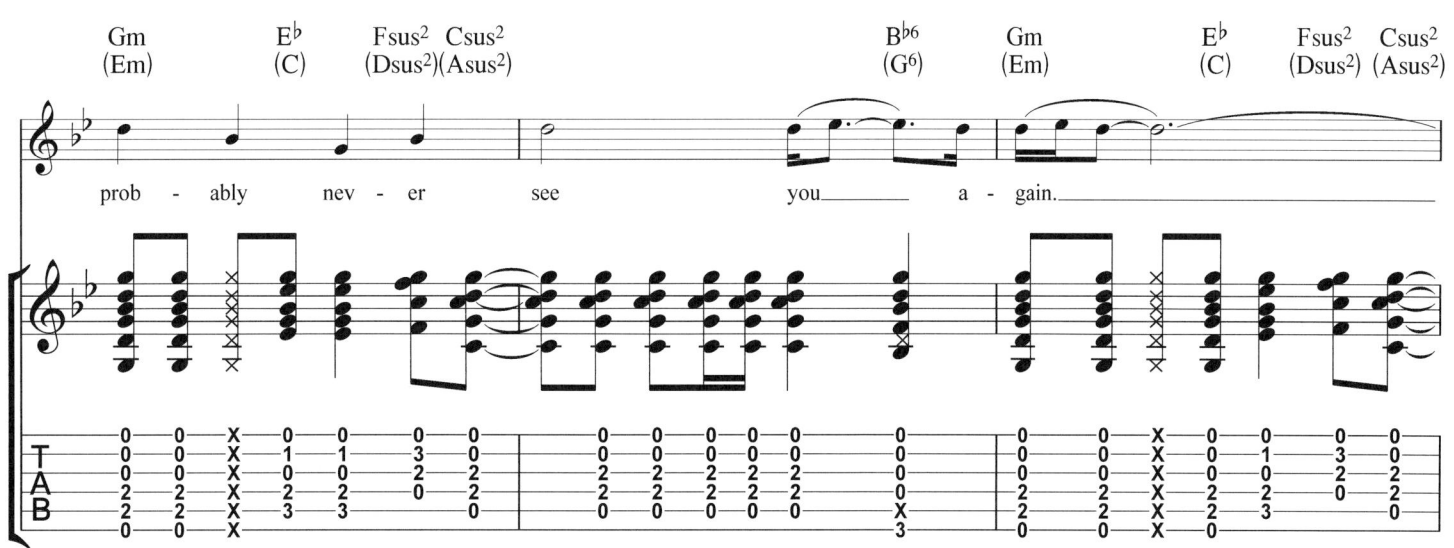

37

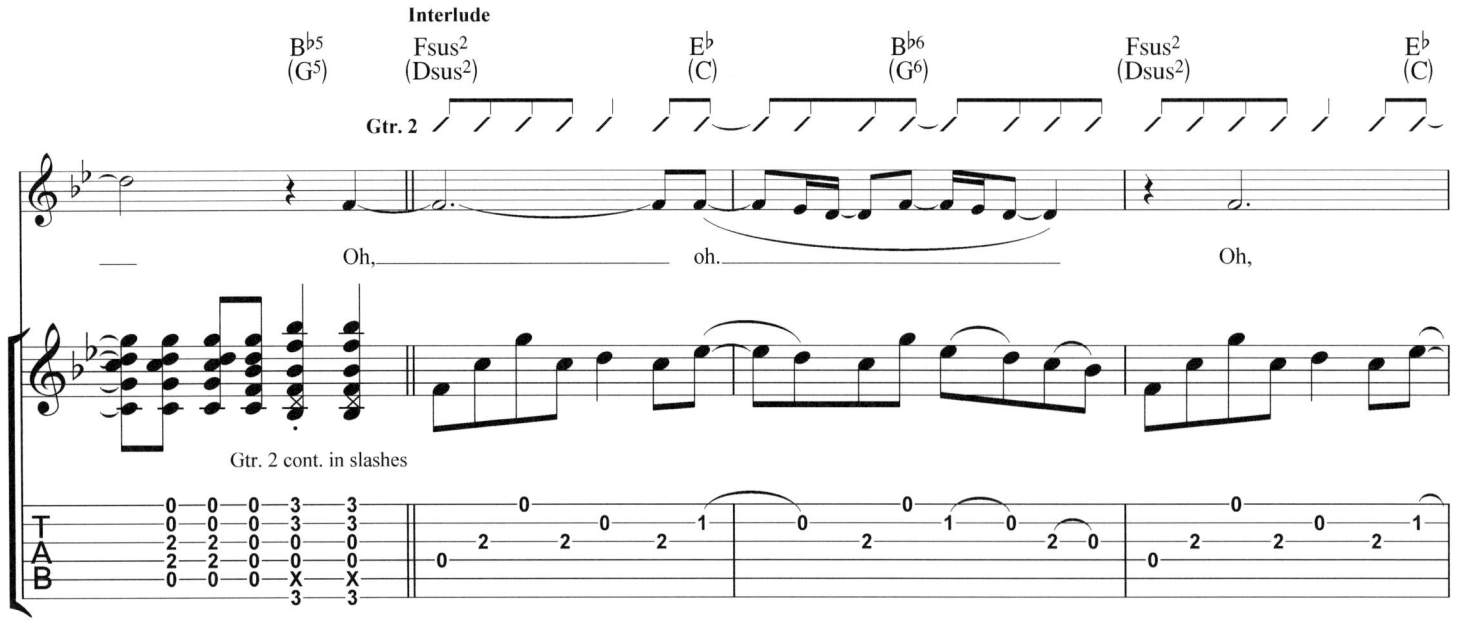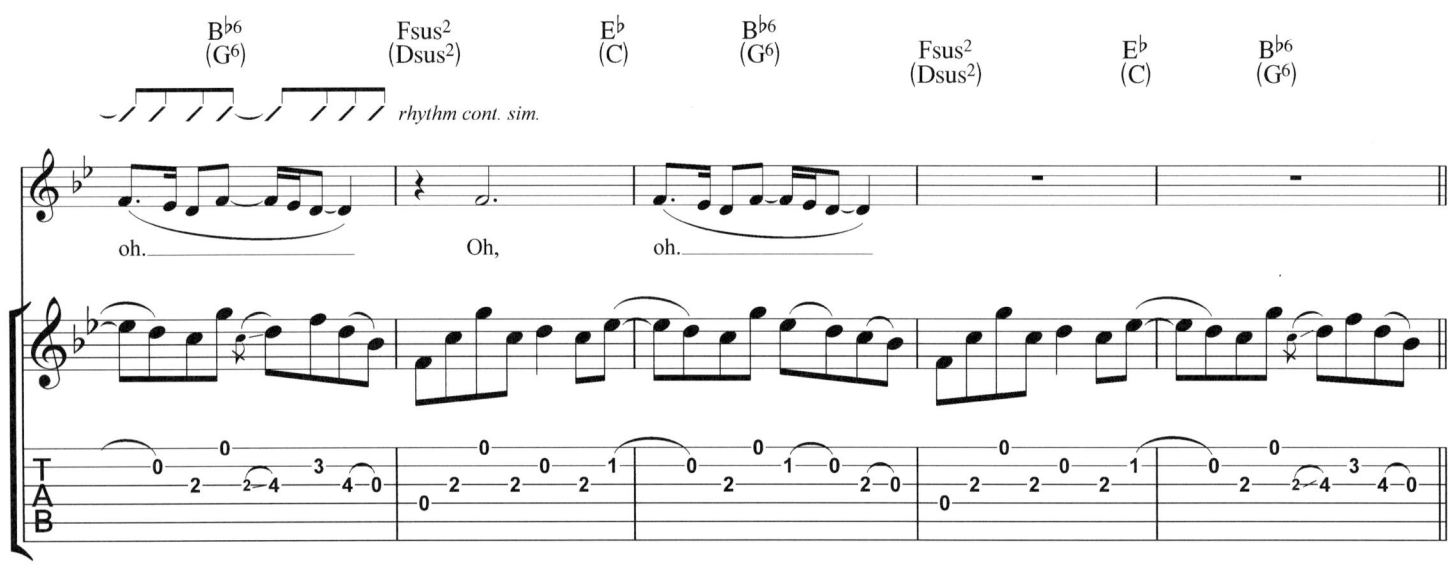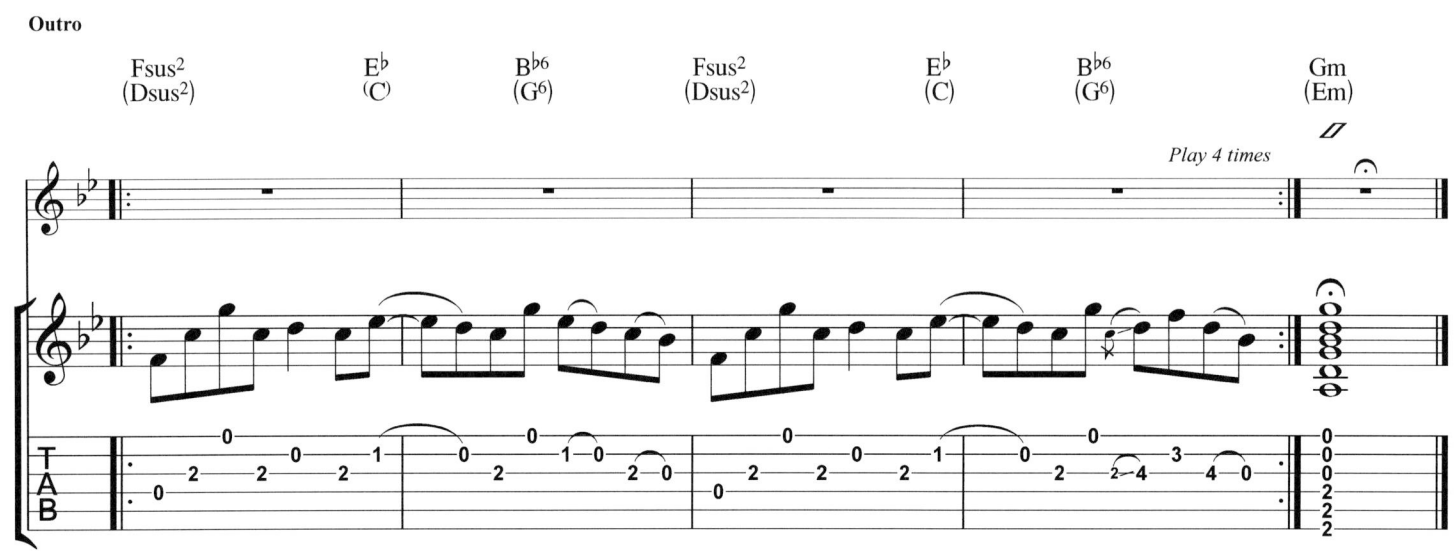

How Soon Is Now?

Words & Music by
Morrissey & Johnny Marr

All Gtrs. Capo 2nd fret.

♩ = 96

*chords implied by harmony throughout

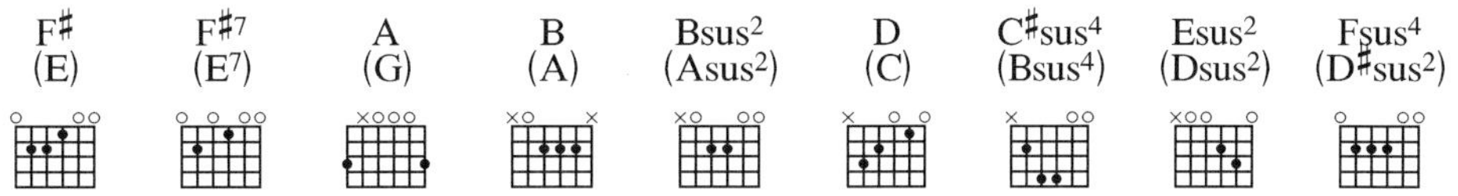

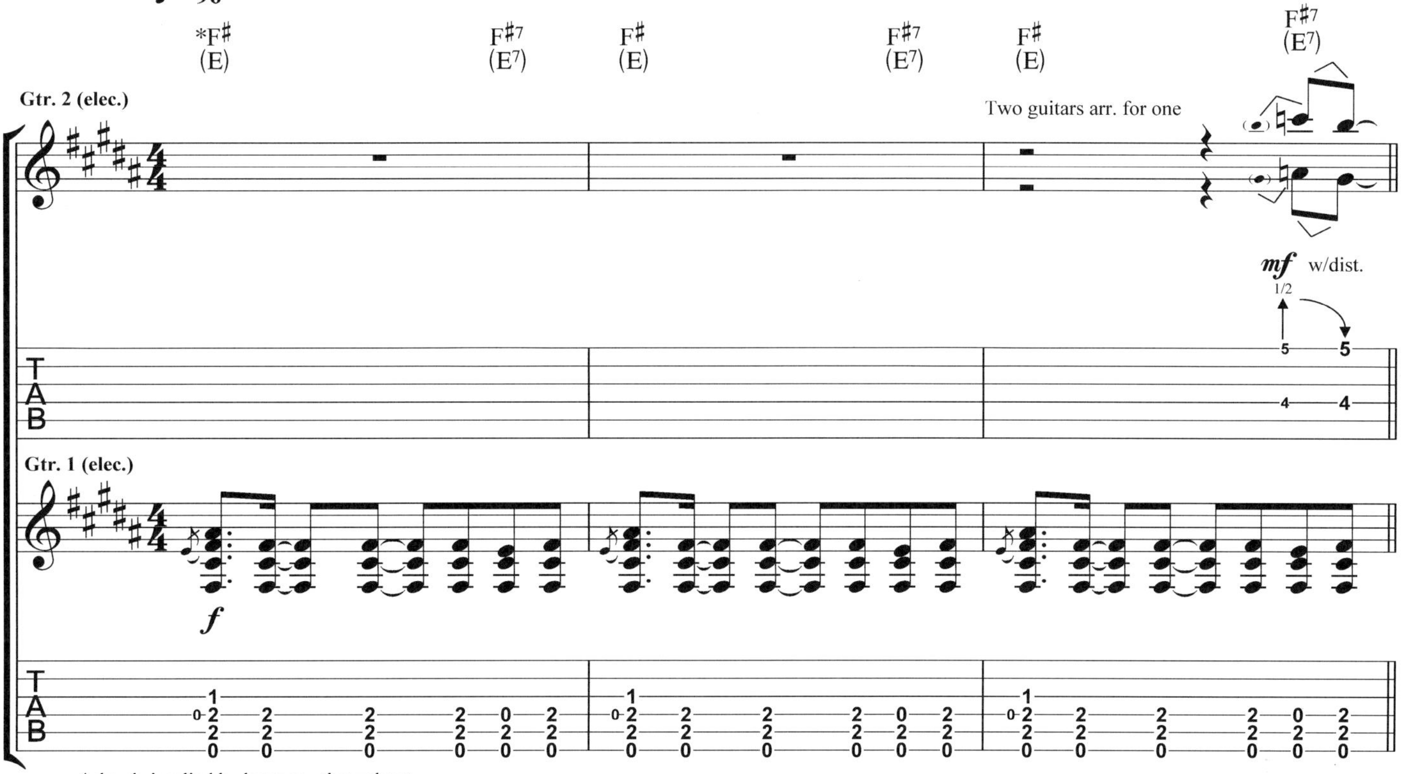

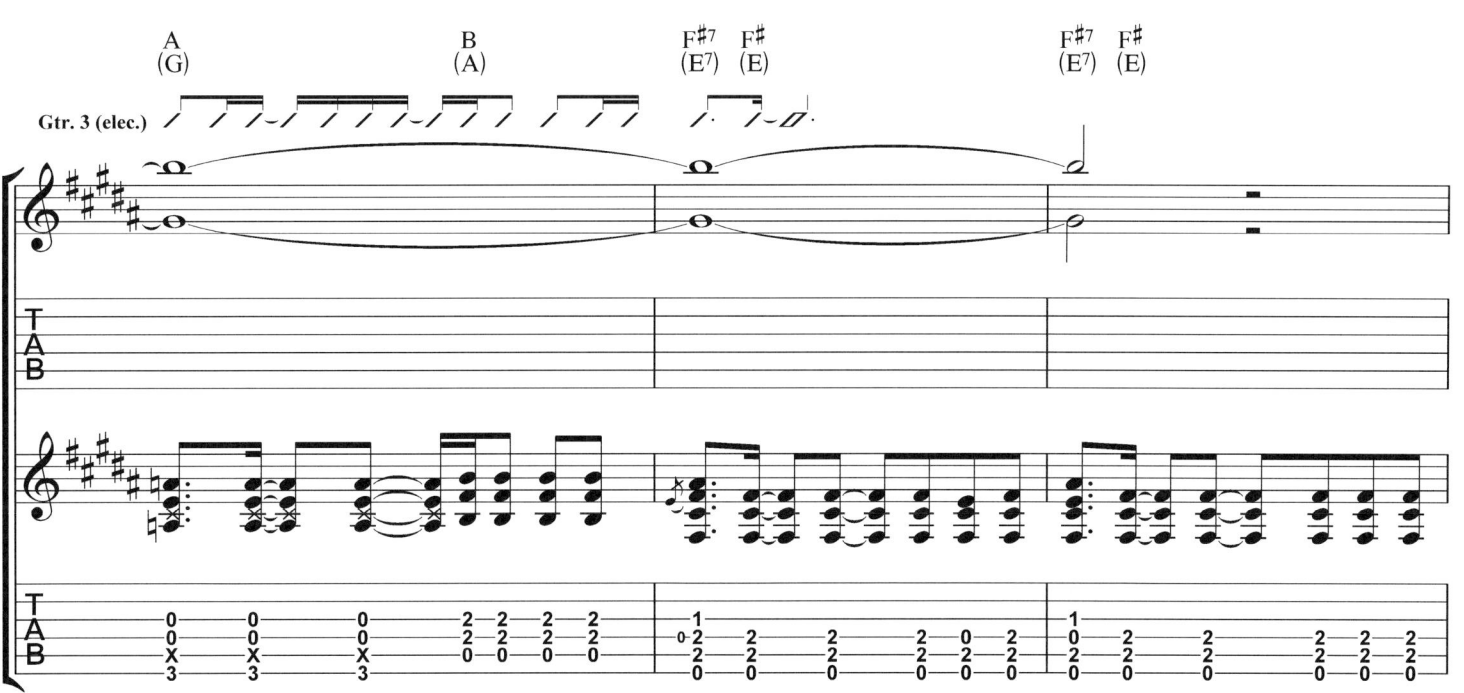

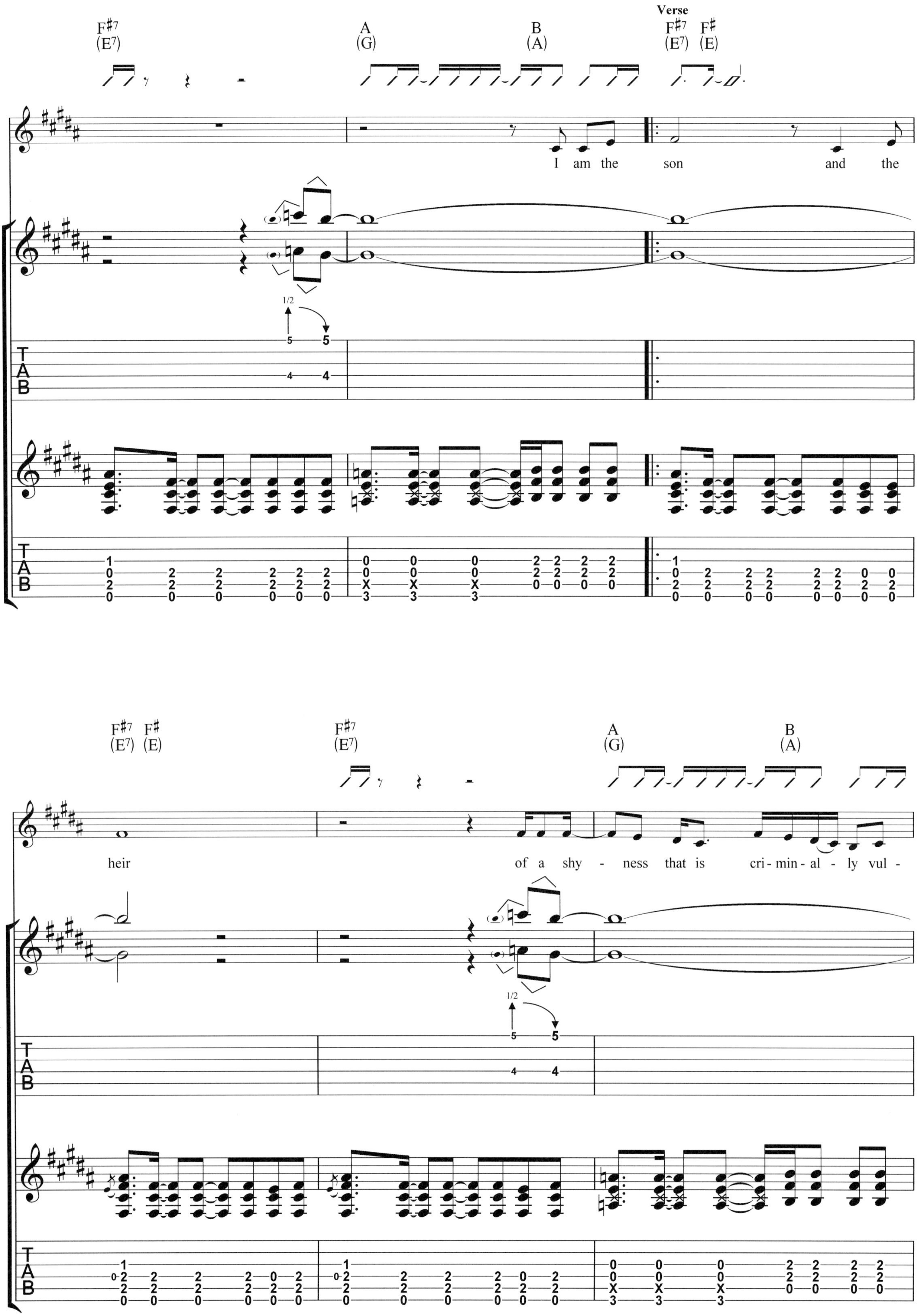
F♯7 (E7)
A (G)
B (A)
Verse
F♯7 (E7) F♯ (E)
I am the son and the
1/2
F♯7 (E7) F♯ (E)
F♯7 (E7)
A (G)
B (A)
heir of a shy - ness that is cri - min - al - ly vul -
1/2

Chorus
Gtrs. 2+3 tacet
A (G)
Bsus2 (Asus2)
C♯sus4 (Bsus4)
Esus2 (Dsus2)
how can you say
I go a - bout things the wrong

F♯ (E)
F♯sus4 (Esus4)
F♯ (E)
Bsus2 (Asus2)
D (C)
way?
I am hu - man and I need to be loved,

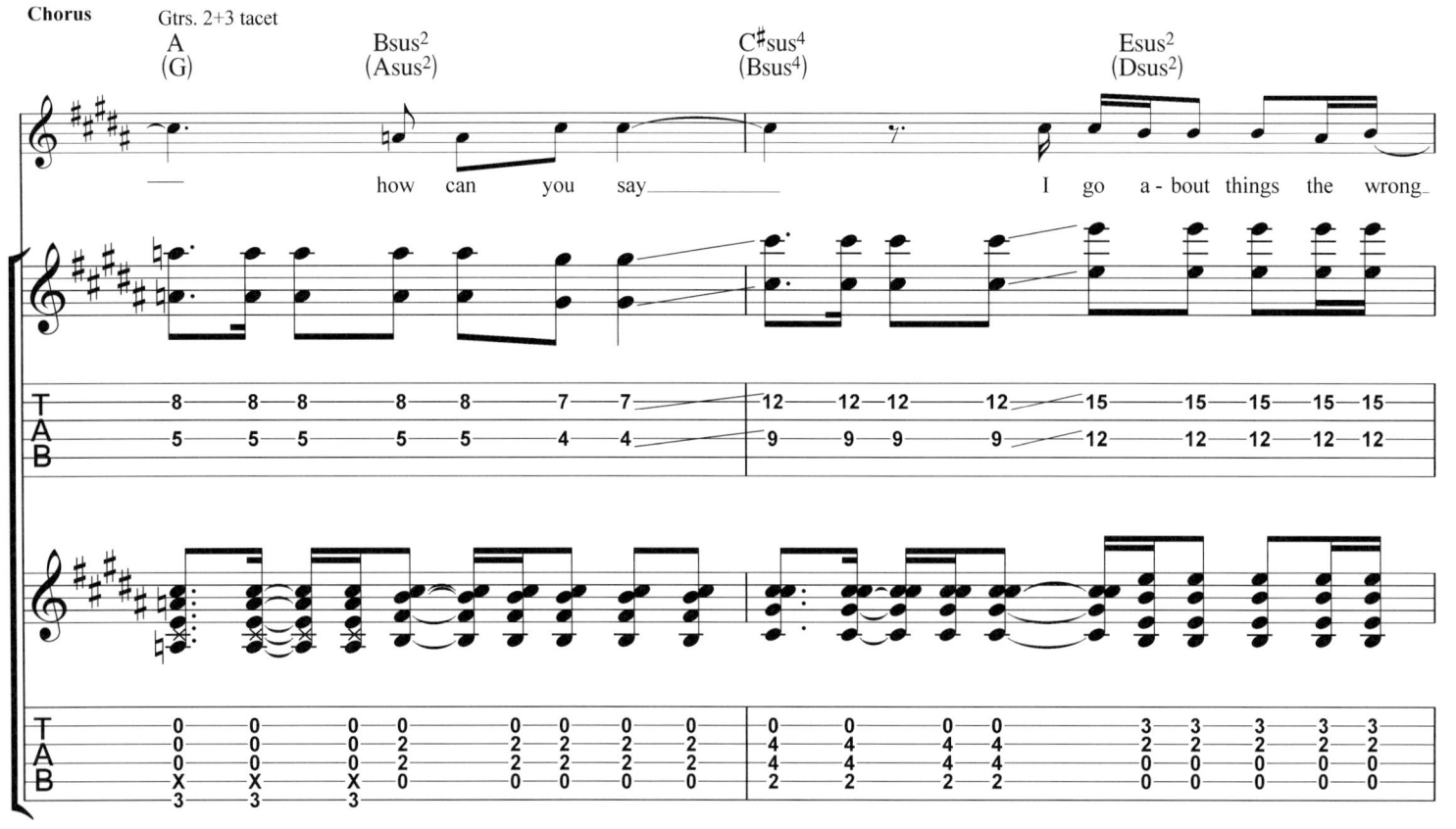

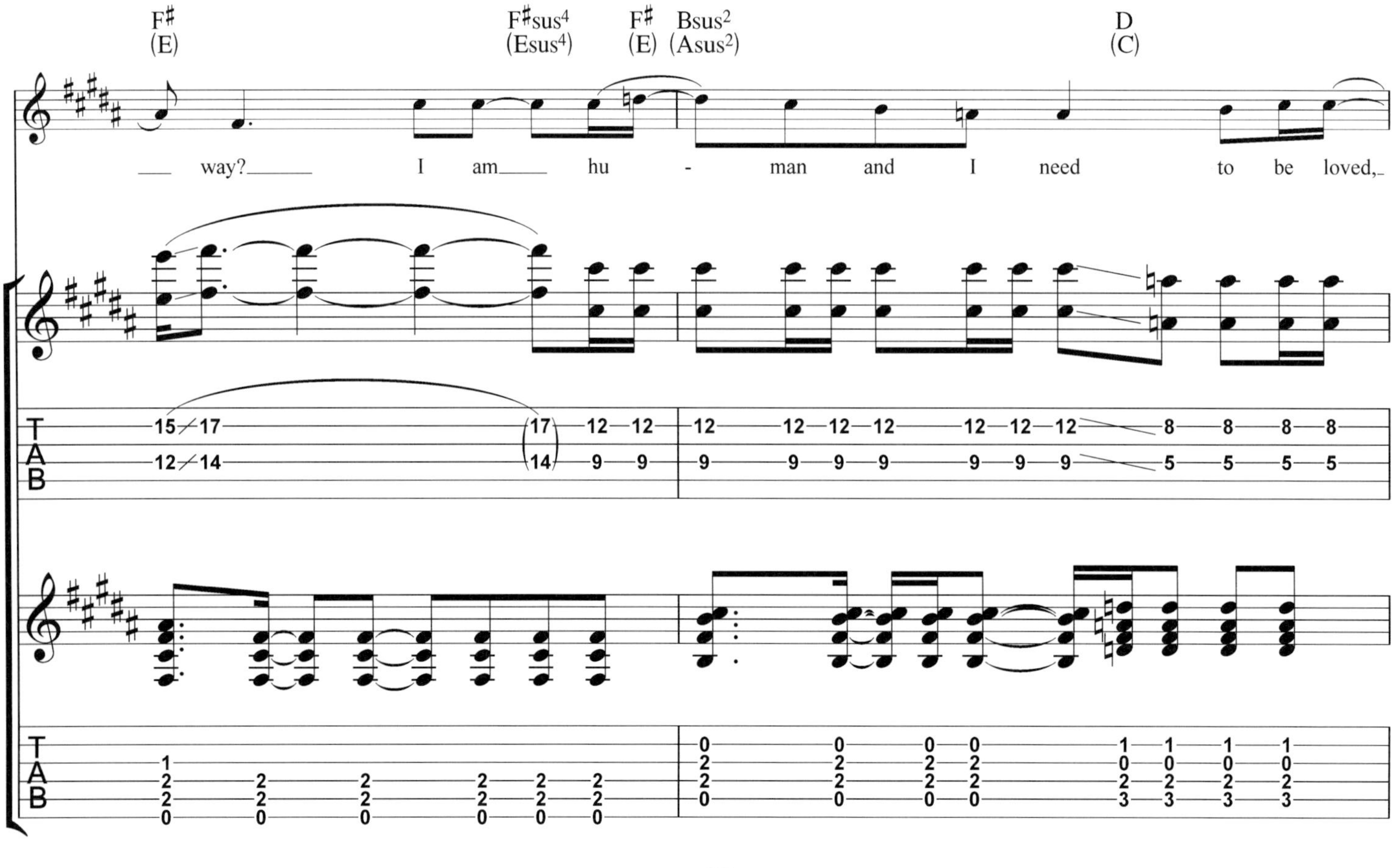

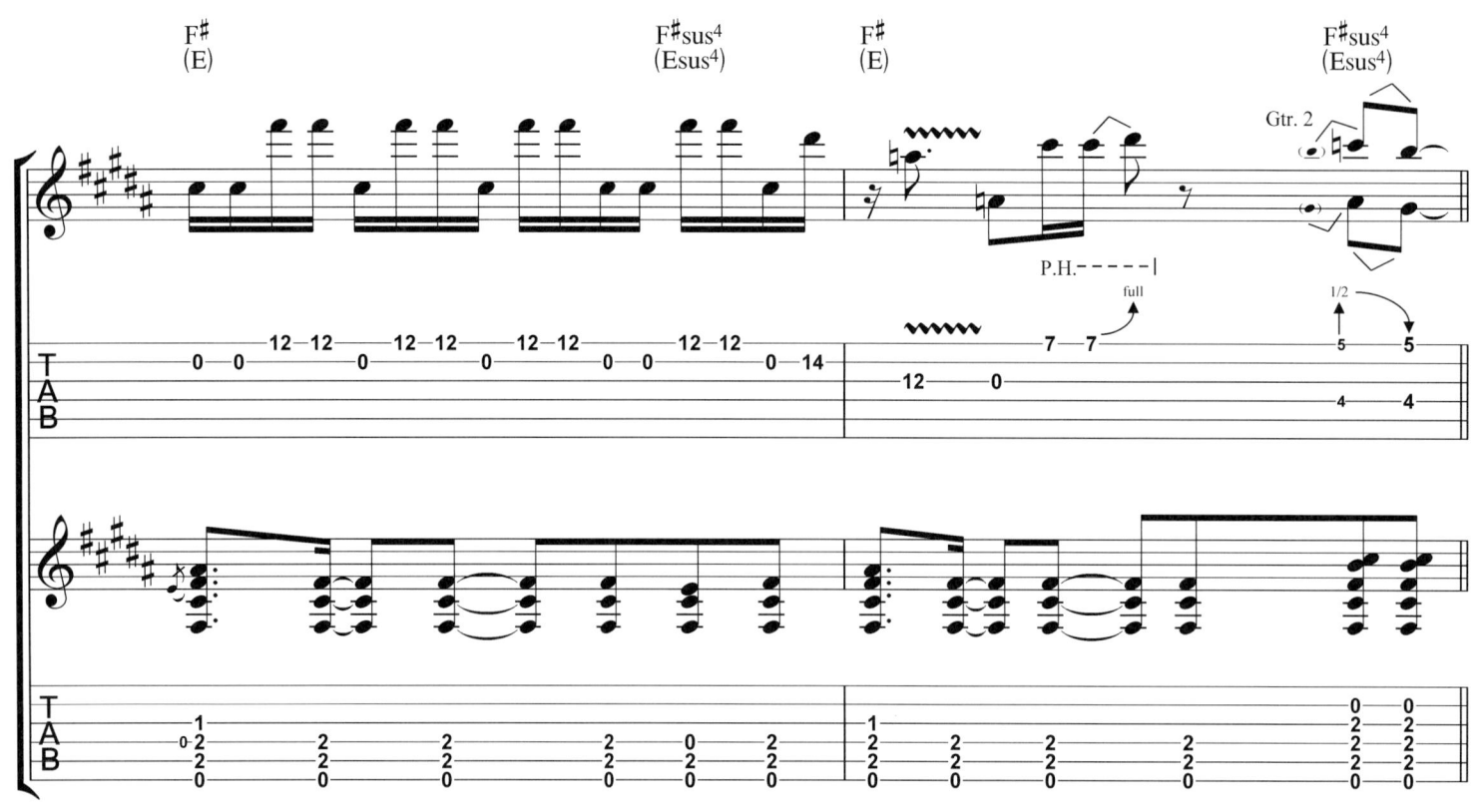
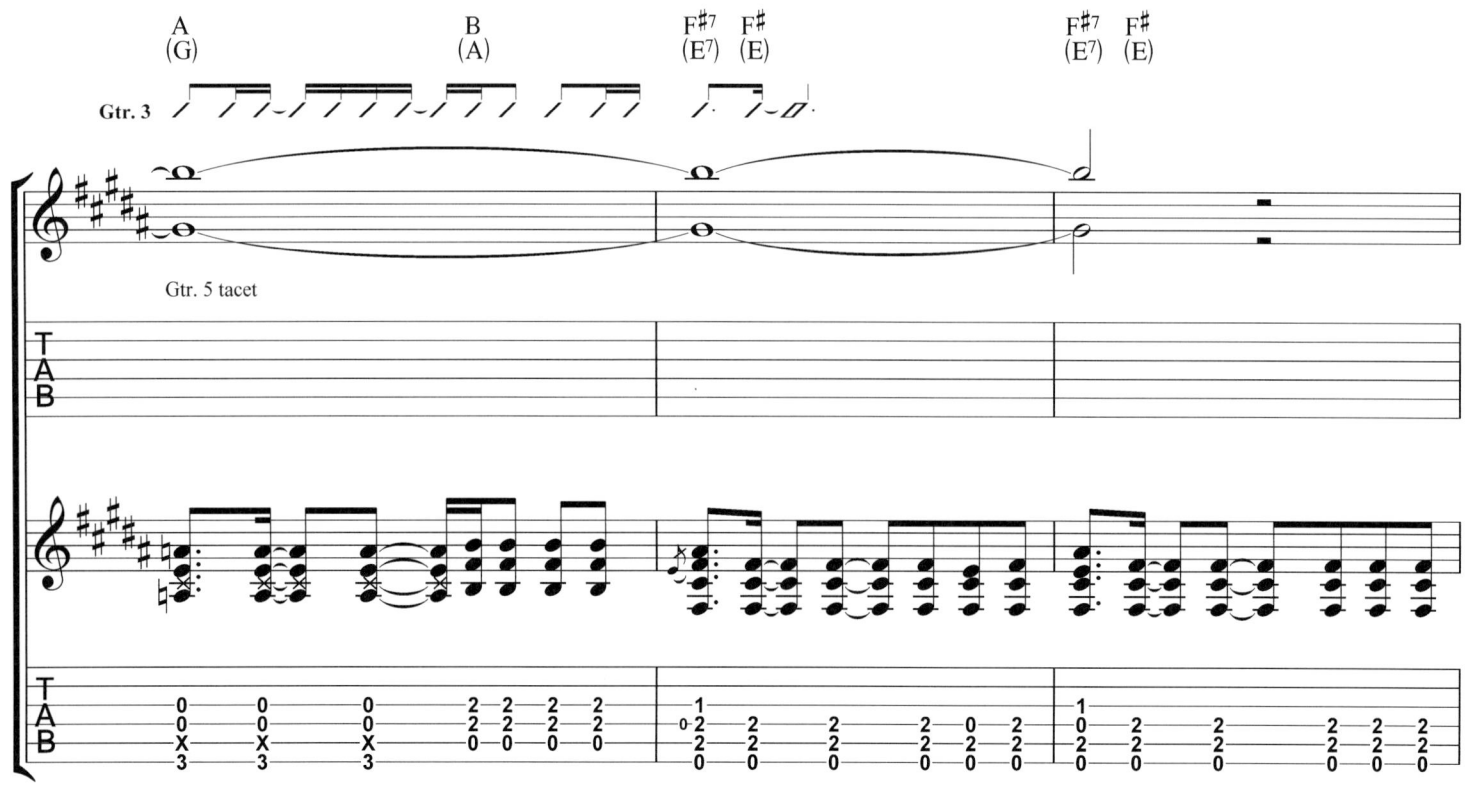

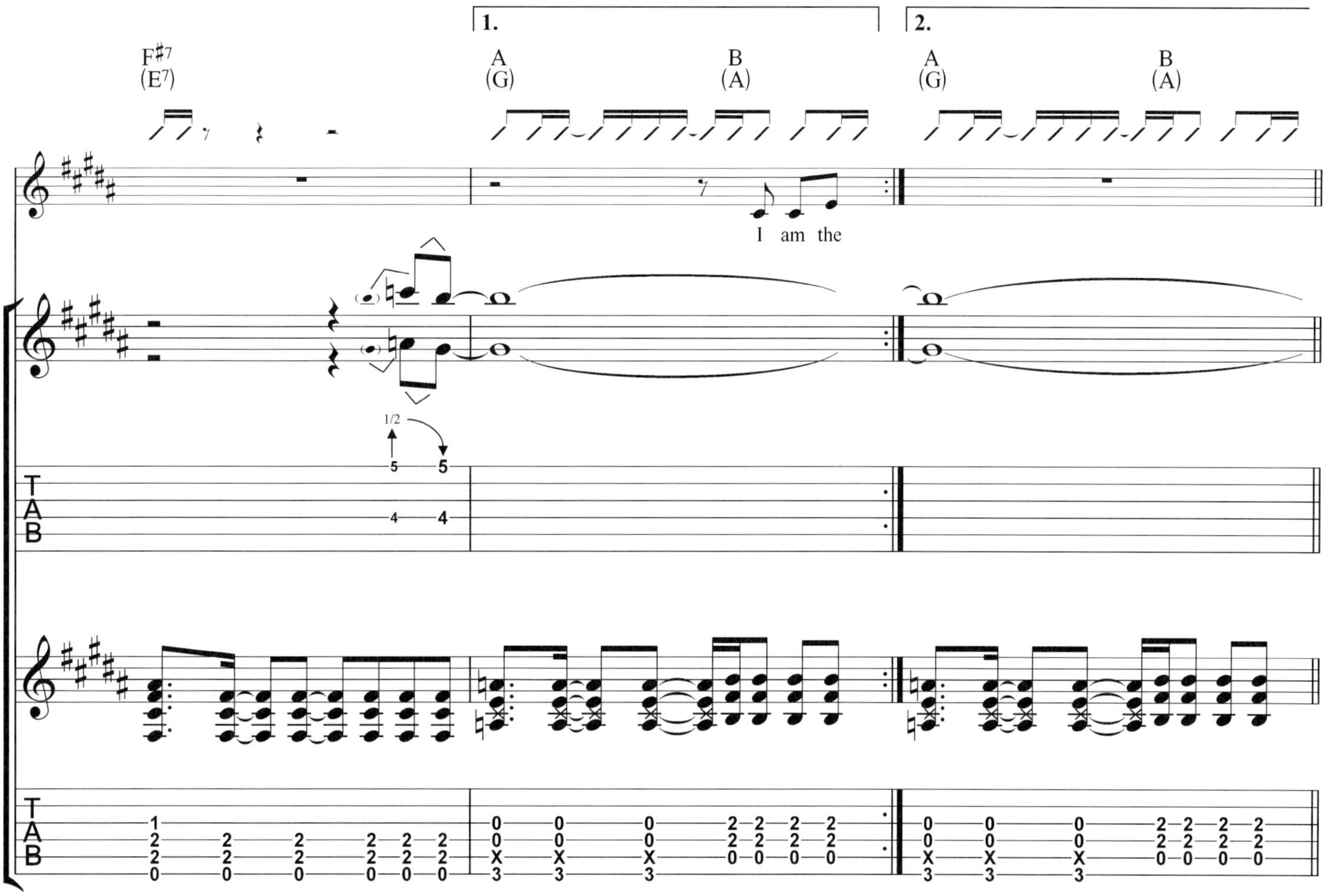

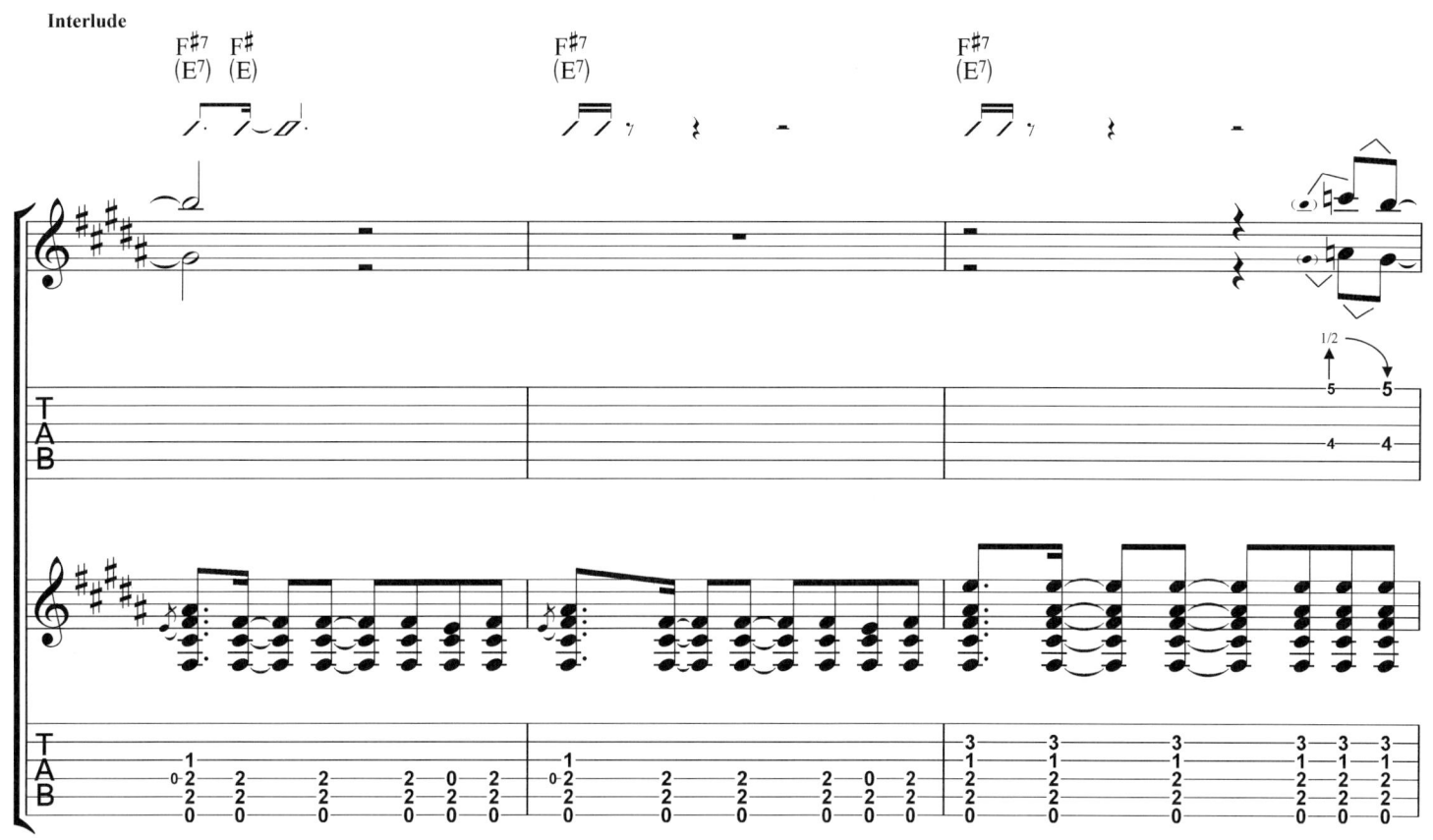

A (G)
B (A)
F♯7 (E7)
F♯ (E)
F♯7 (E7)
F♯7 (E7)
A (G)
B (A)
Bsus2 (Asus2)
There's a club, if you'd like to go?
Gtr. 4
cont. sim.
1/2

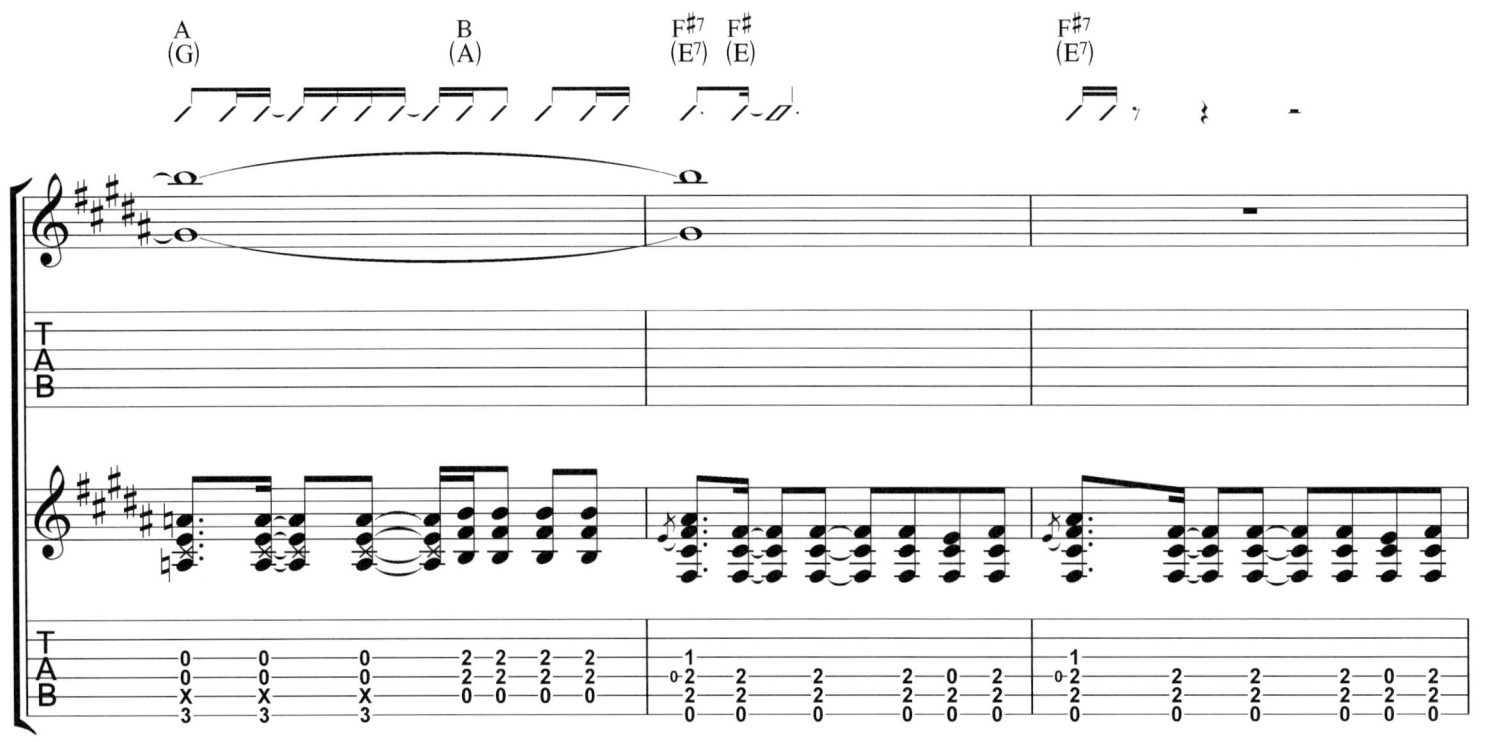

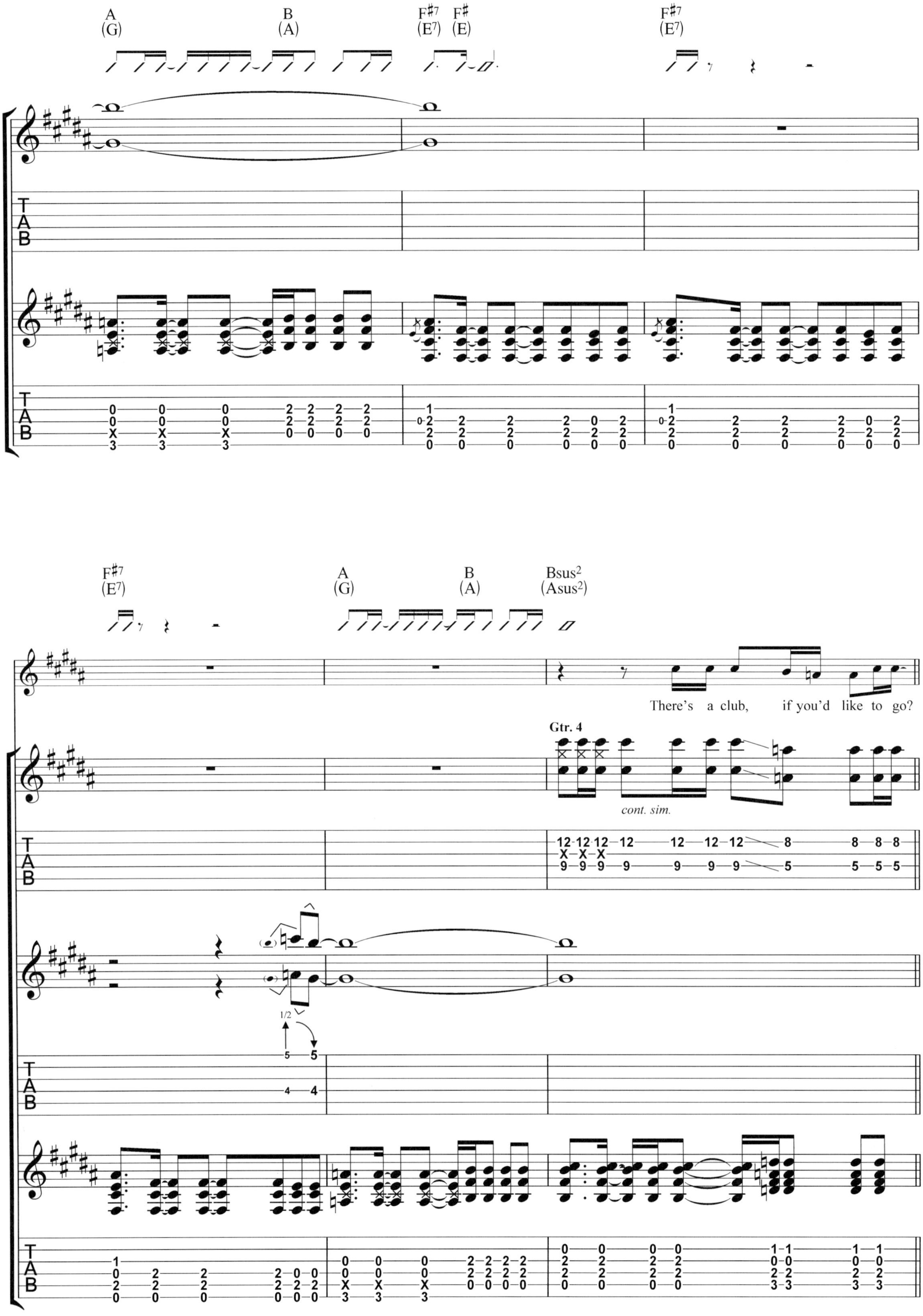

Chorus
A (G)
Bsus2 (Asus2)
C♯sus4 (Bsus4)
Esus2 (Dsus2)
You could meet some-bo-dy that real-ly loves
well, when ex-act-ly do you mean?
F♯ (E)
F♯sus4 (Esus4)
F♯ (E)
Bsus2 (Asus2)
D (C)
you. So you go and you stand on your own,
See, I've al-rea-dy wait-ed too
TAB

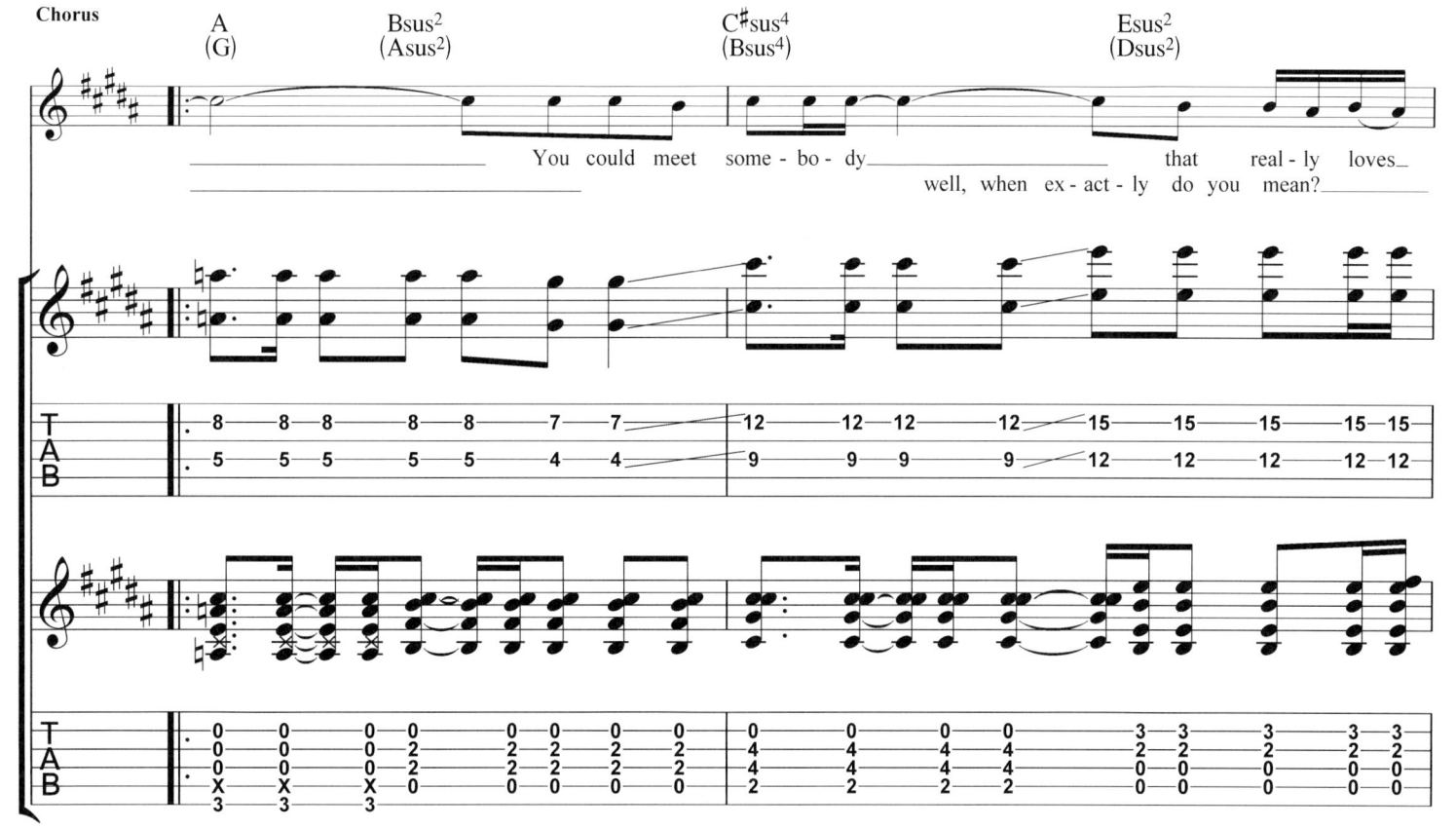

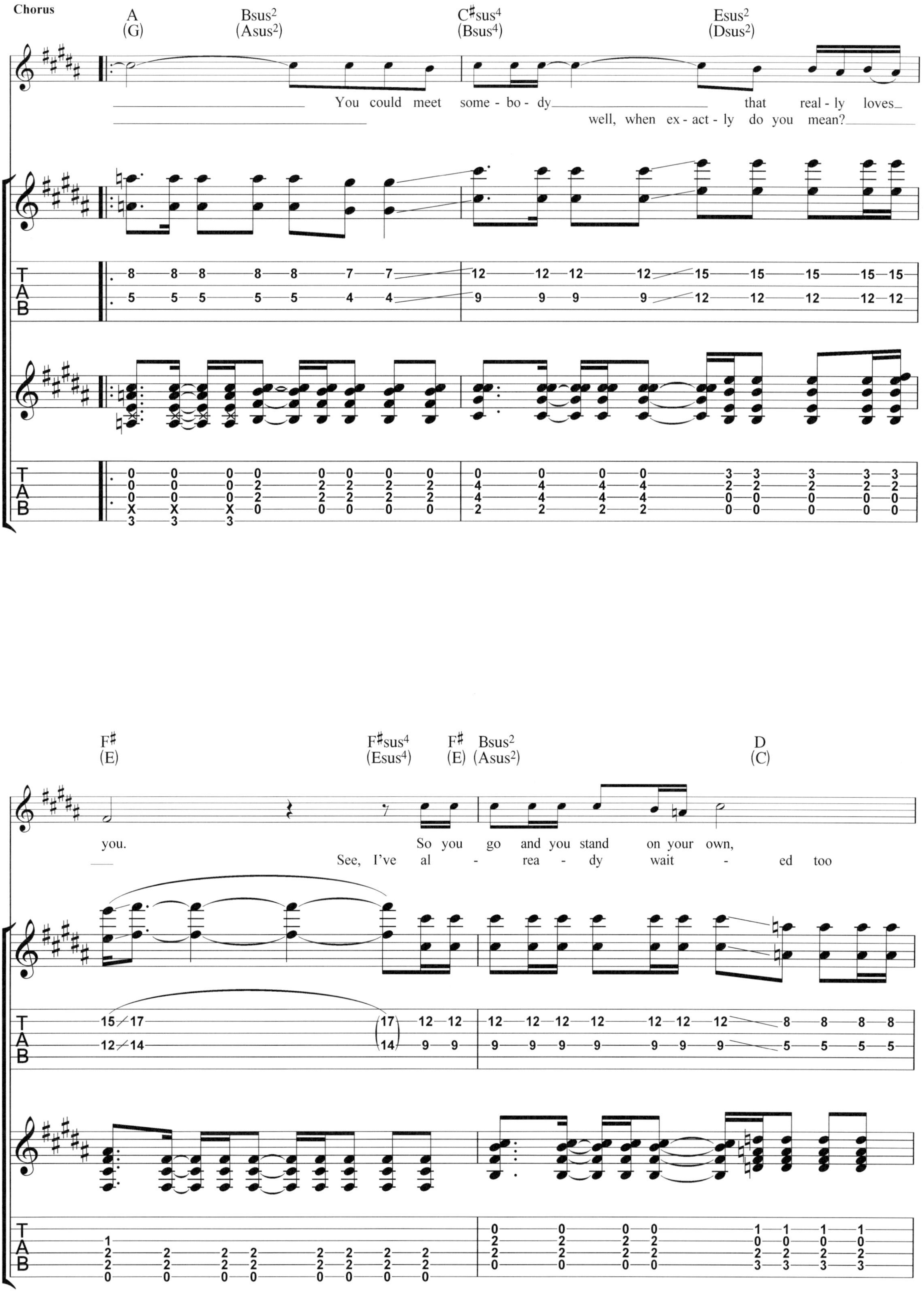

1.
Bsus2
(Asus2)
Gtr. 6 tacet
2.
Bsus2
(Asus2)
Gtr. 6 tacet
When you say it's gon-na hap-pen now,
Gtr. 4
cont. sim.
cont. sim.
Chorus (Instrumental)
A
(G)
Bsus2
(Asus2)
C♯sus4
(Bsus4)
Esus2
(Dsus2)
F♯
(E)
F♯sus4
(Esus4)

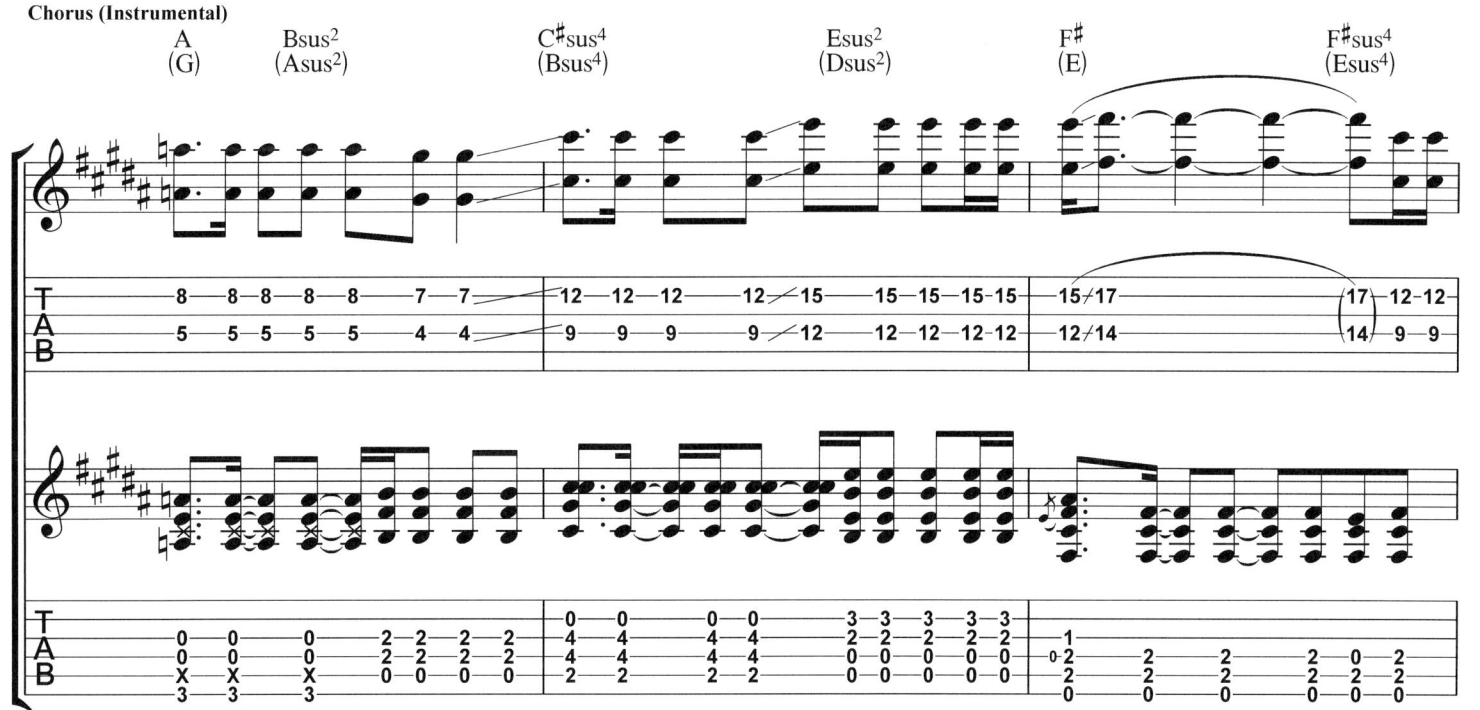

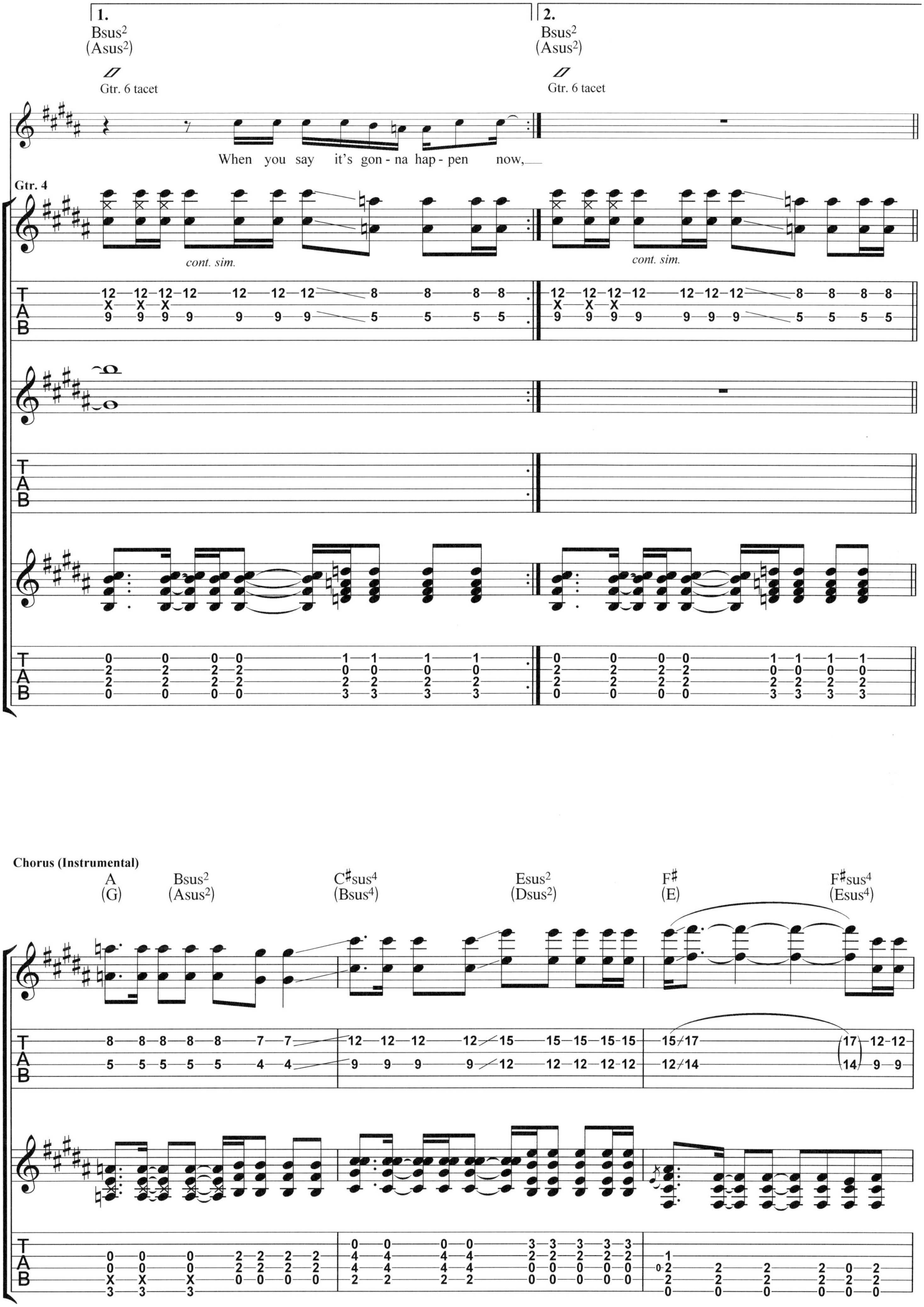

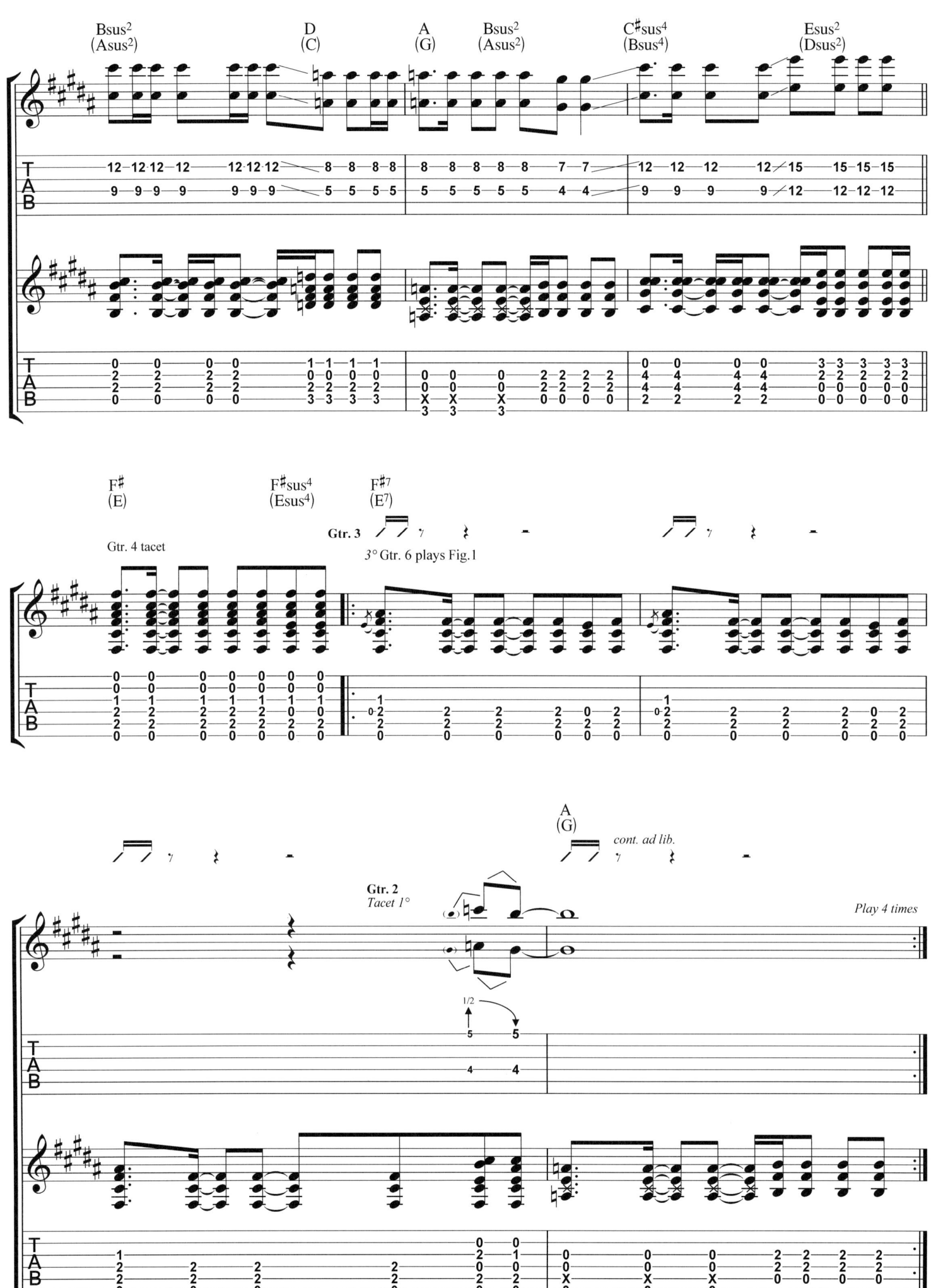

Chorus
Bsus2 (Asus2)
A (G)
Bsus2 (Asus2)
Gtr. 3 tacet
You shut your mouth, how can you say
Gtr. 4
cont. sim.
C♯sus4 (Bsus4)
Esus2 (Dsus2)
F♯ (E)
F♯sus4 (Esus4)
F♯ (E)
I go a-bout things the wrong way? I am hu-

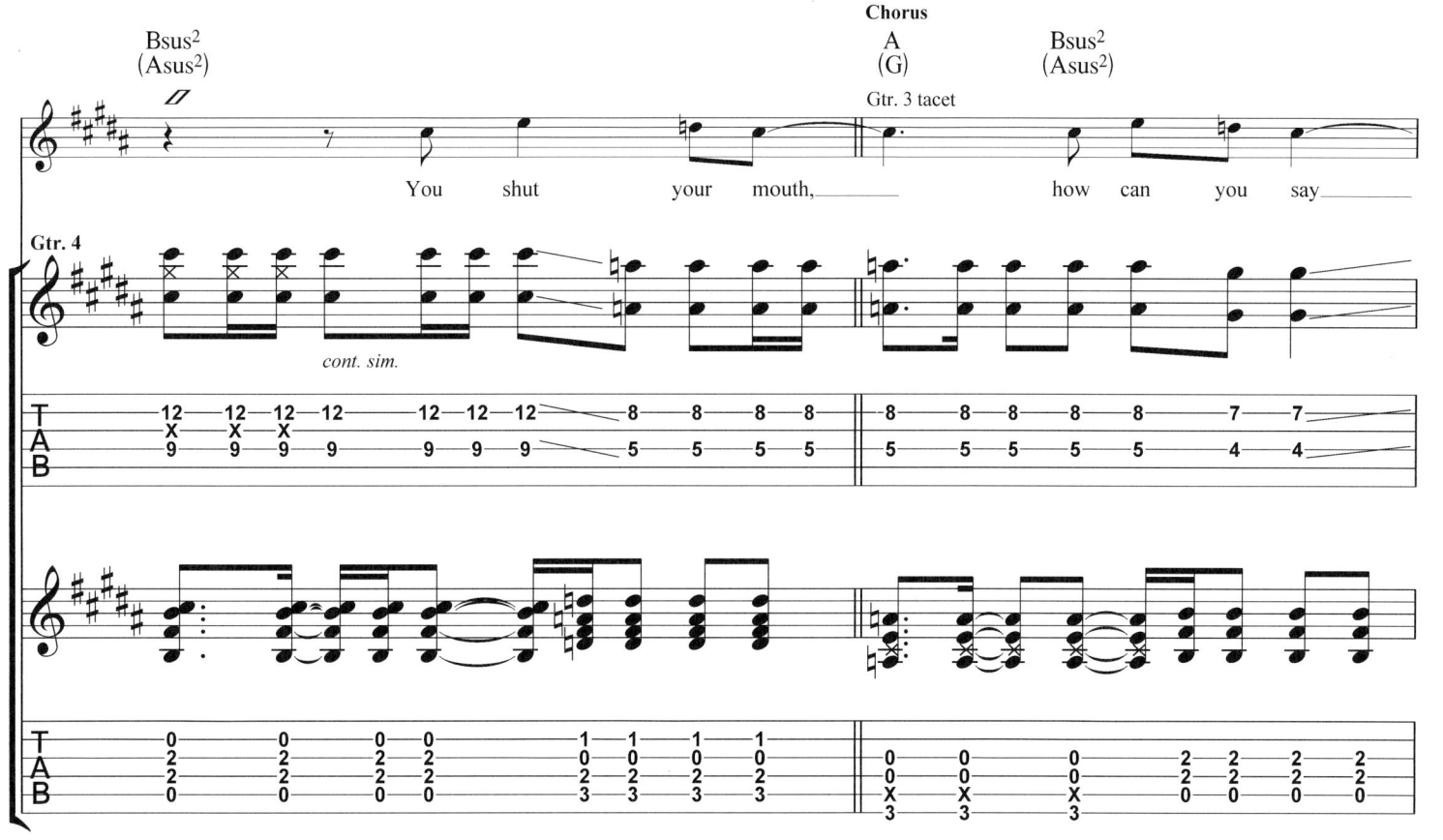

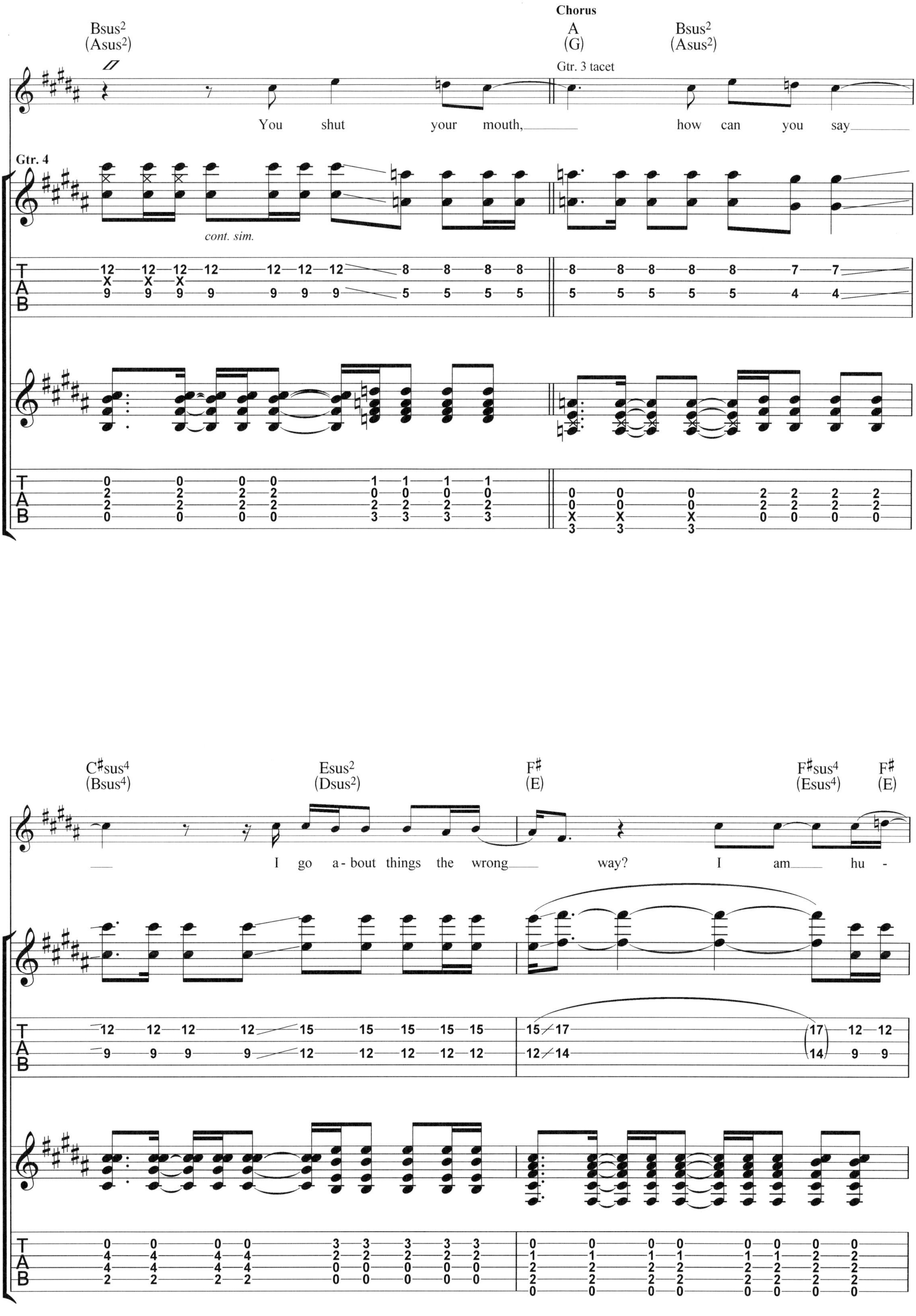

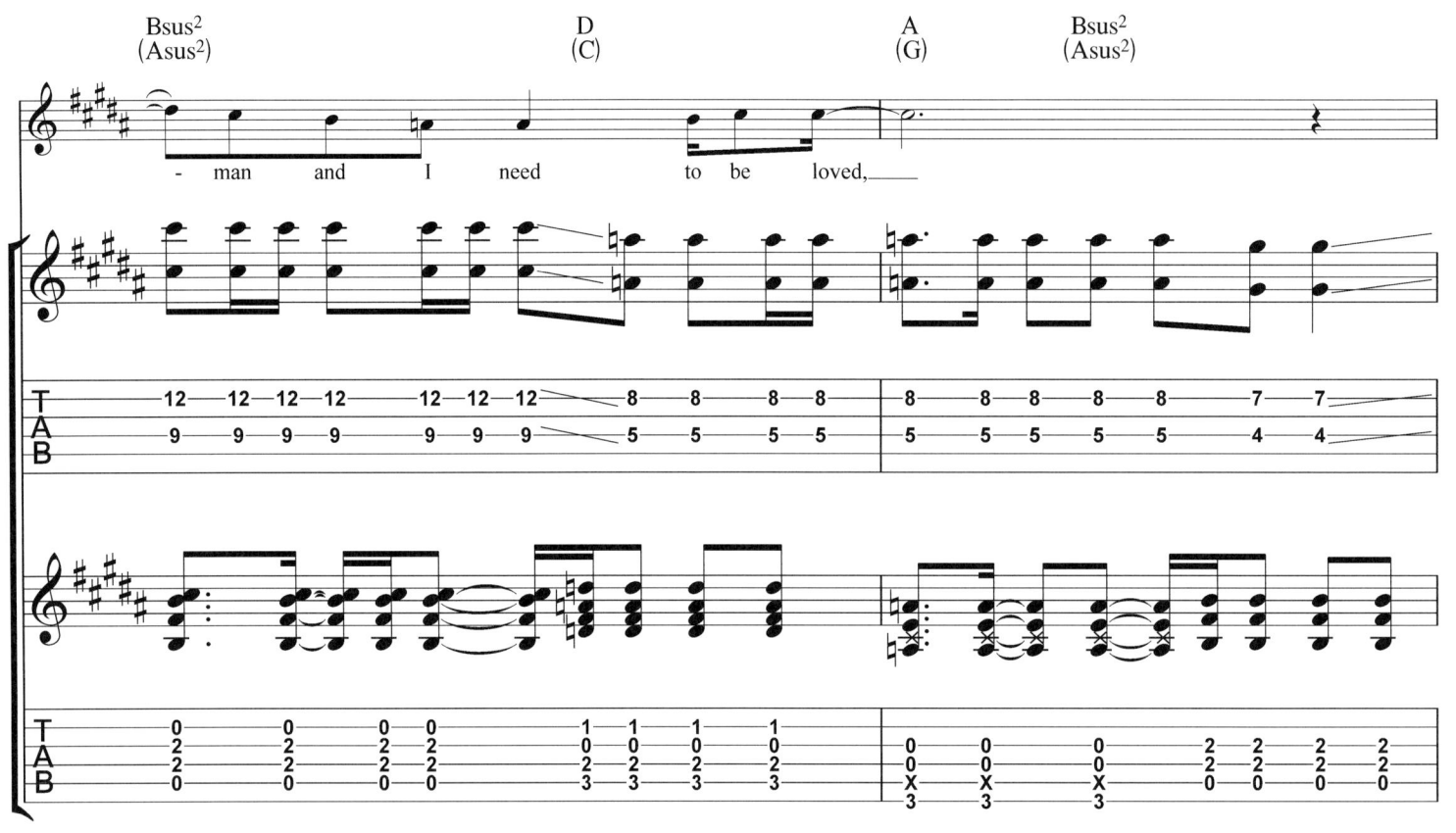

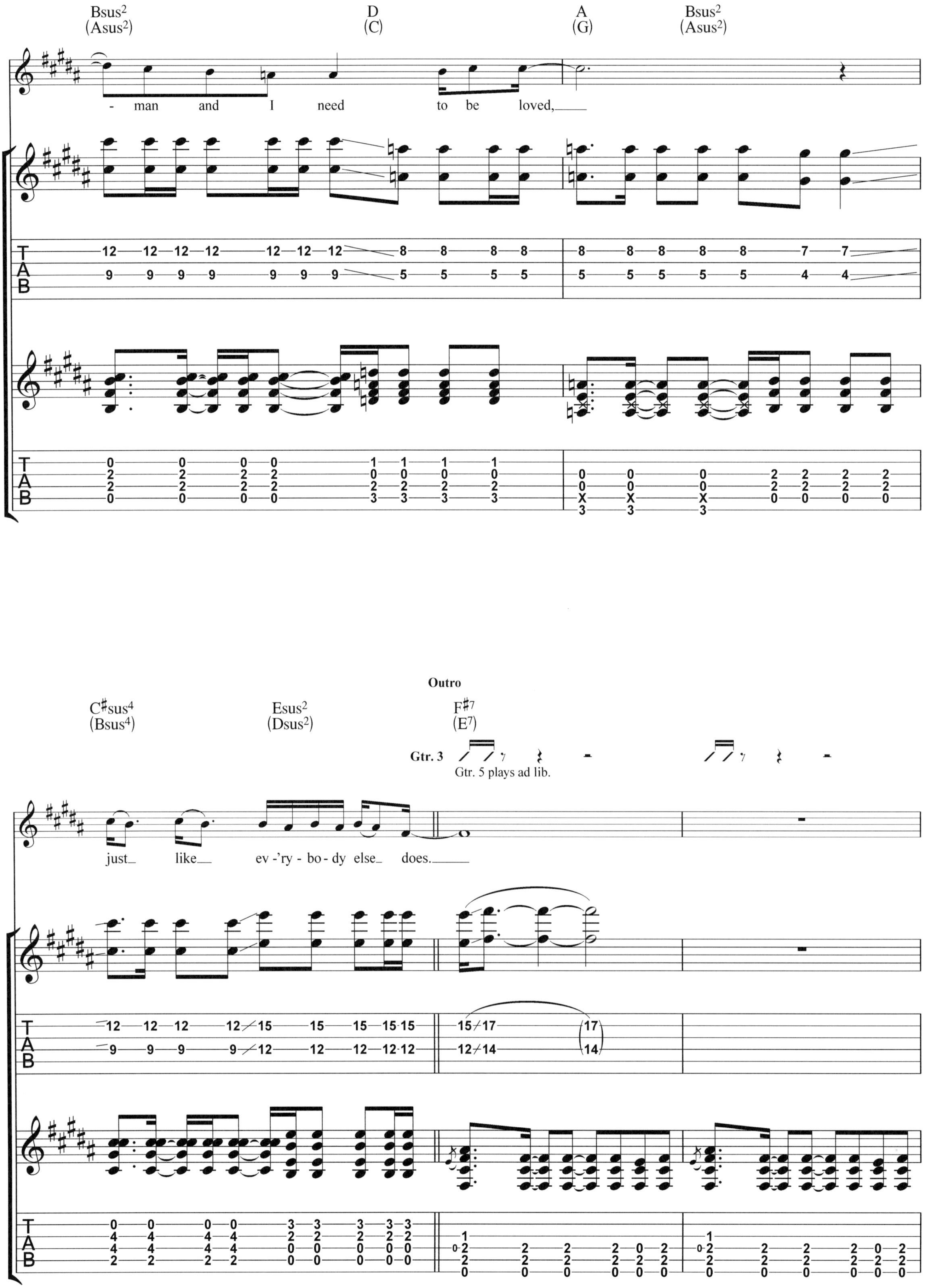
Bsus2 (Asus2)
D (C)
A (G)
Bsus2 (Asus2)
- man and I need to be loved,
Outro
C♯sus4 (Bsus4)
Esus2 (Dsus2)
F♯7 (E7)
Gtr. 3
Gtr. 5 plays ad lib.
just like ev-'ry-bo-dy else does.

A
(G)
B
(A)
1/2

A
(G)
B
(A)
Repeat to fade
Gtr. 6 plays Fig.1
1/2

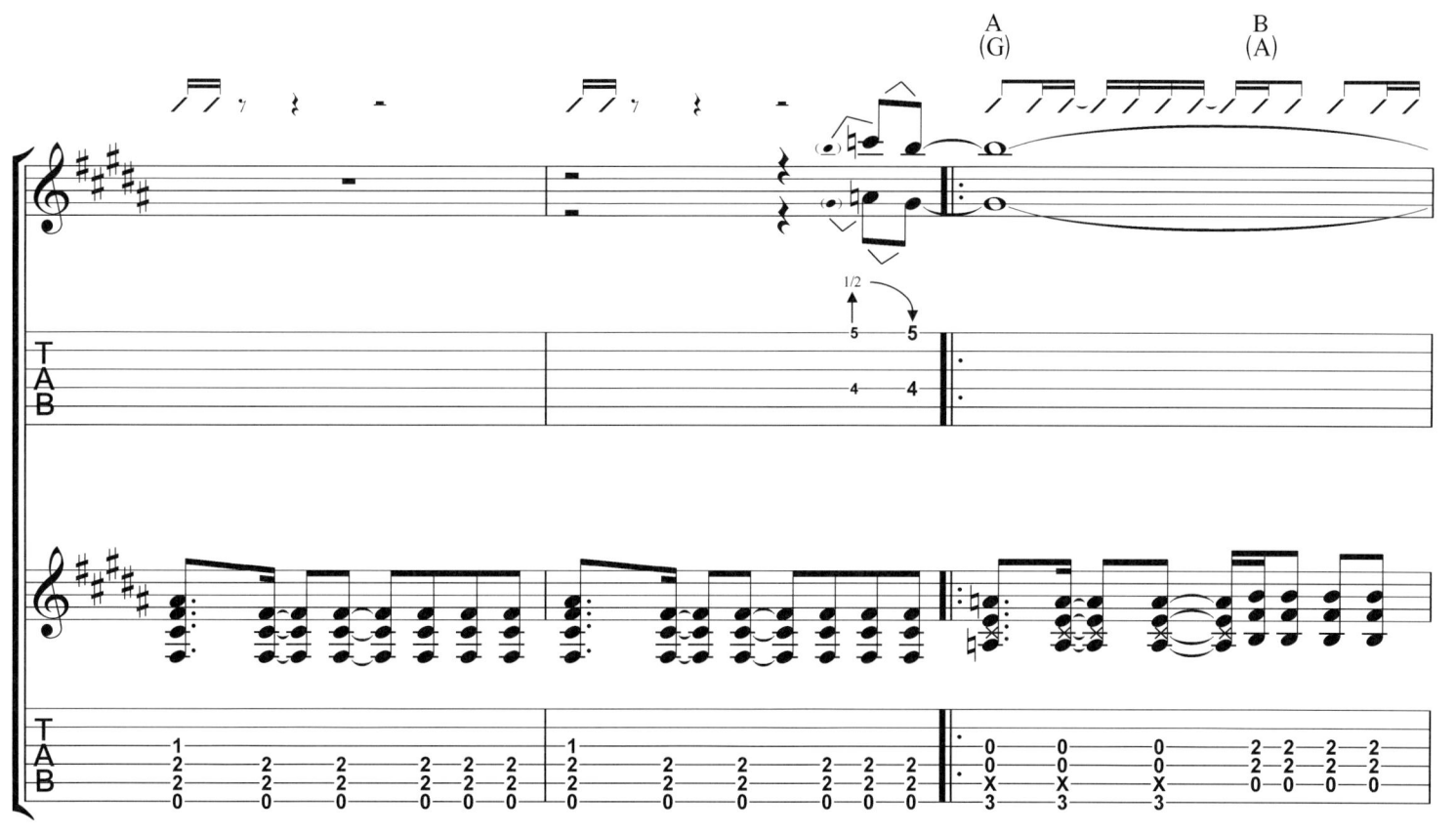

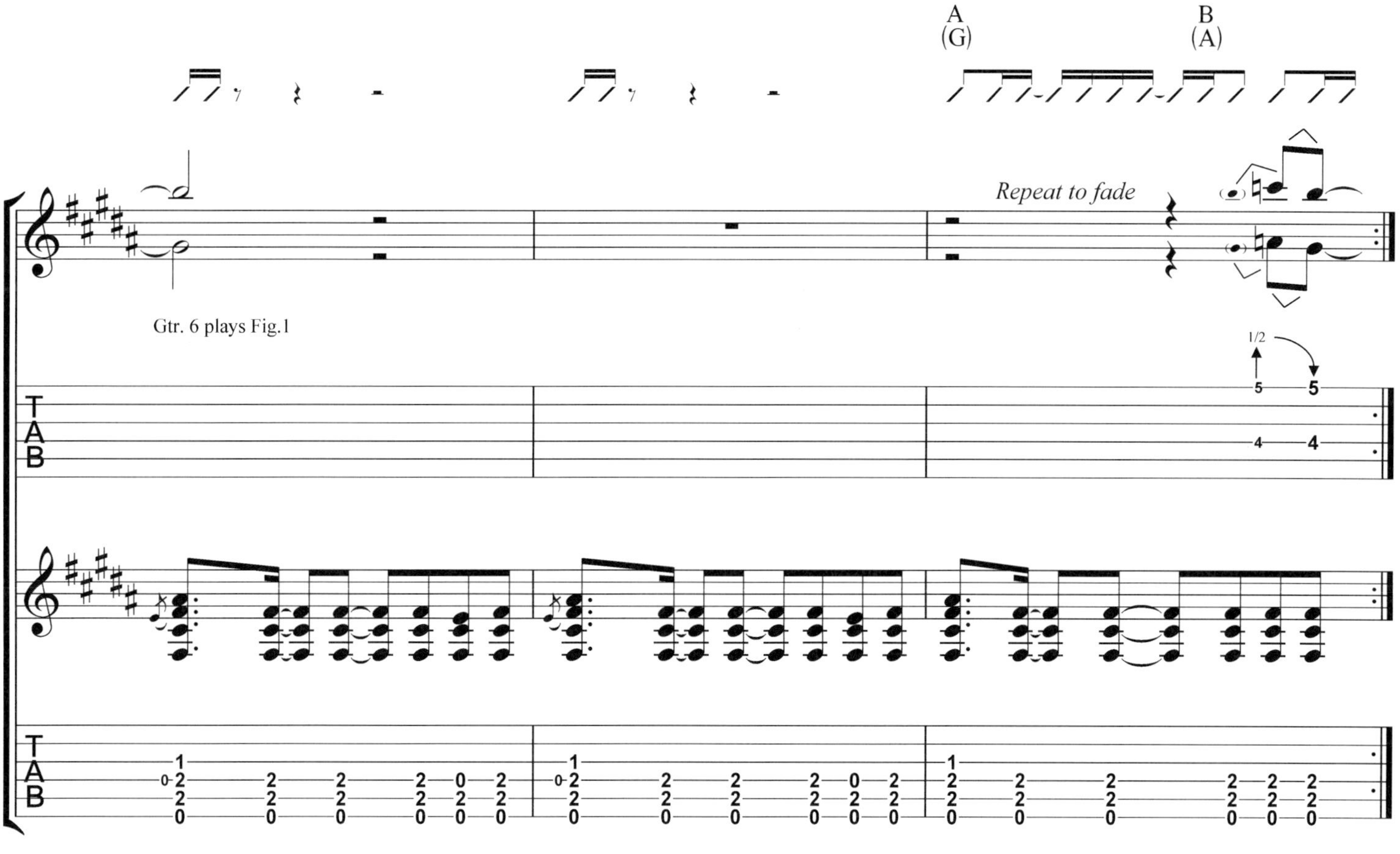

I Started Something I Couldn't Finish

Words & Music by
Morrissey & Johnny Marr

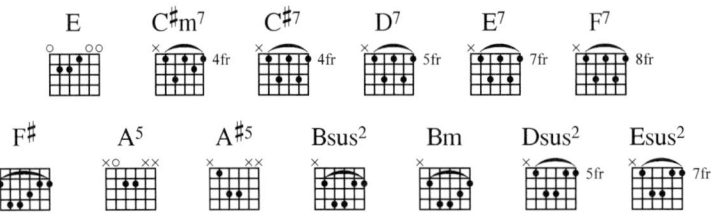

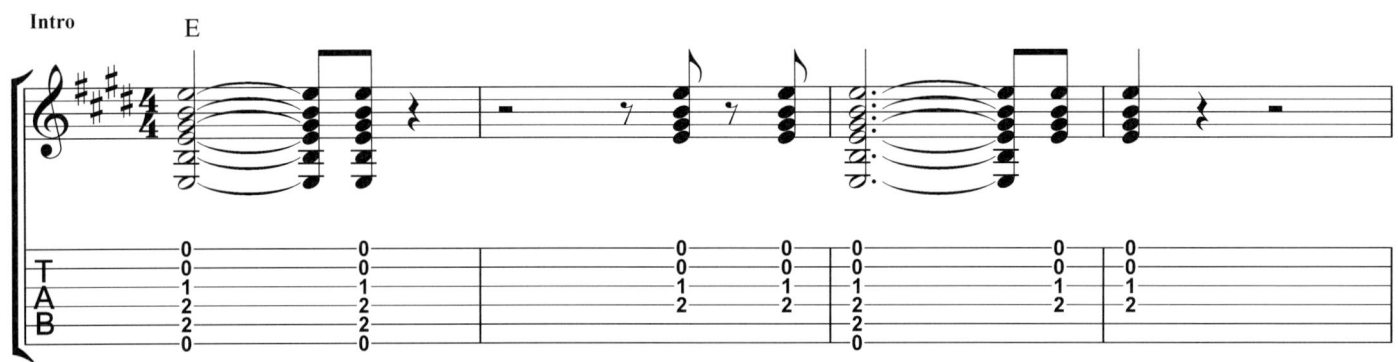

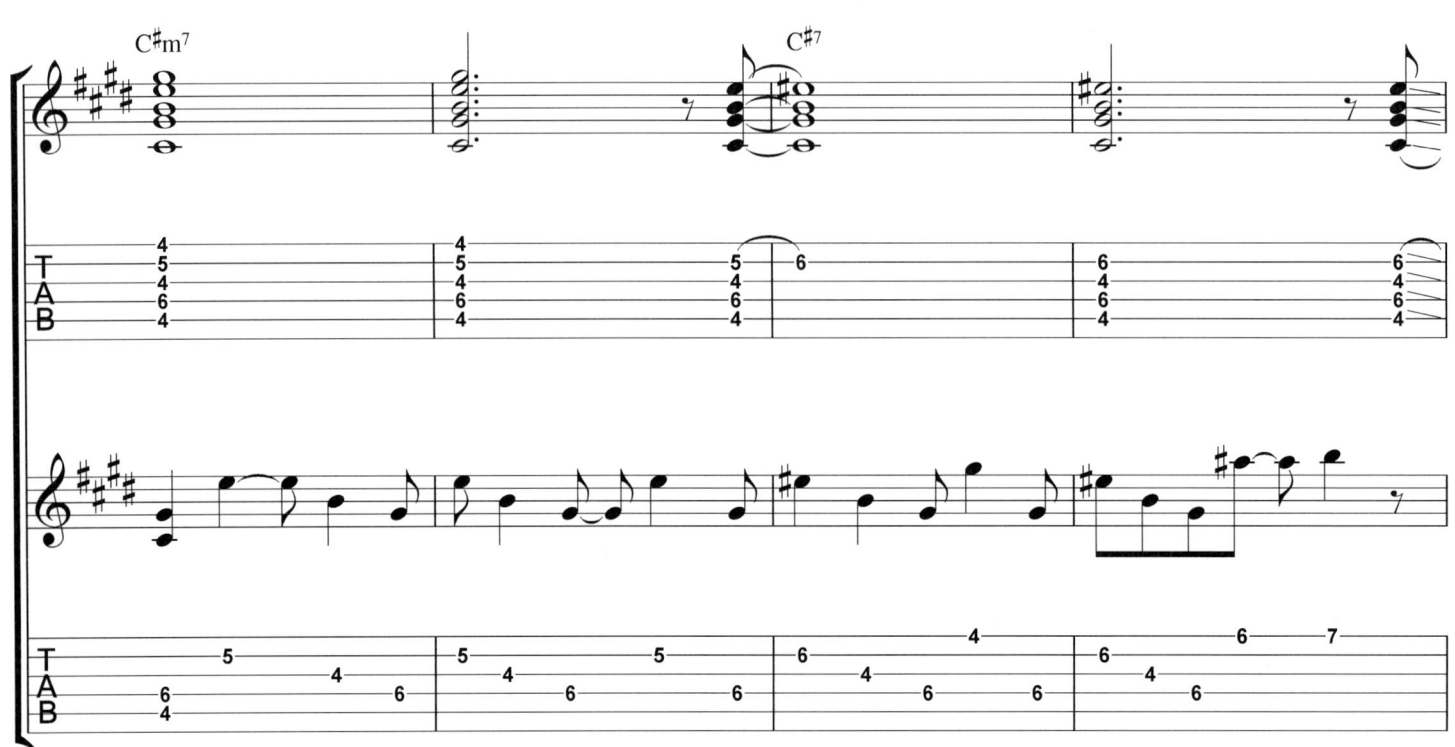

D7 E7 F7 F♯ A5 A♯5
Verse
Bsus2 Bm Dsus2 Esus2
1. The lanes_ were si - lent, there was no - thing, no_ no - thing___ a - round_ for miles._
(2.) grabbed you by__ the guild - ed___ beams, uur,______ that's what tra - di - tion means._
(3.) grabbed you by__ the guild - ed beams, uur, that's what tra - di - tion means._

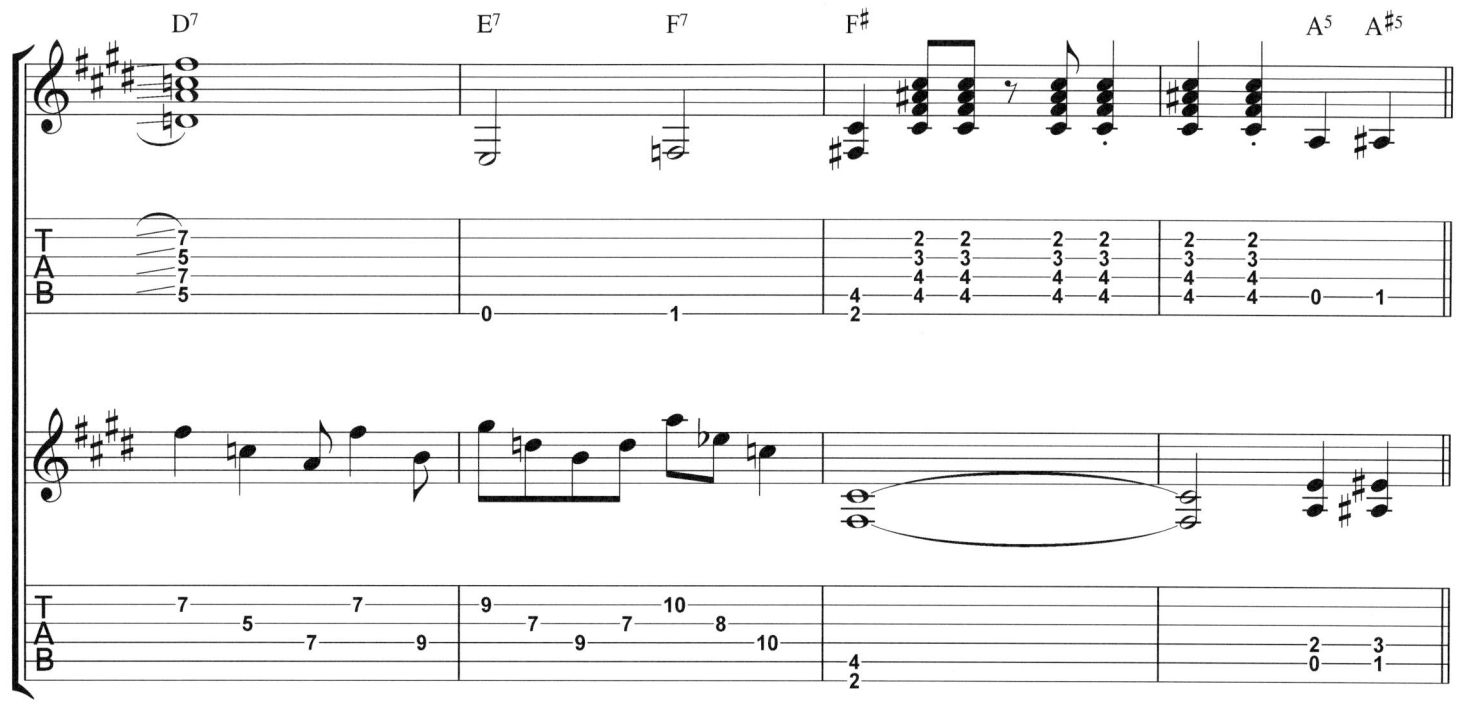

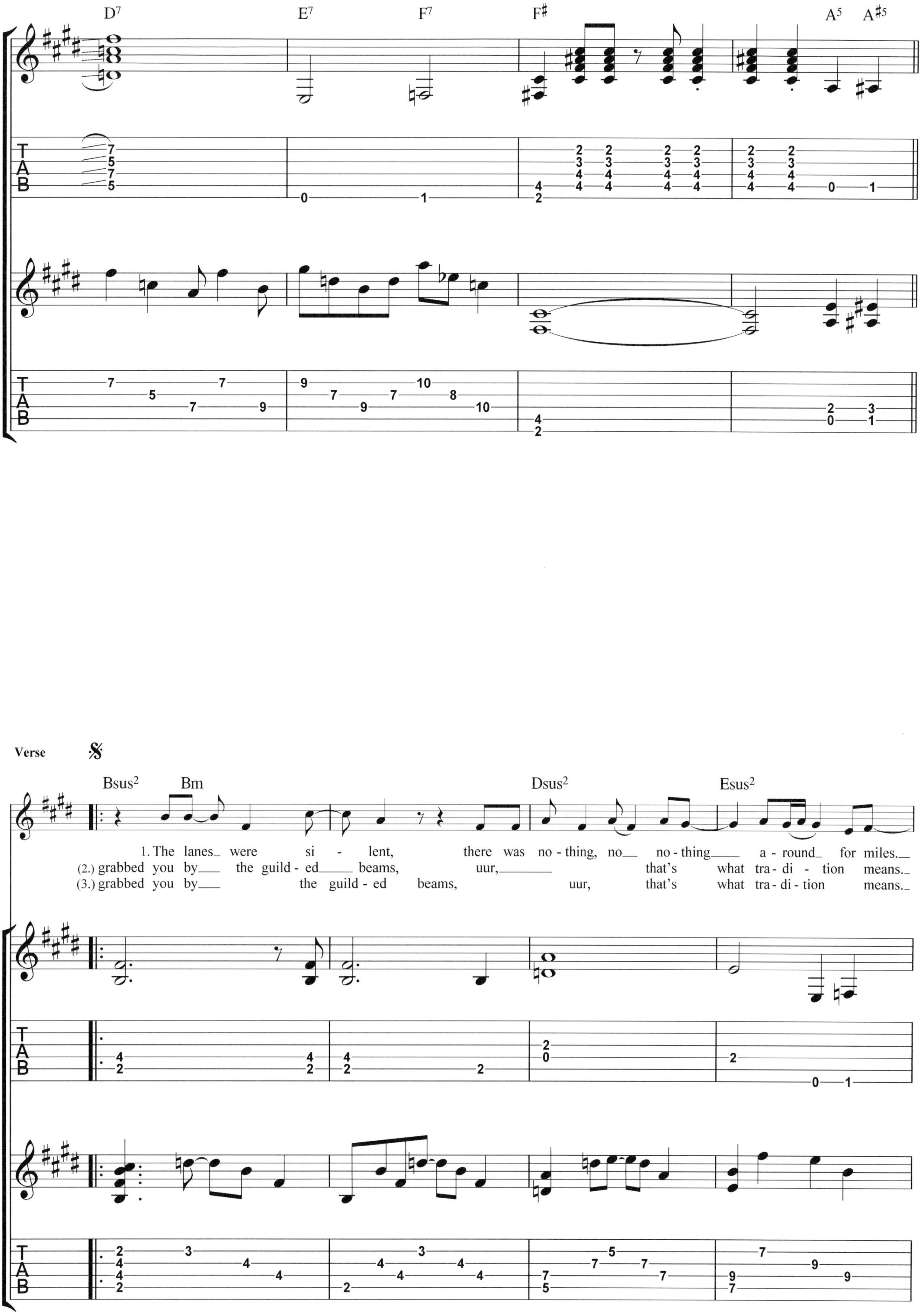

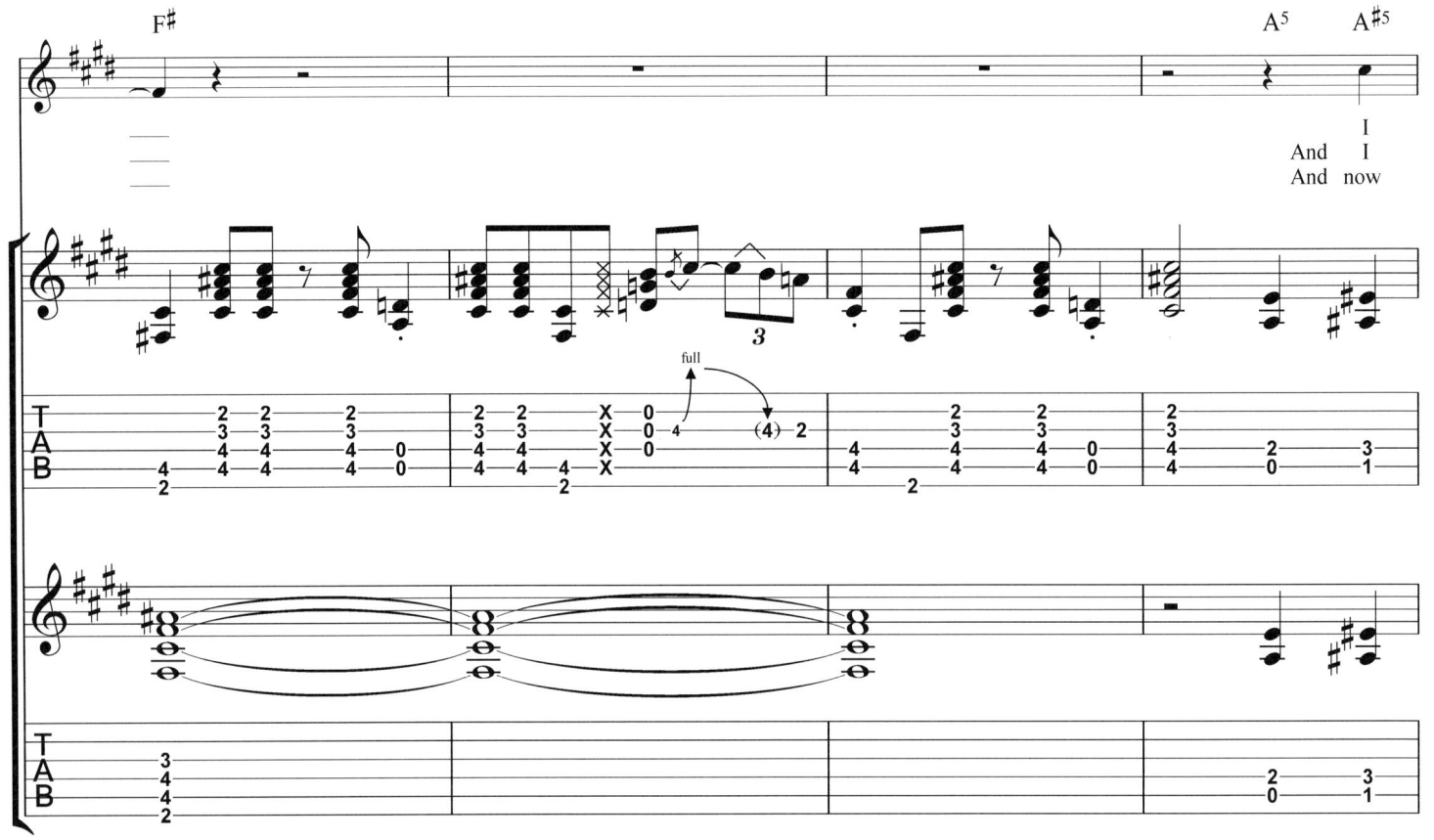

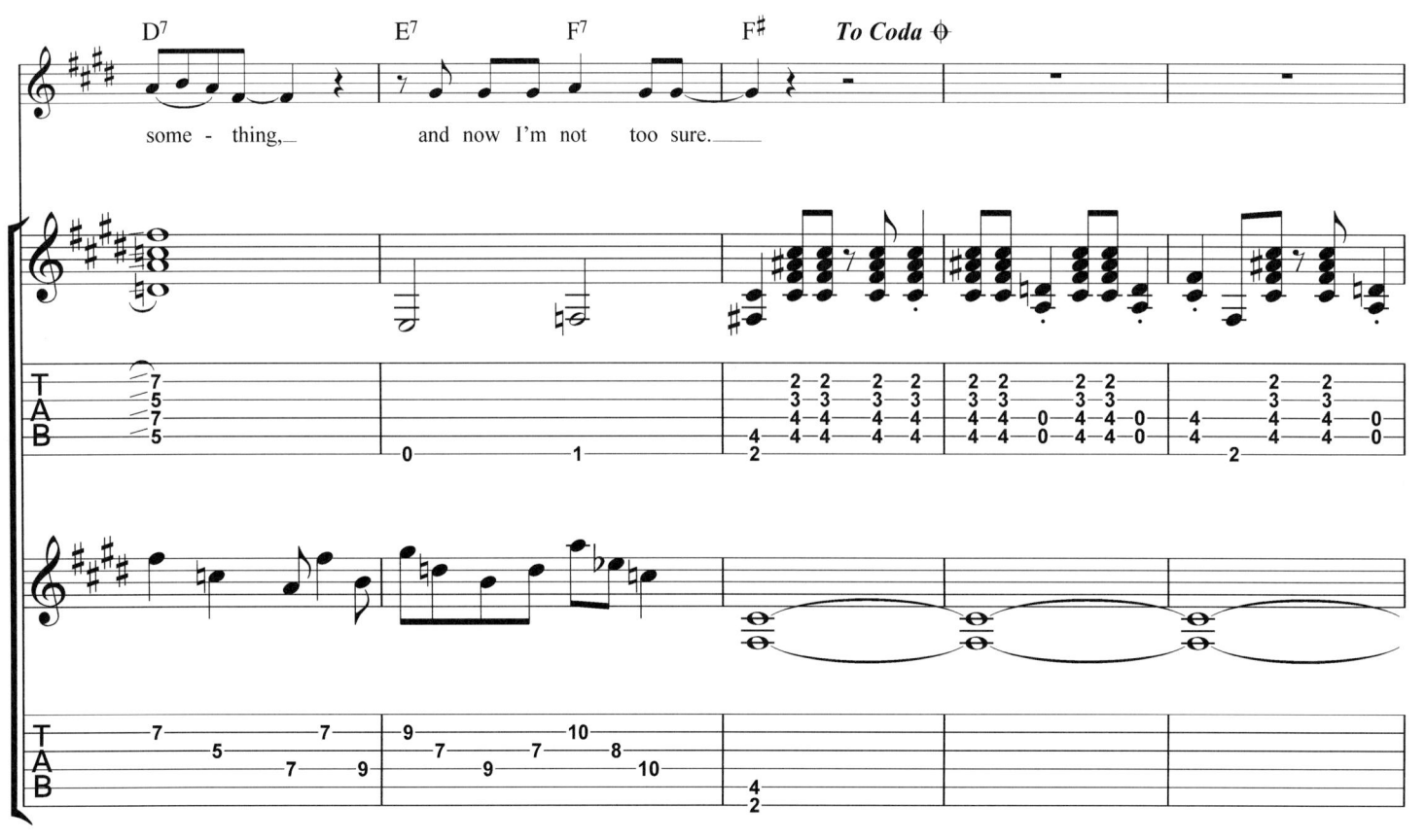

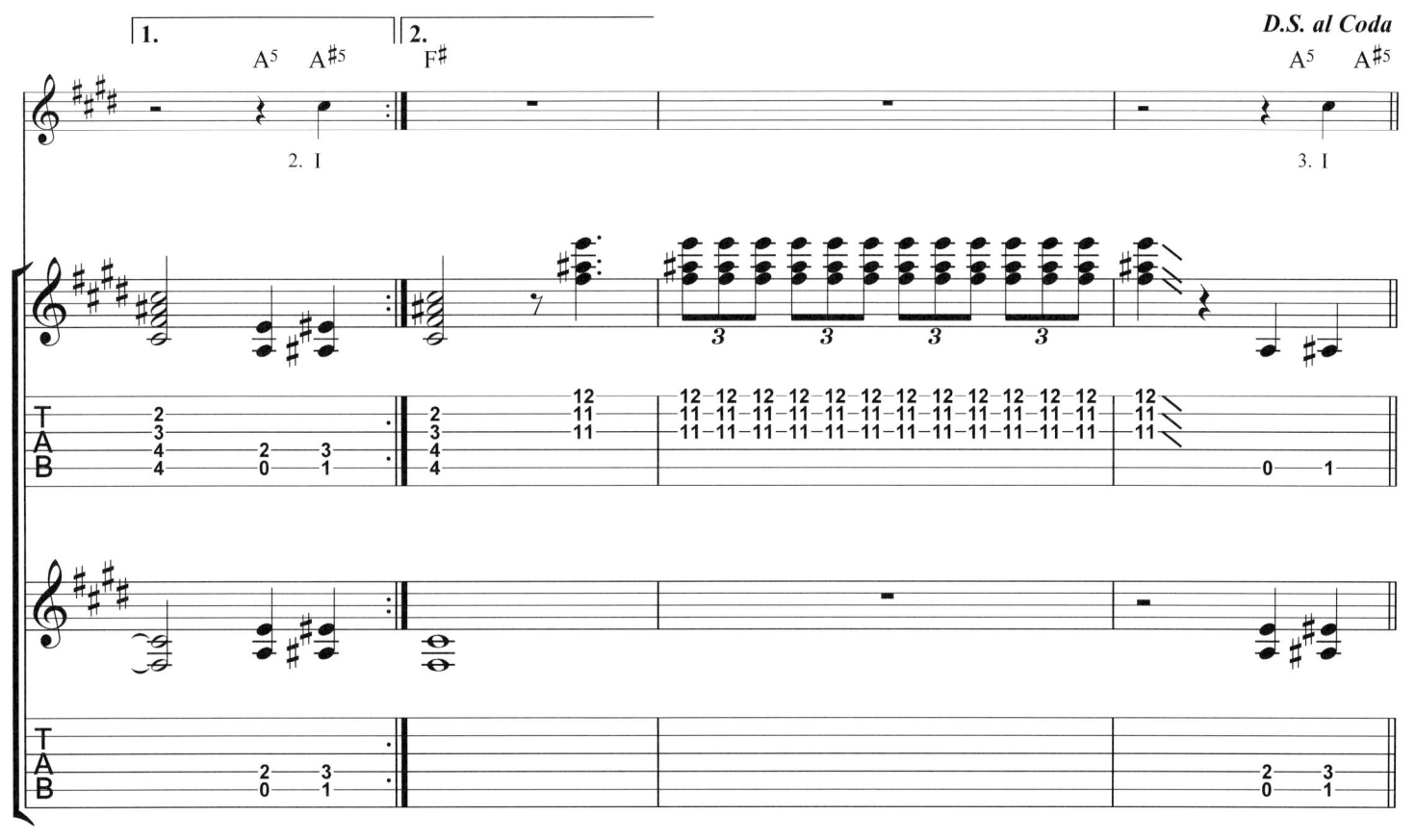
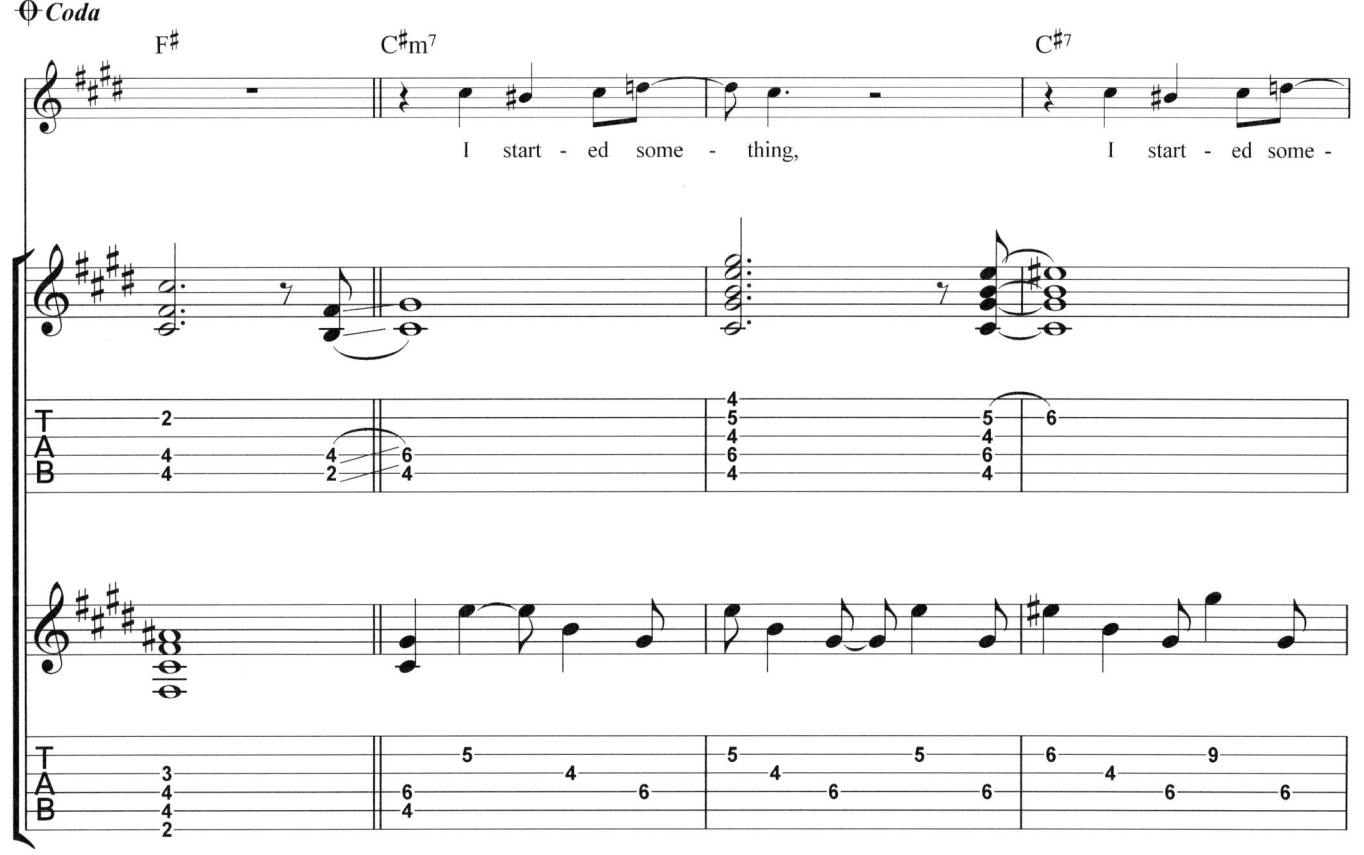

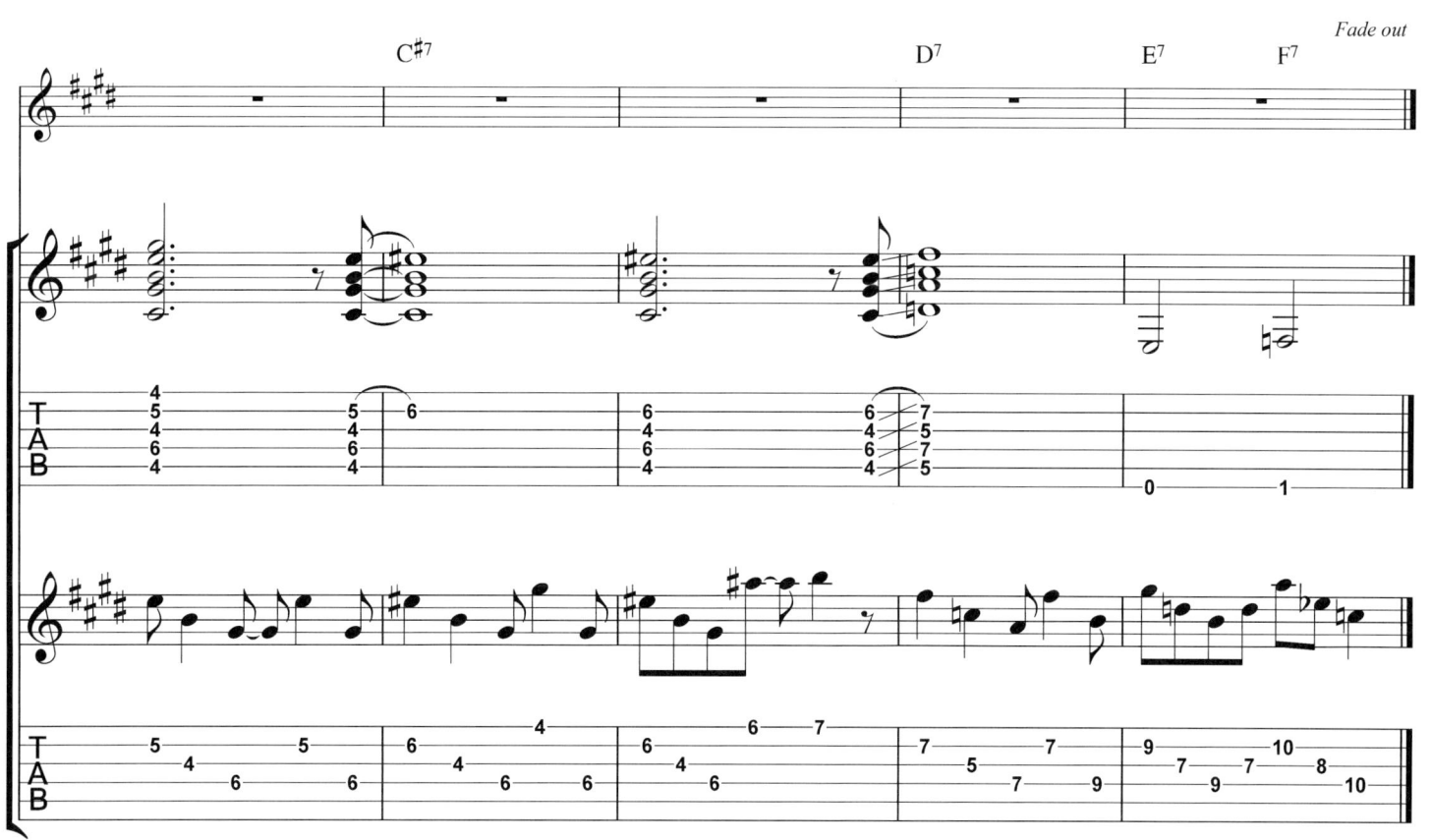

Last Night I Dreamt That Somebody Loved Me

Words & Music by
Morrissey & Johnny Marr

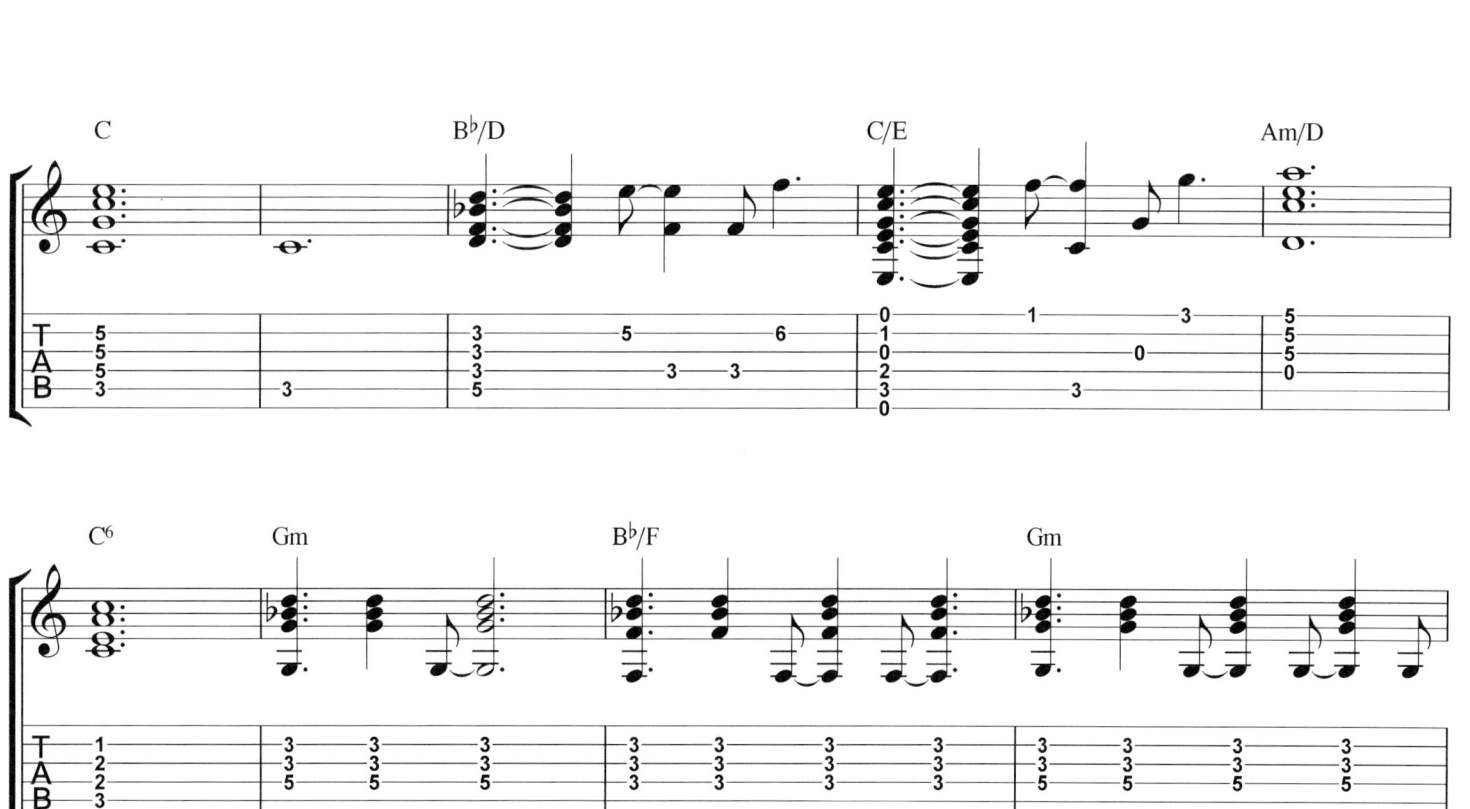
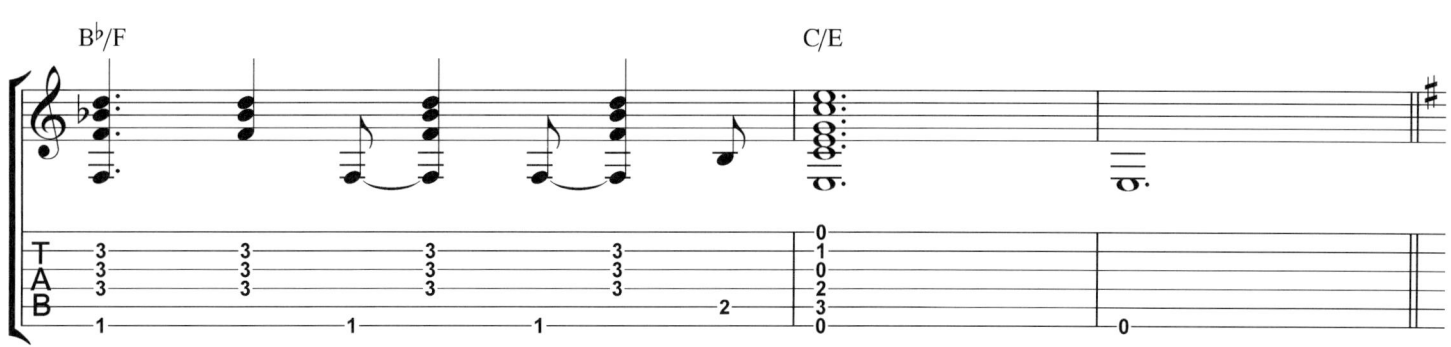
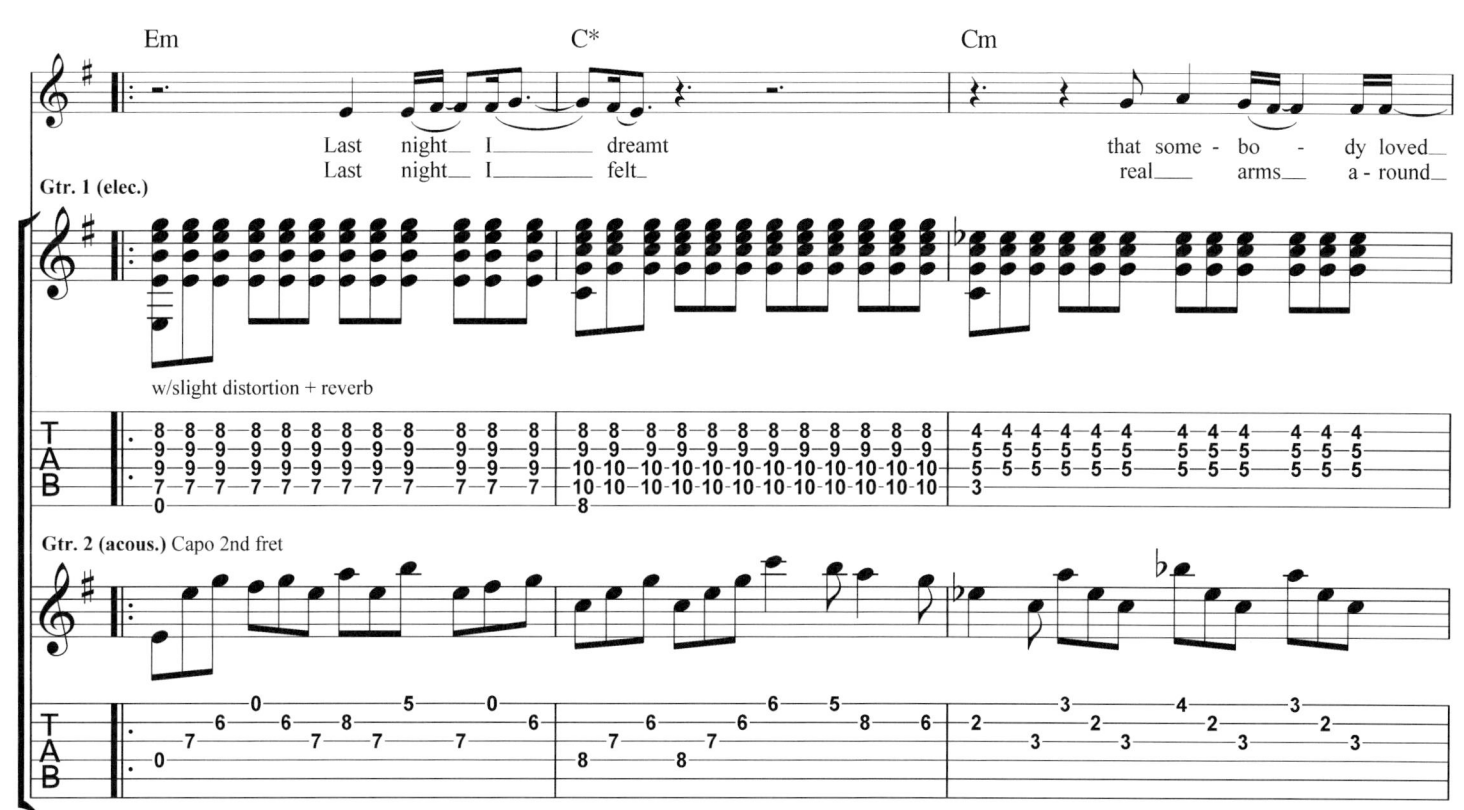

65

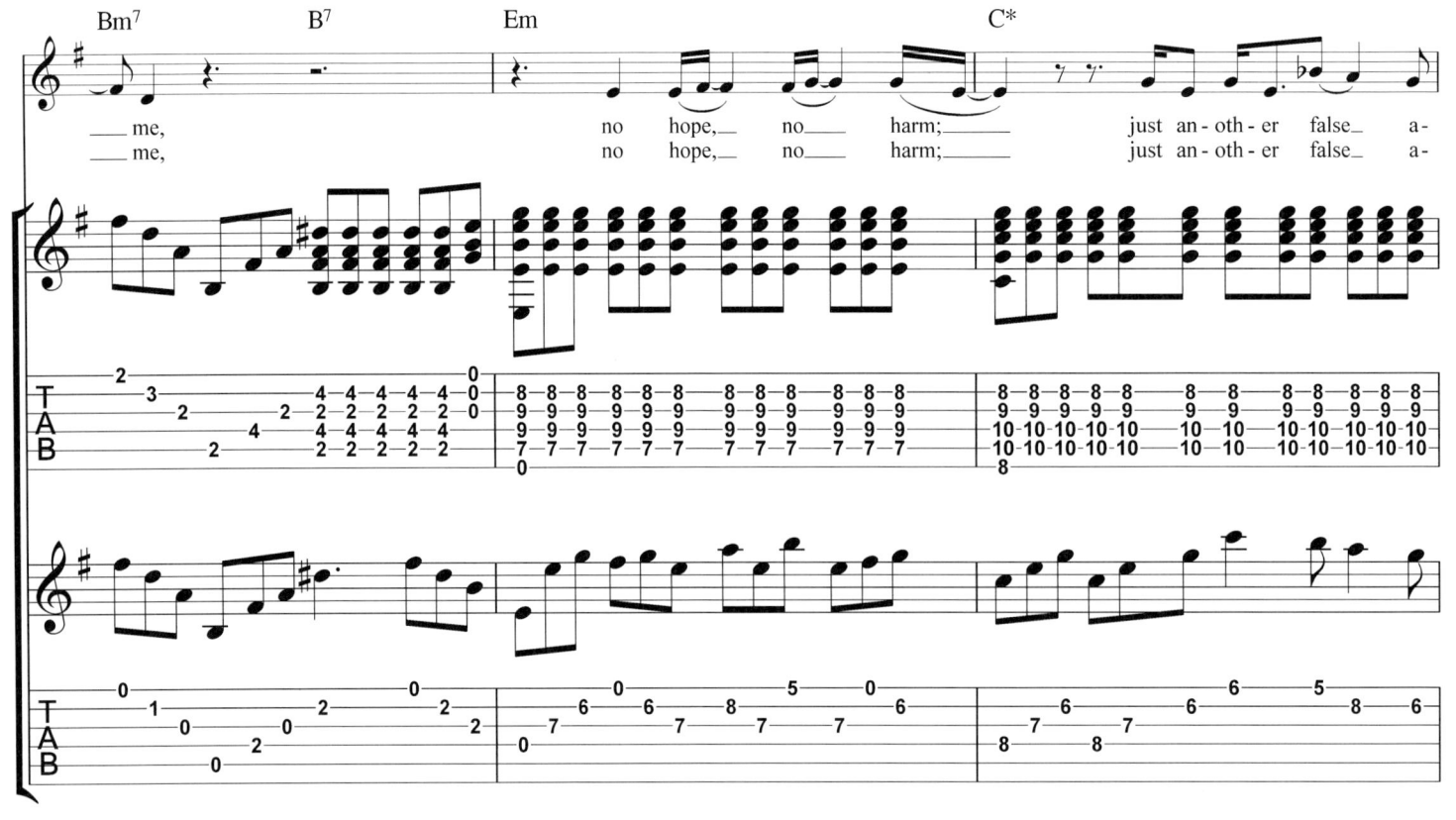
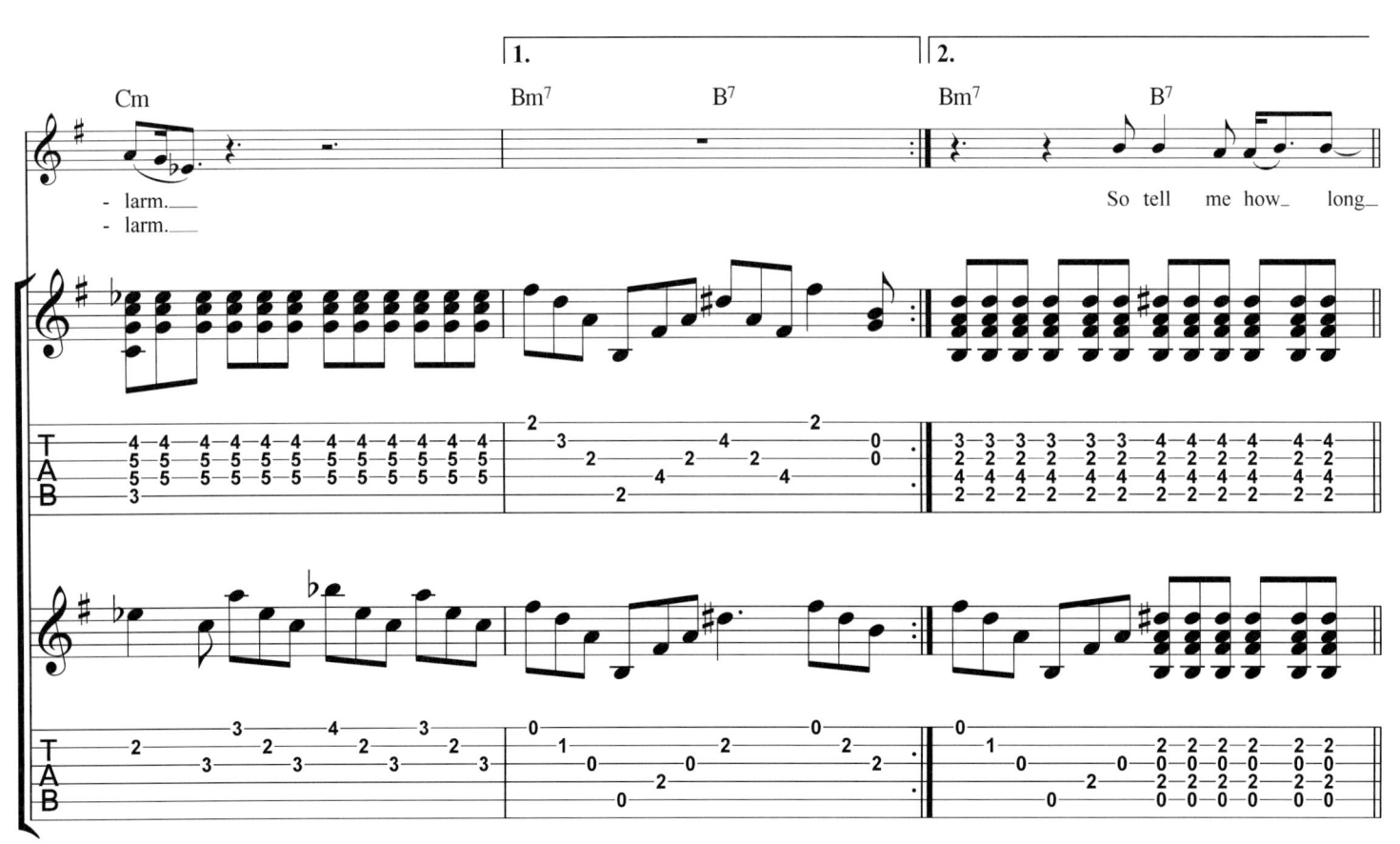

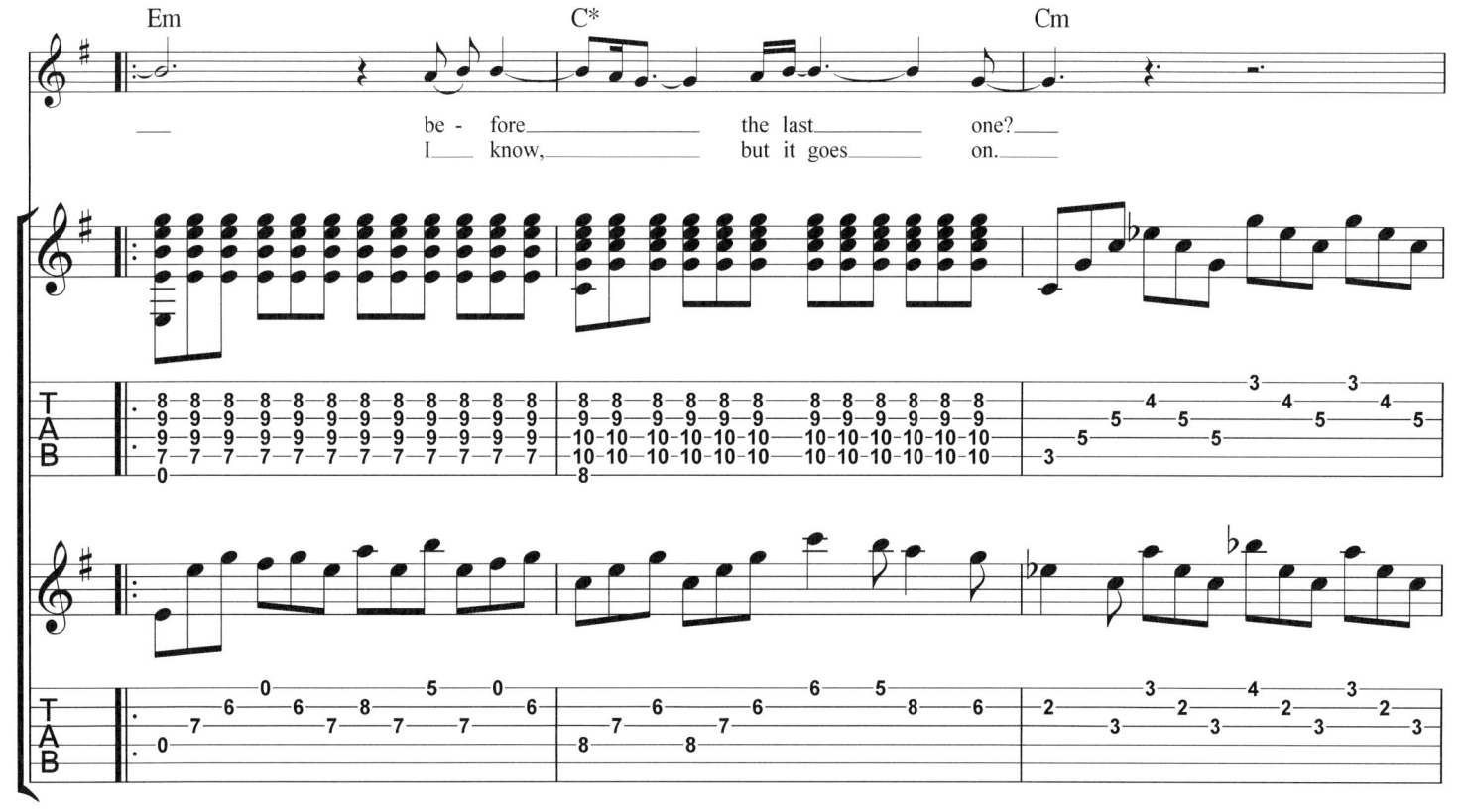
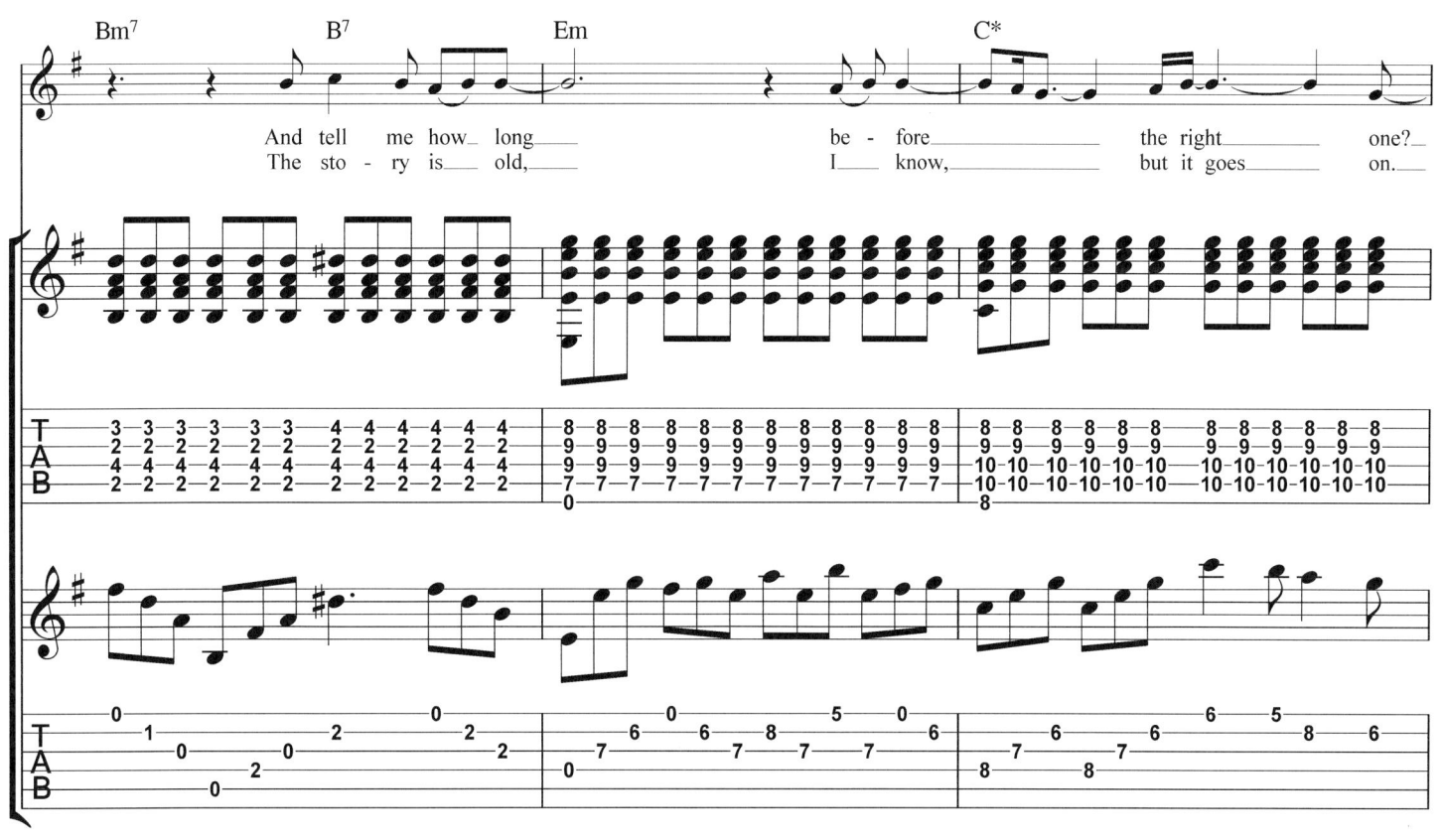

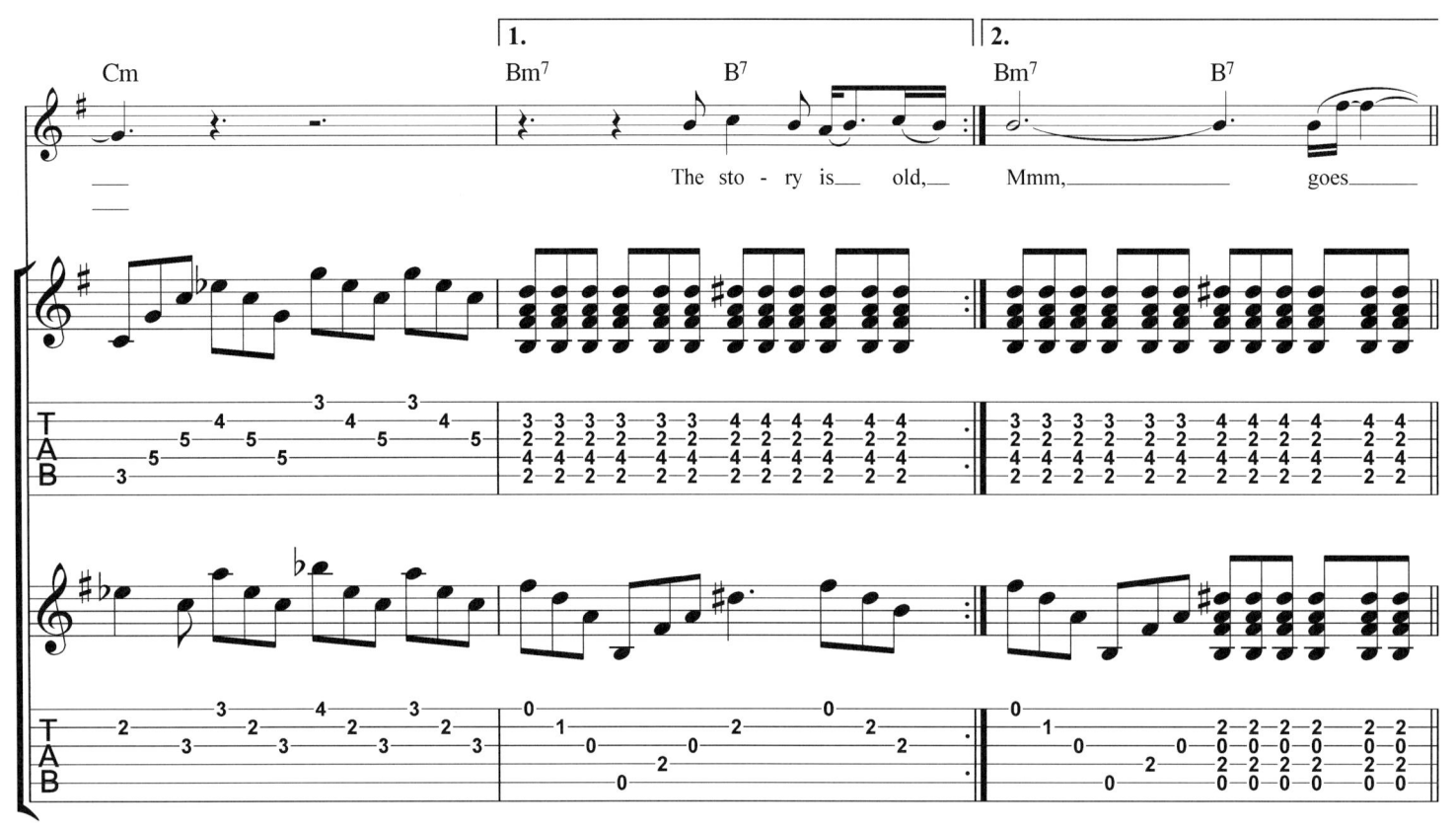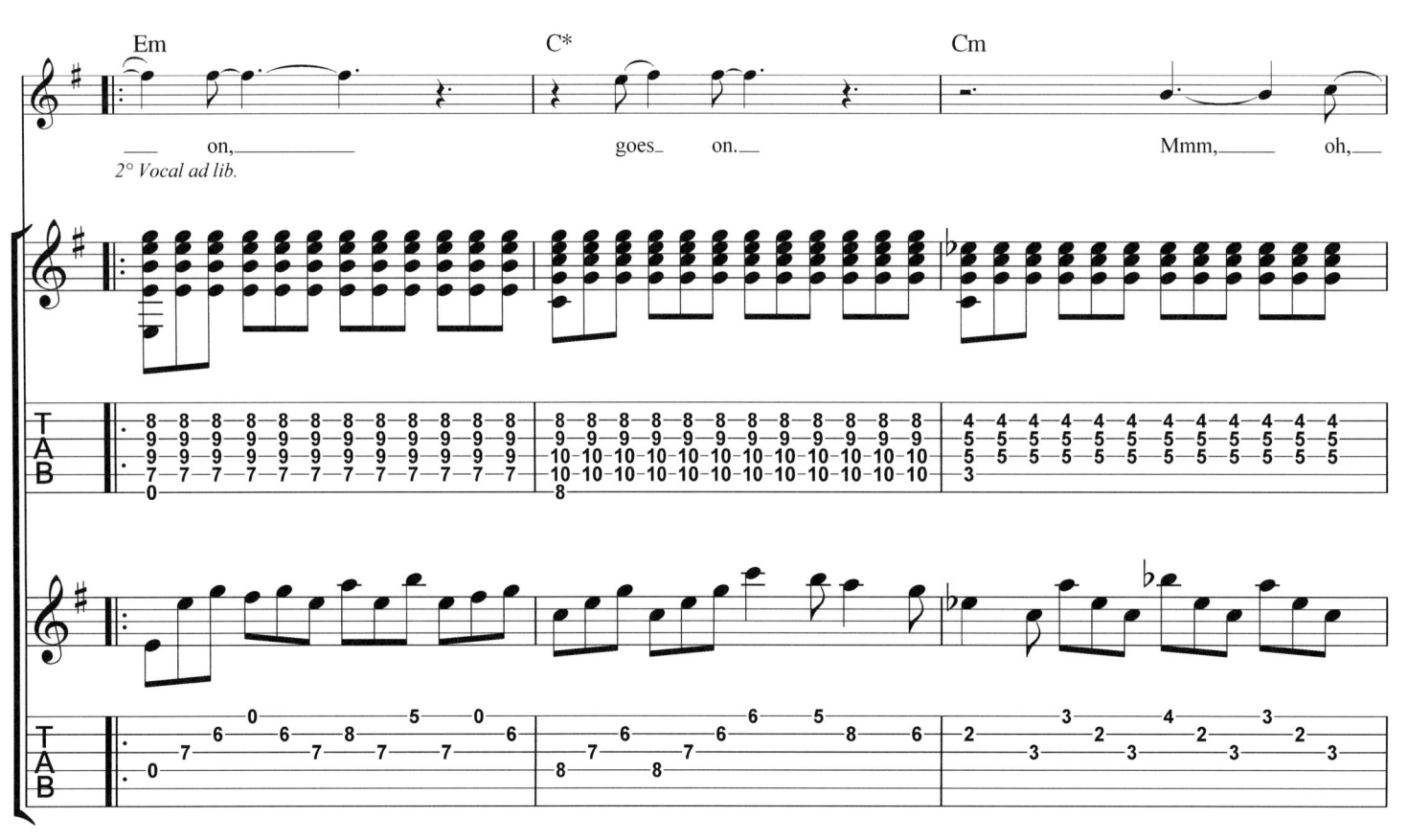

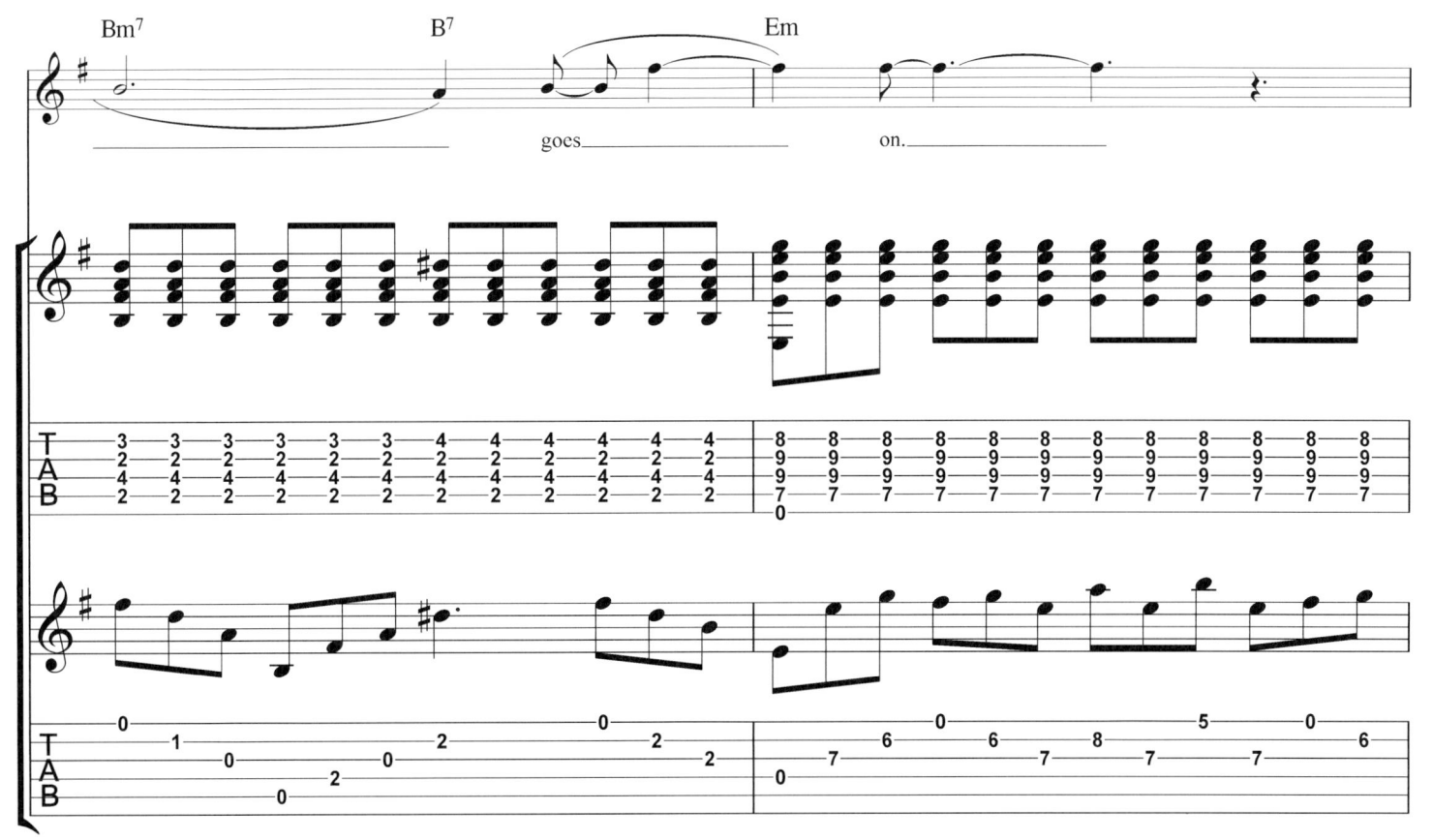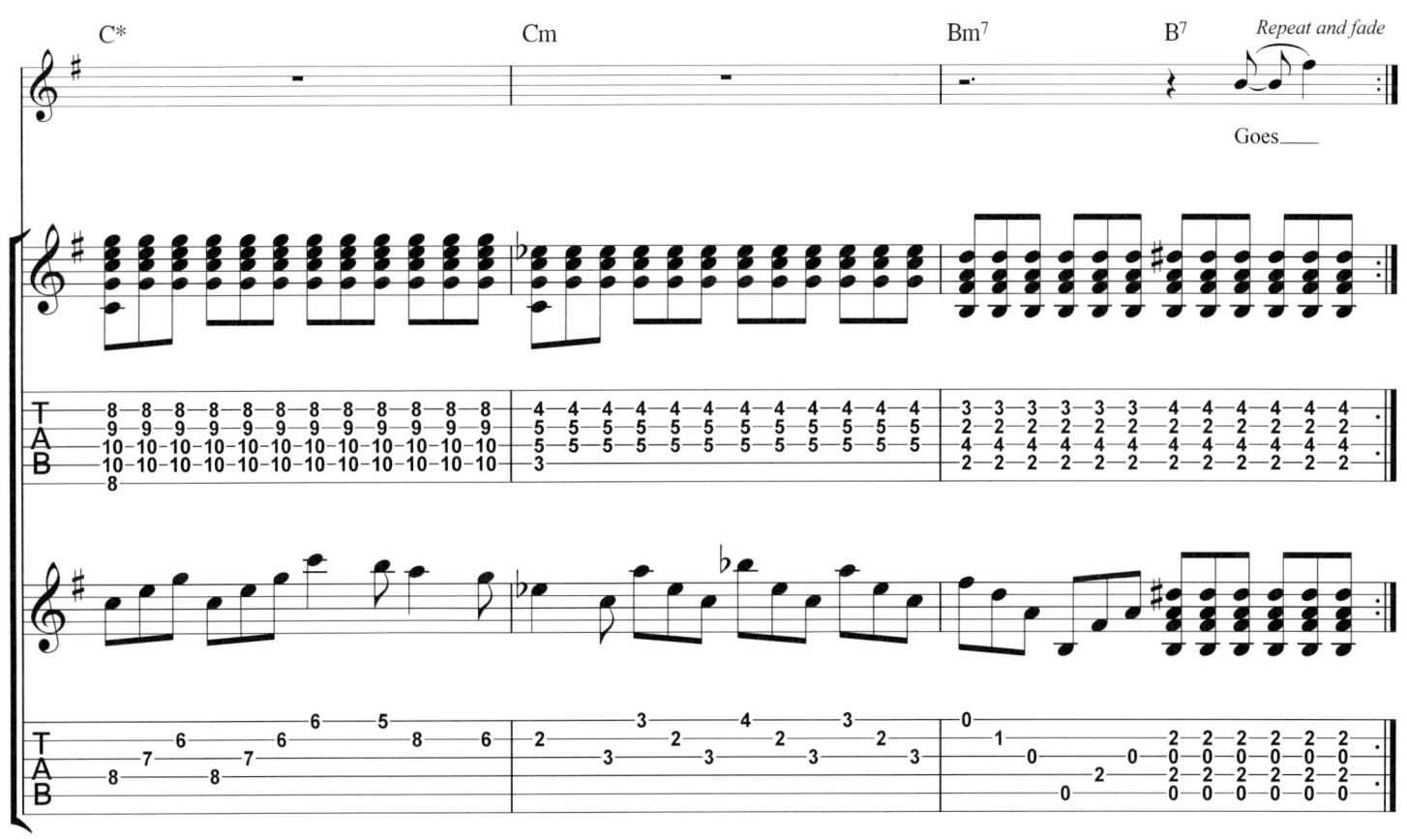

Panic

**Words & Music by
Morrissey & Johnny Marr**

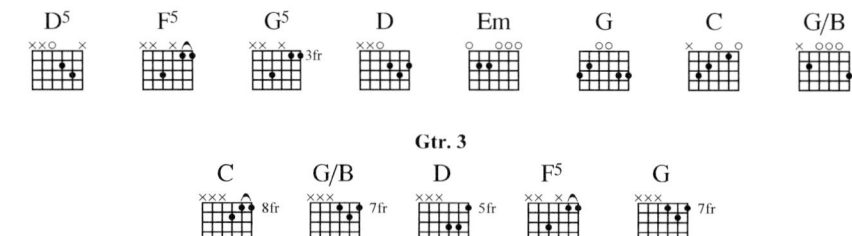

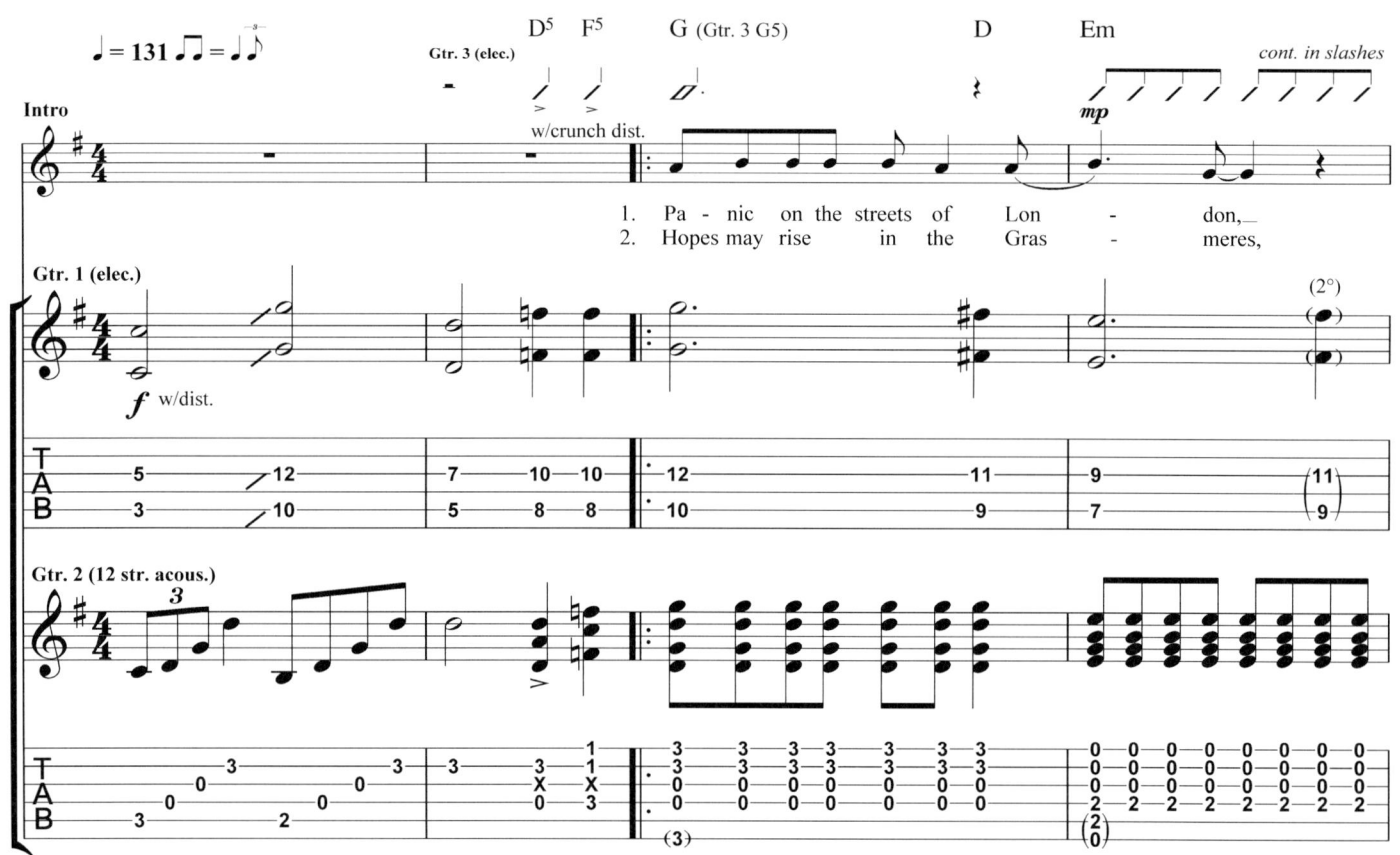

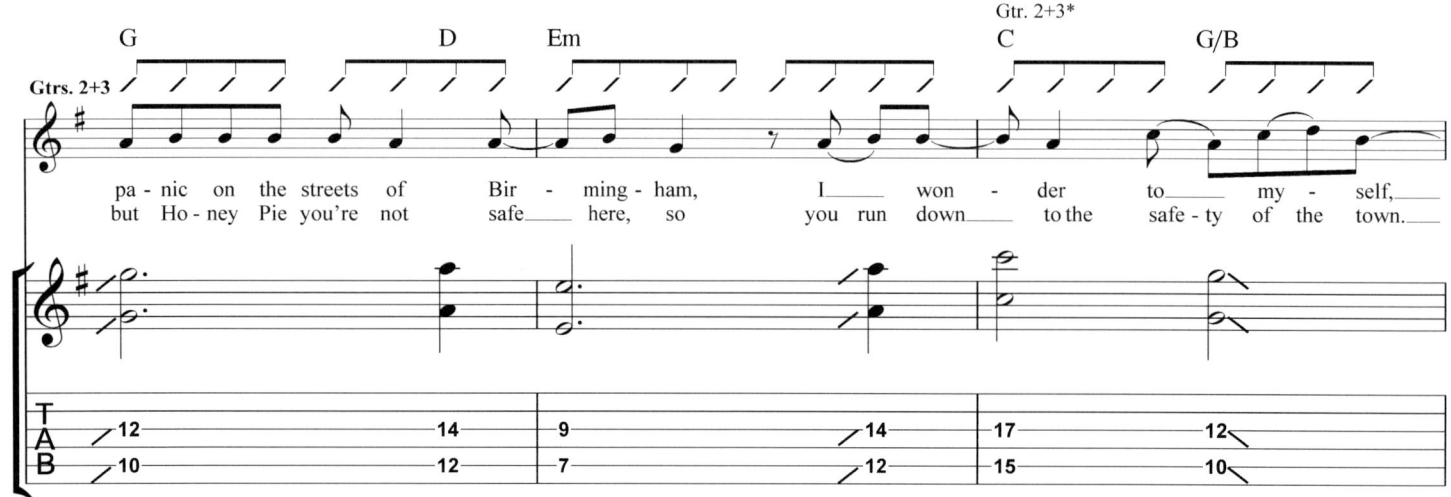

© Copyright 1986 Marr Songs Limited/Artane Music Incorporated.
Chrysalis Music Limited (50%)/Universal Music Publishing Limited (50%).
All Rights Reserved. International Copyright Secured.

B♭ ② 11fr
B ② 12fr
C♯ ② 14fr
D ② 15fr
G D Em G D Em
Gtr. 2
cont. sim.
3. Burn down the dis - co, hang the bless - ed D. J. be - cause the
Gtr. 3 tacet
Gtr. 2 + 3*
even ♪s
G/B D G D Em
mu - sic that they con - stant - ly play, it says no - thing to me a - bout my life.
* Gtr. 3 plays held chords (see chords boxes)
G D Em C G/B D F5
Hang the bless - ed D. J. be - cause the mu - sic they con - stant - ly play on the

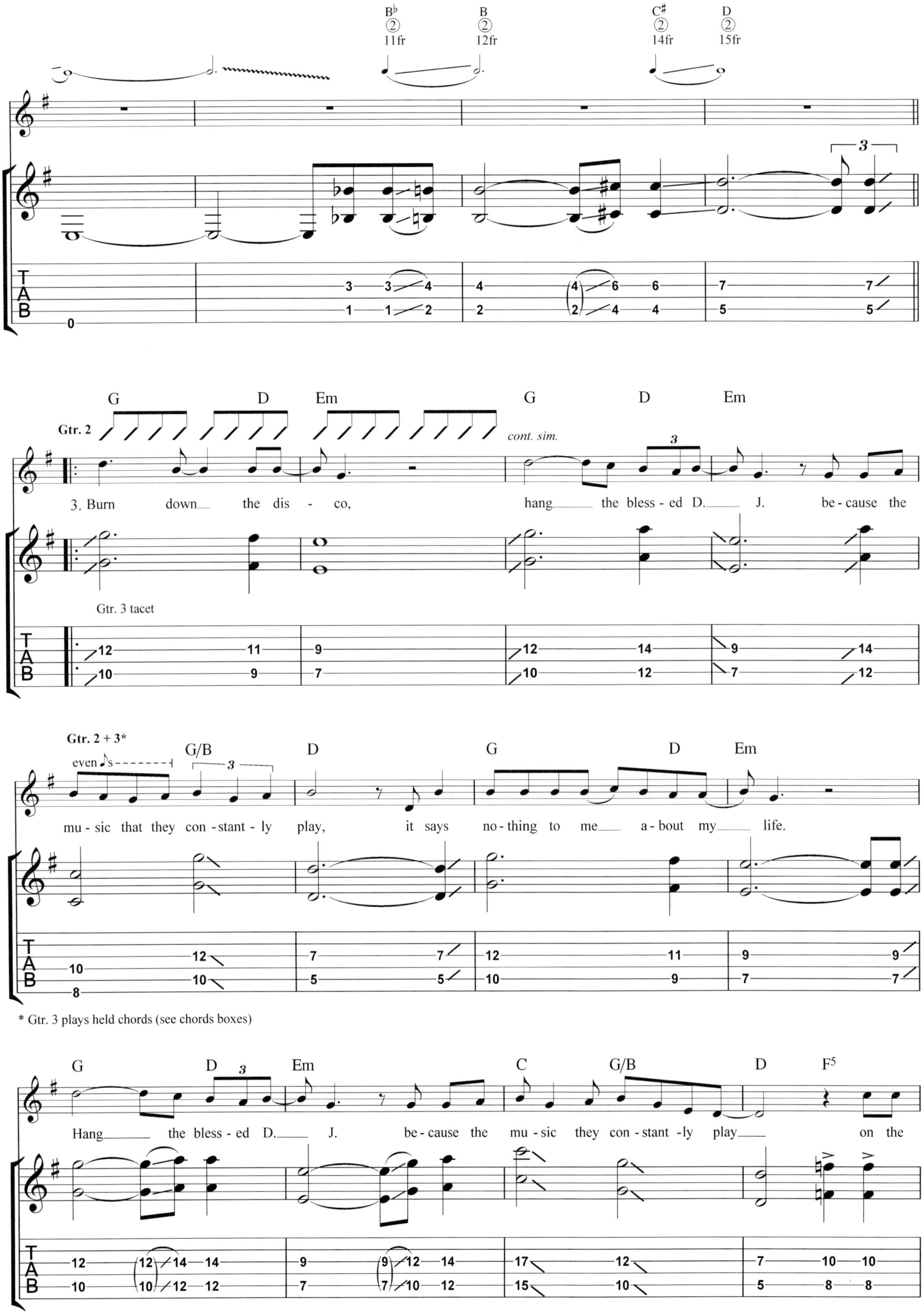

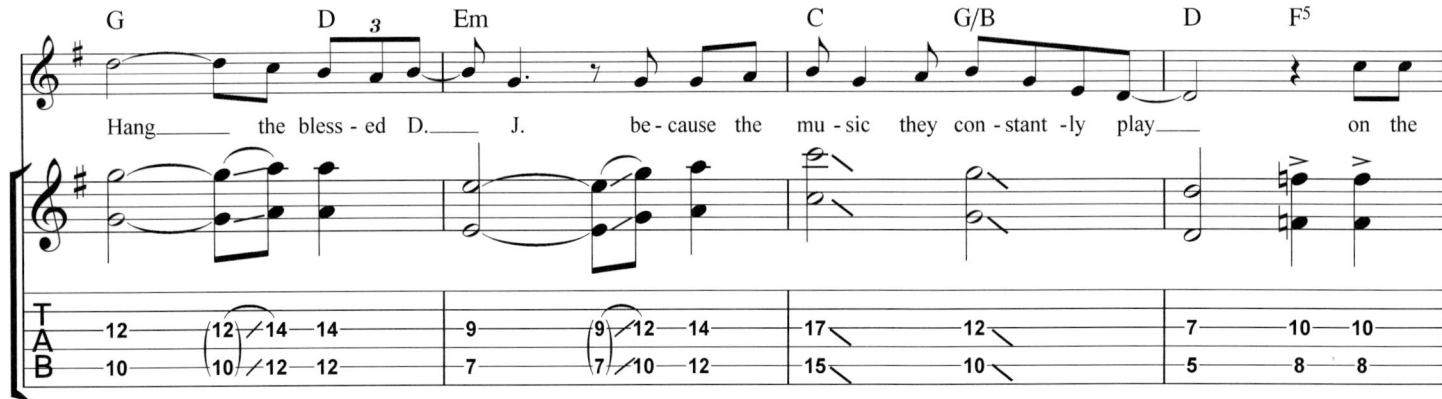

Shakespeare's Sister

Words & Music by
Morrissey & Johnny Marr

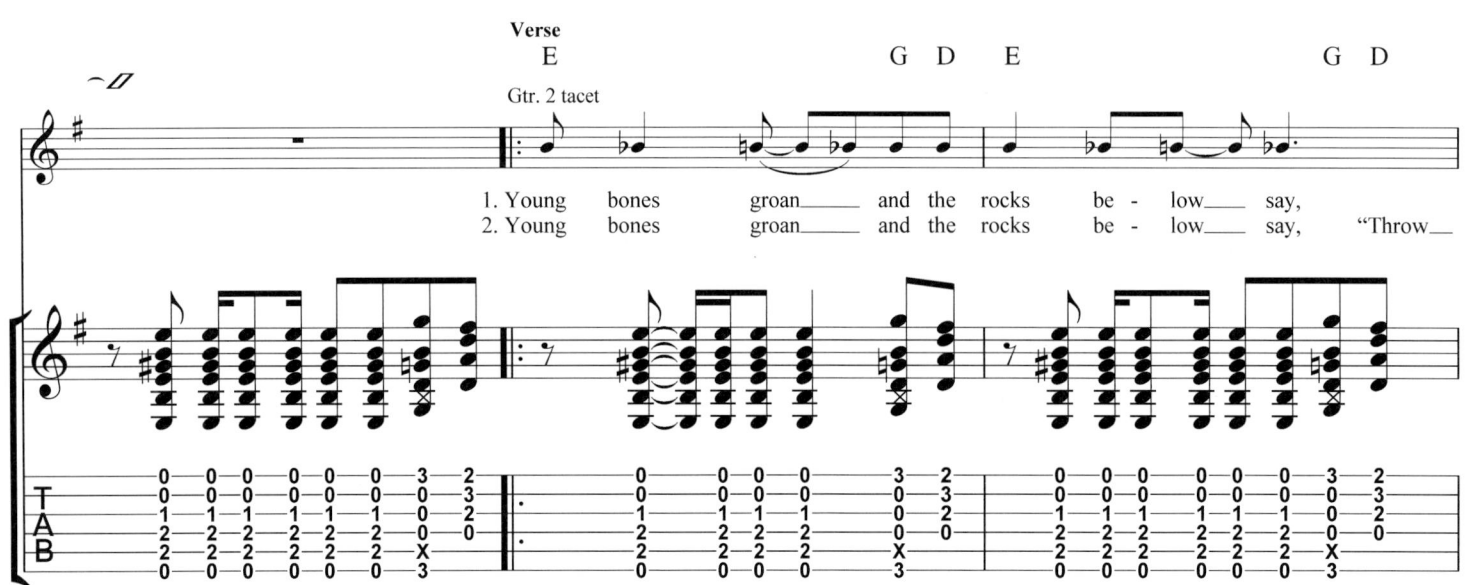

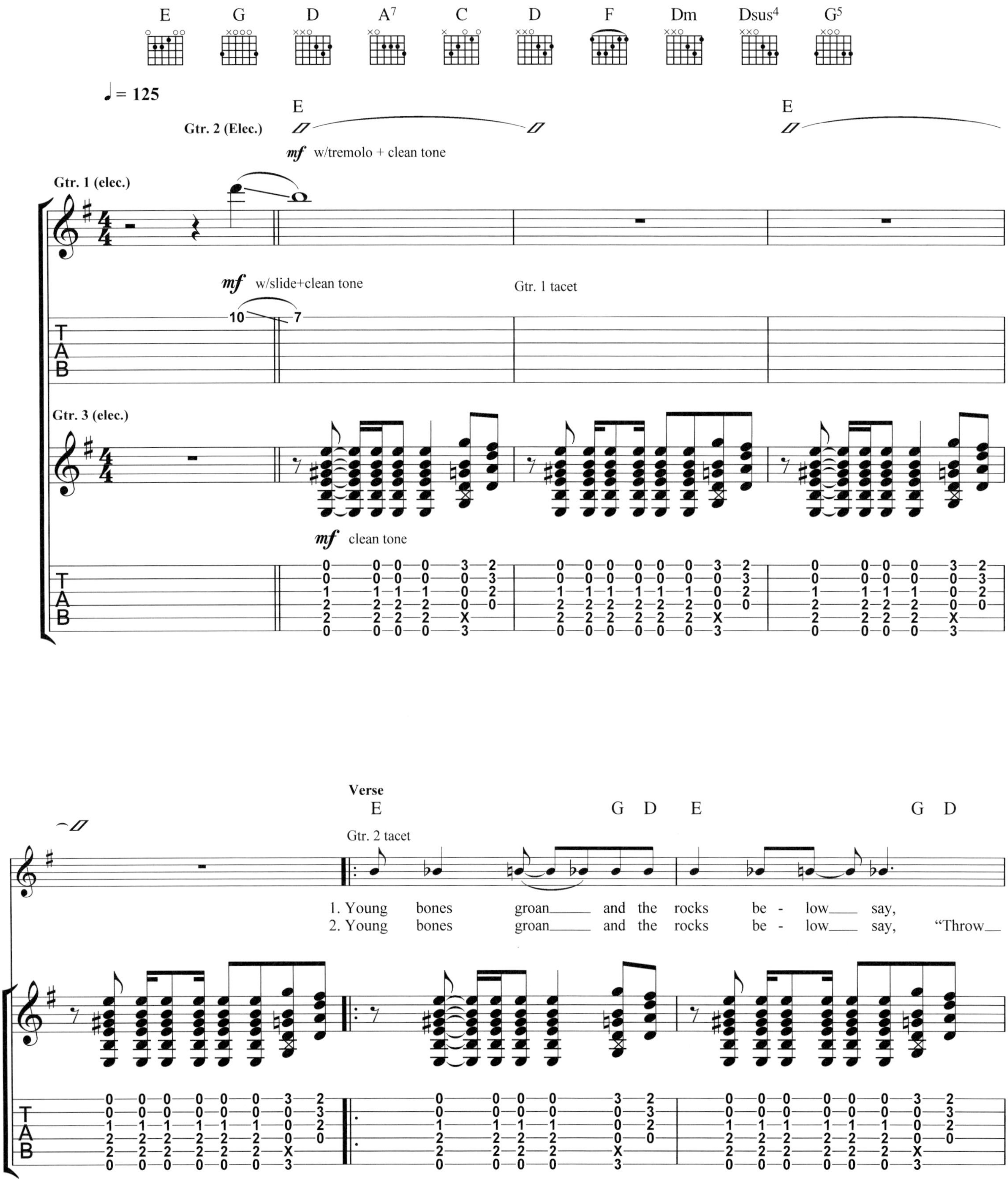

E G D E G D A7
"Throw your skin - ny bo - dy down son." But I'm go - ing to meet the one I love,
your white bo - dy down." But I'm go - ing to meet the one I love,
Gtr. 1
w/slide
C D E
Gtr. 2 (elec.)
so please don't stand in my way. Be - cause I'm
at last, at last, at last. I'm

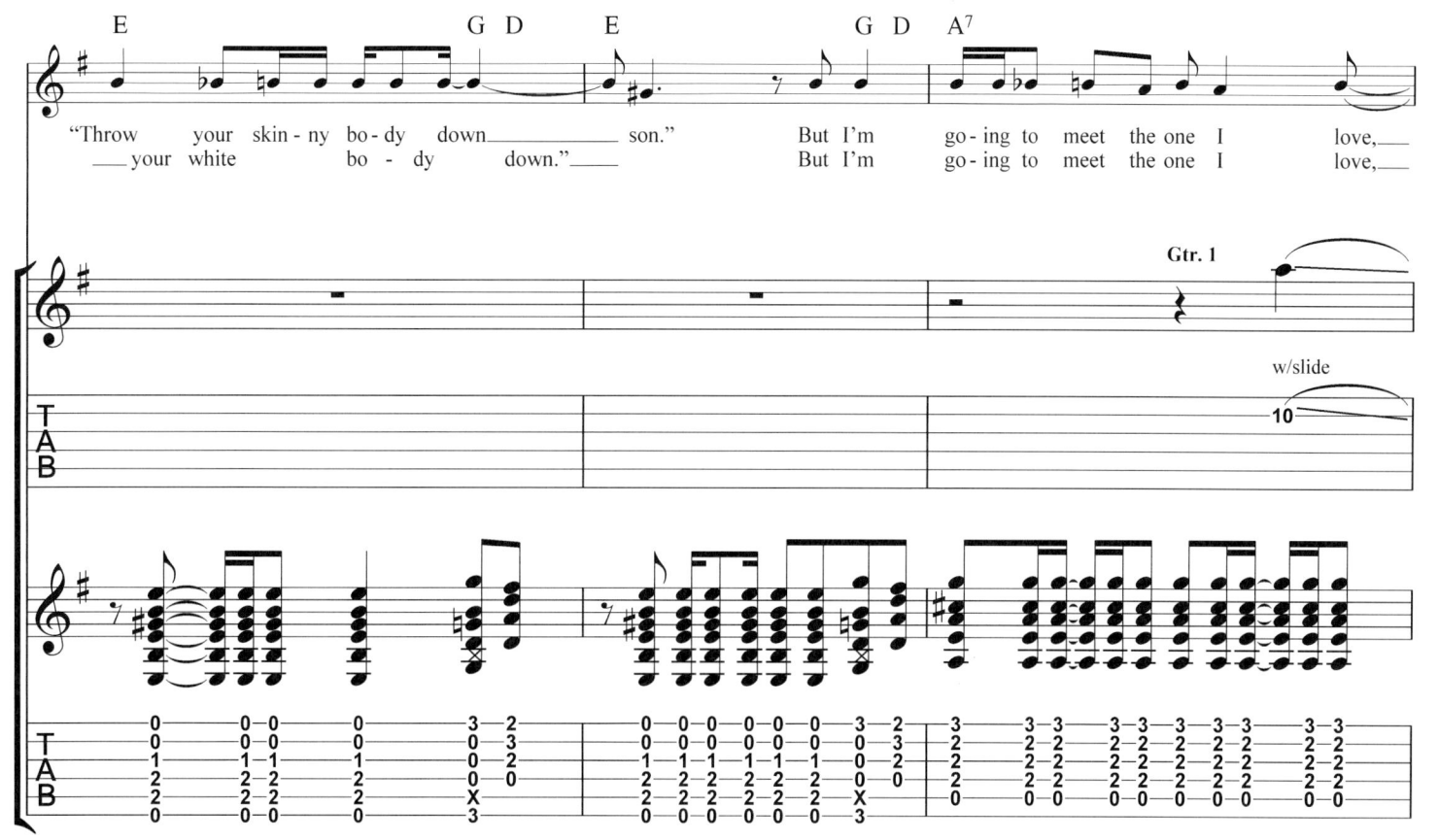

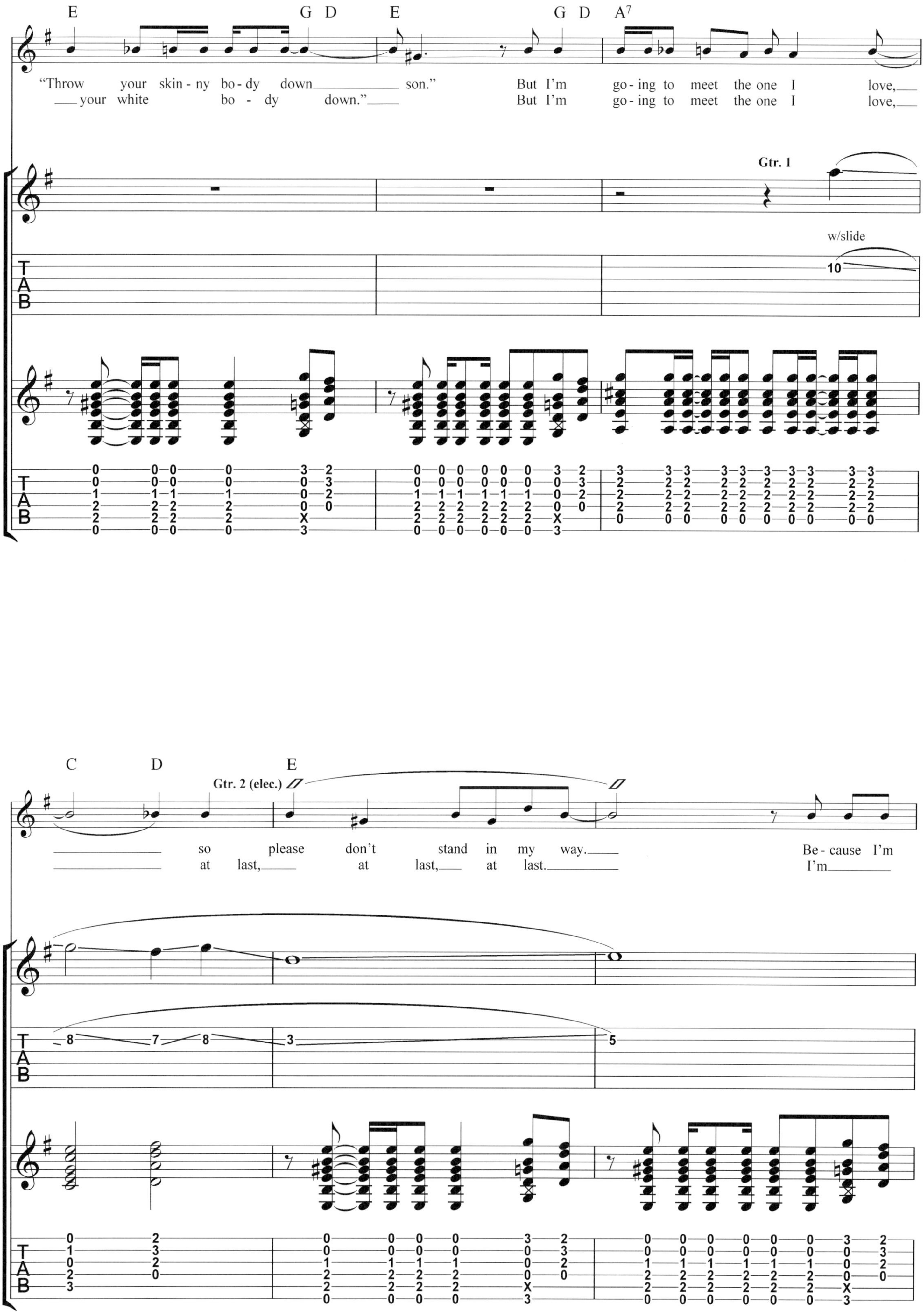

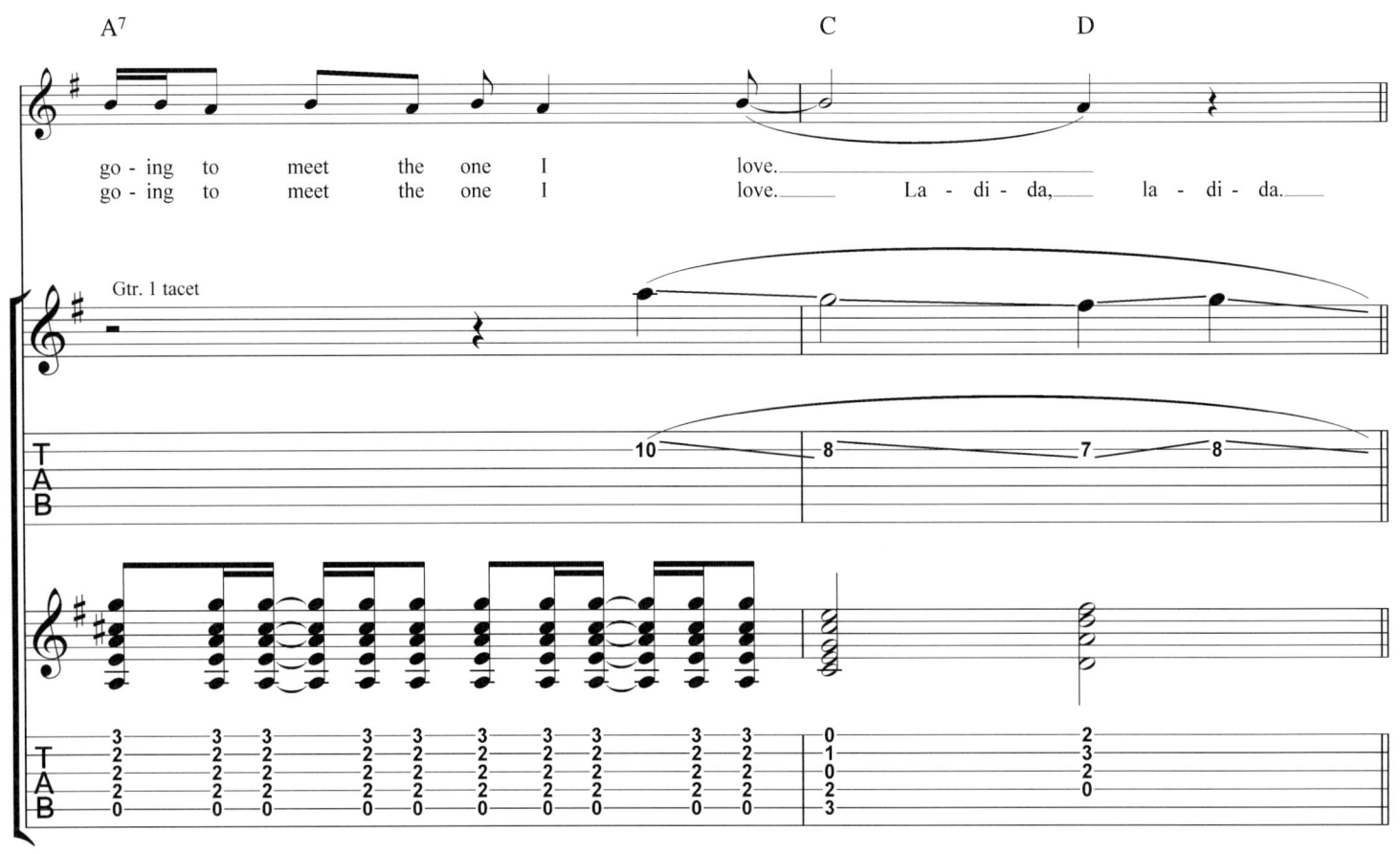

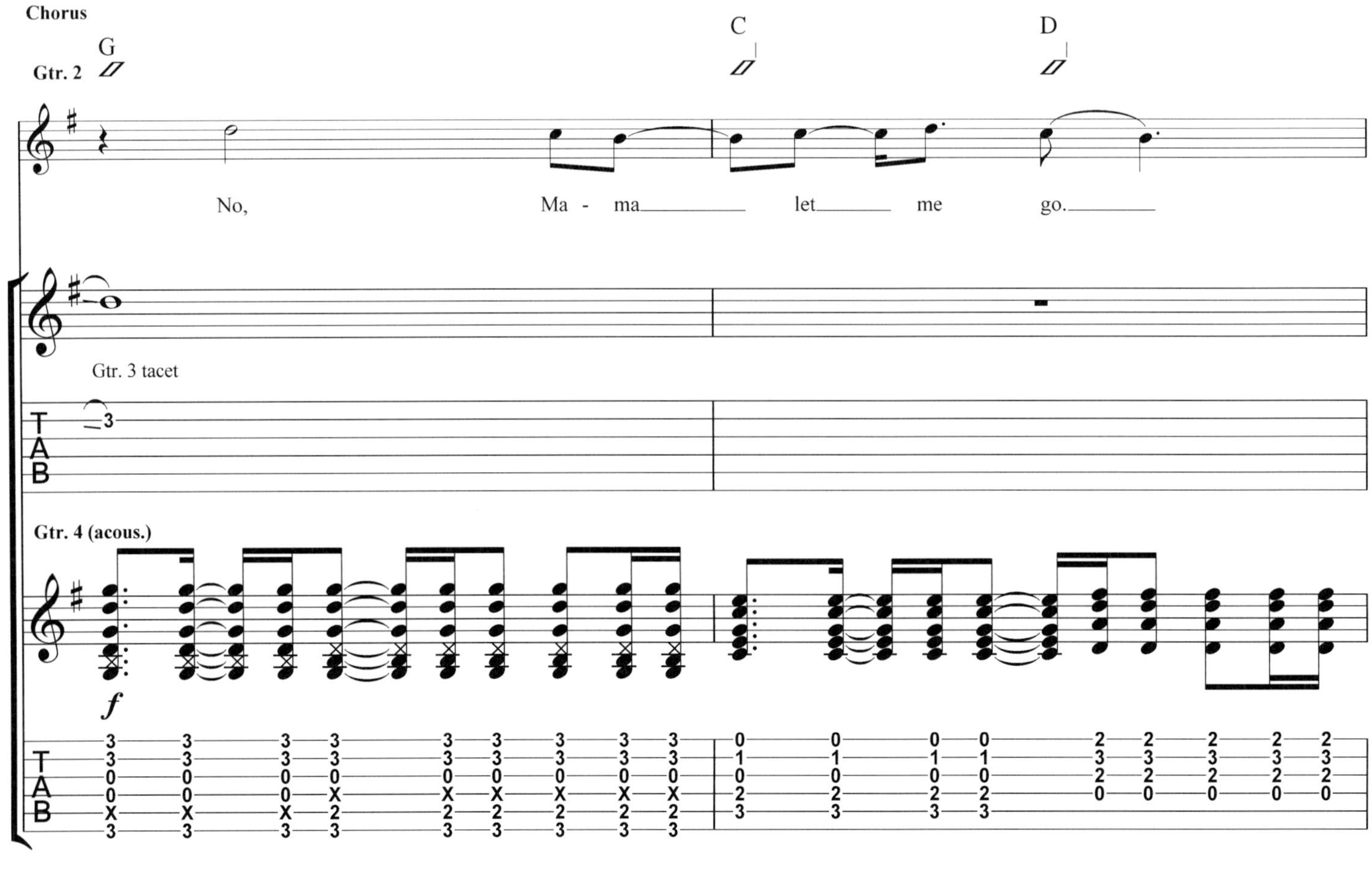

1.
E
Gtr. 4 tacet
Gtr. 3
mf
2.
Bridge
C
F
Gtr. 2 tacet
Ooh, la, la, la. La, la,
Gtr. 5 (elec.)
mf w/chorus + clean tone
Gtr. 3 tacet
Gtr. 4 (acous.)

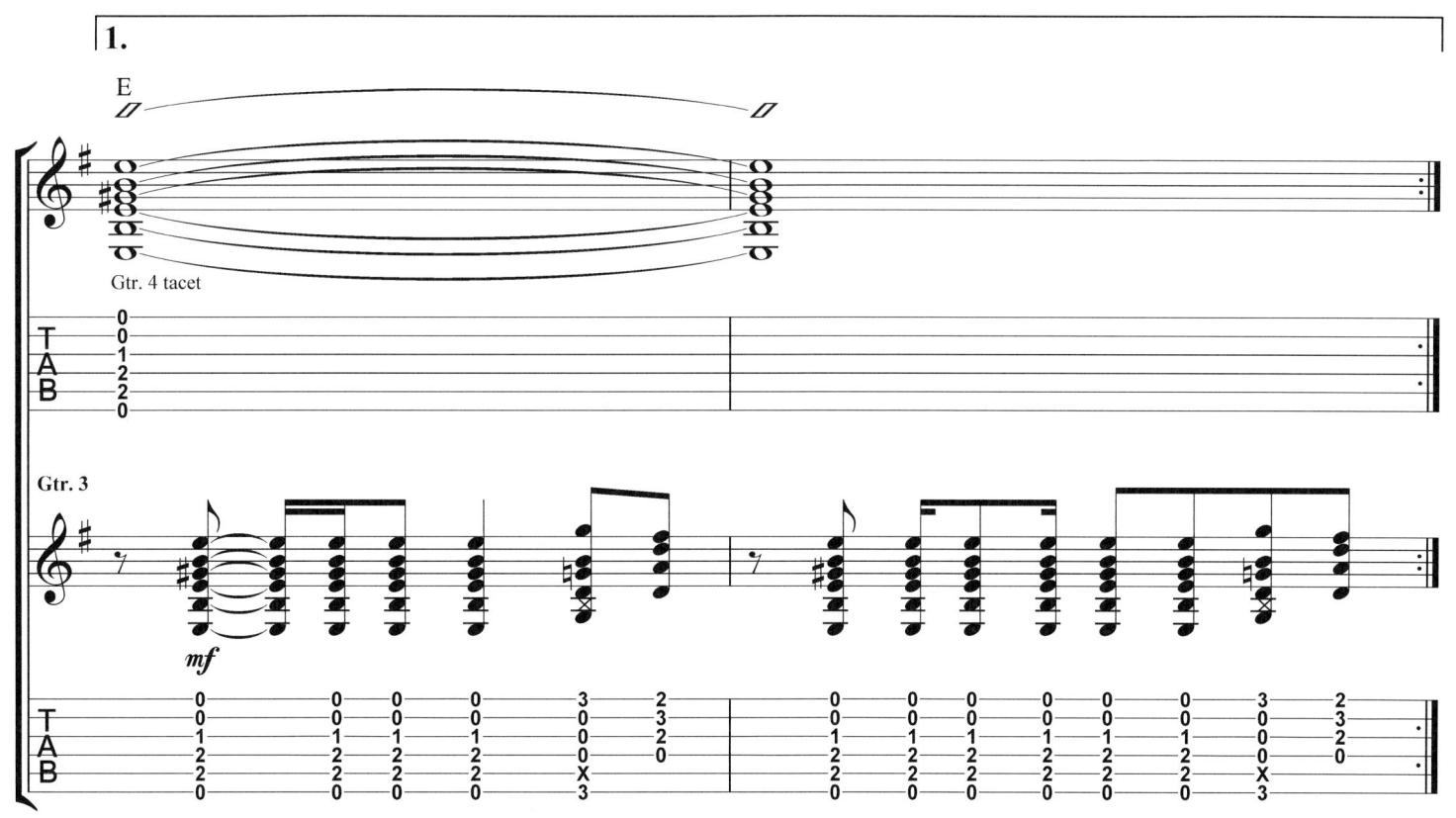

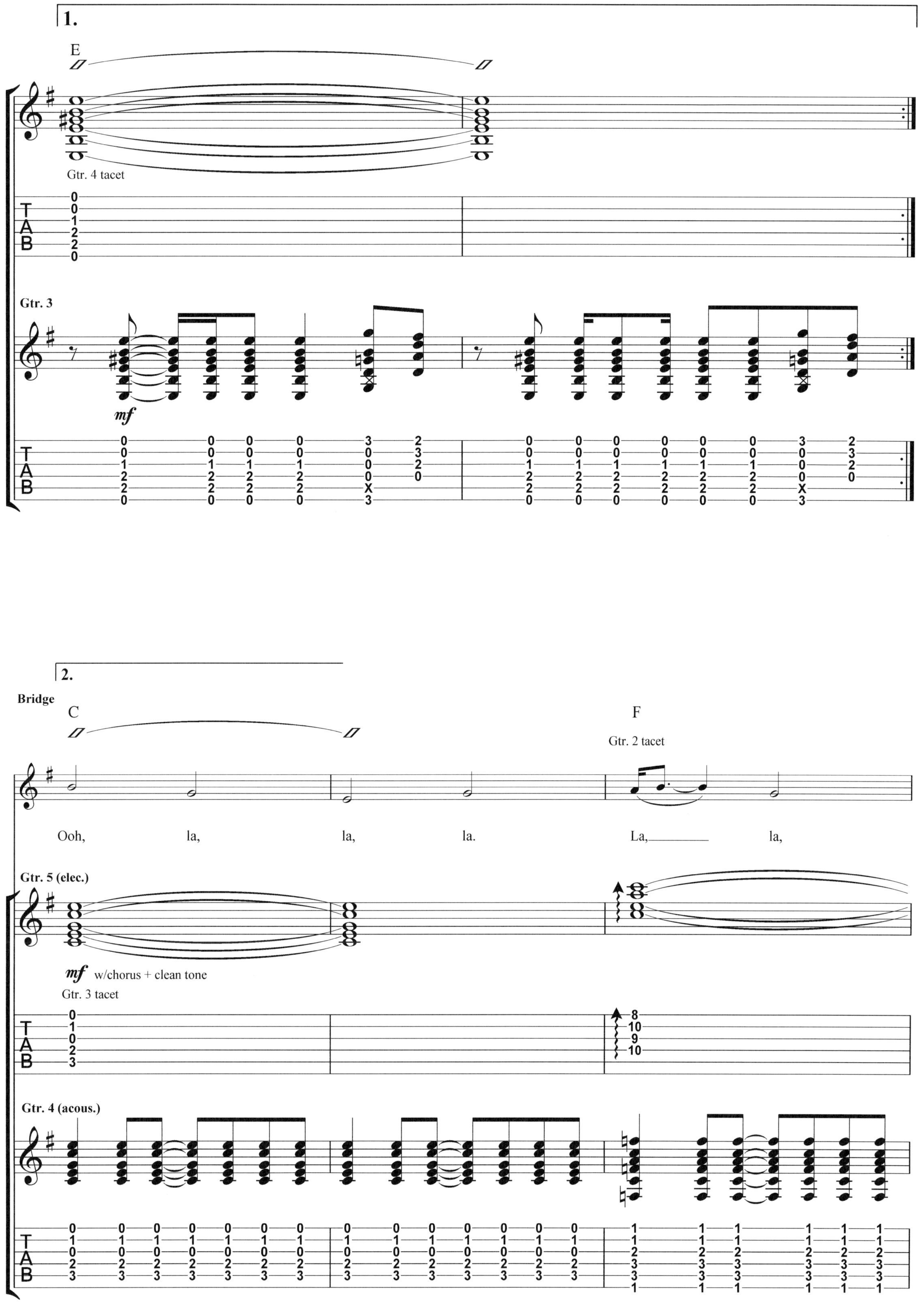

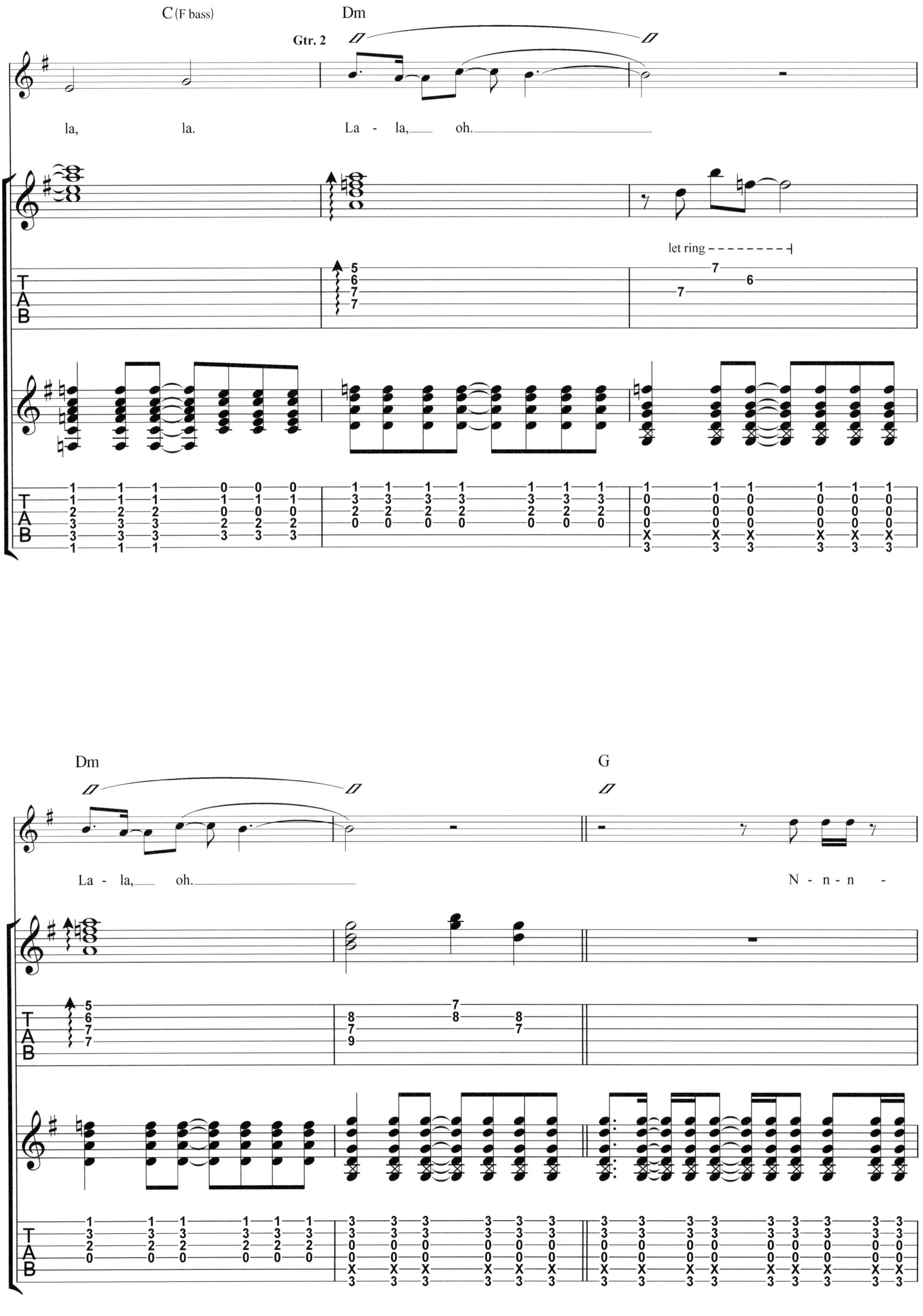
C(F bass)
Dm
Gtr. 2
la, la. La - la, oh.
let ring
Dm
G
La - la, oh.
N - n - n -

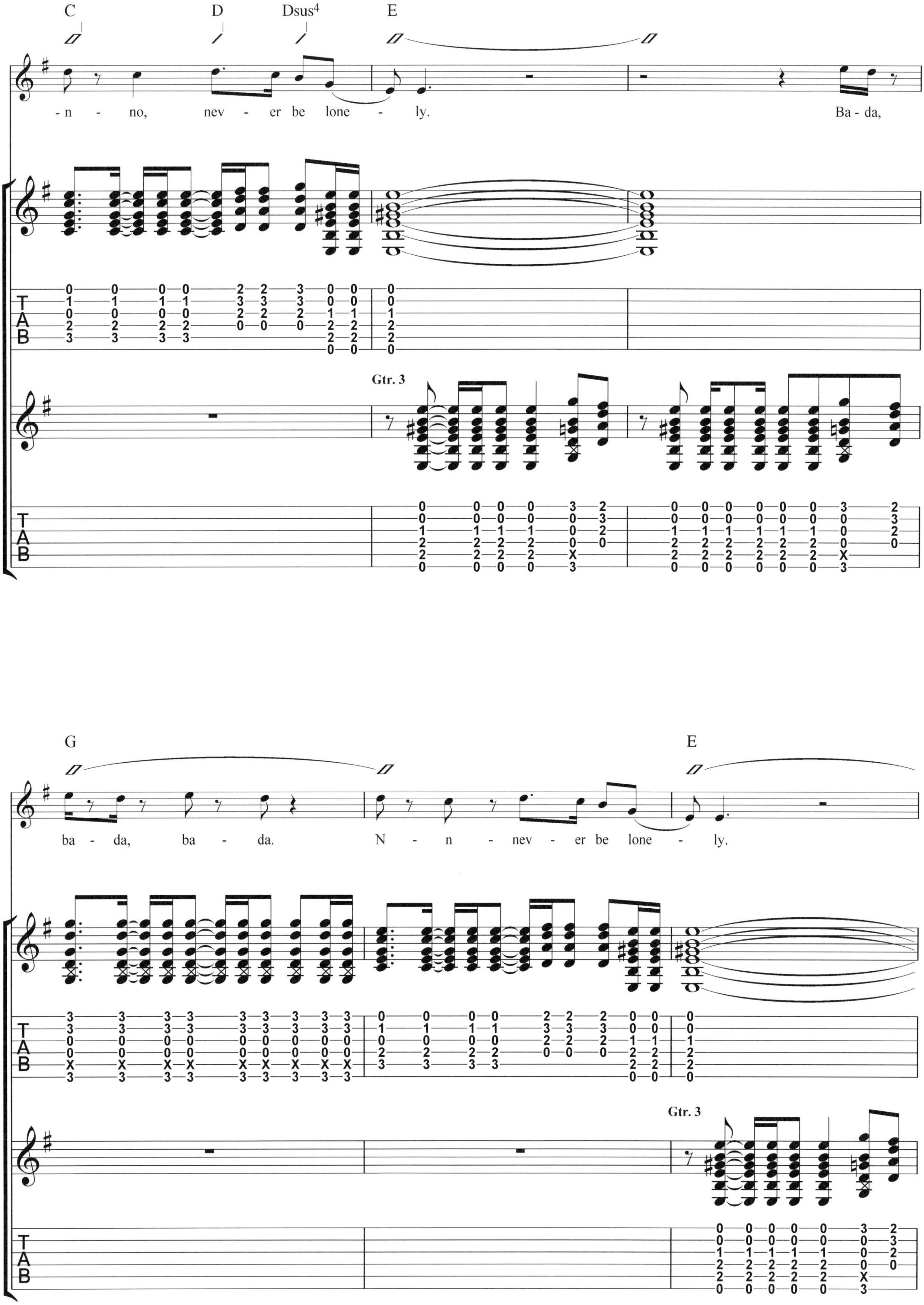
C D Dsus4 E
-n - no, nev - er be lone - ly. Ba - da,
Gtr. 3
G E
ba - da, ba - da. N - n - nev - er be lone - ly.
Gtr. 3

E
G D E

Verse
E
G D A7
Gtr. 2 tacet
3. I thought that if you had an a-cous-tic gui-tar then it
Gtr. 1
w/slide

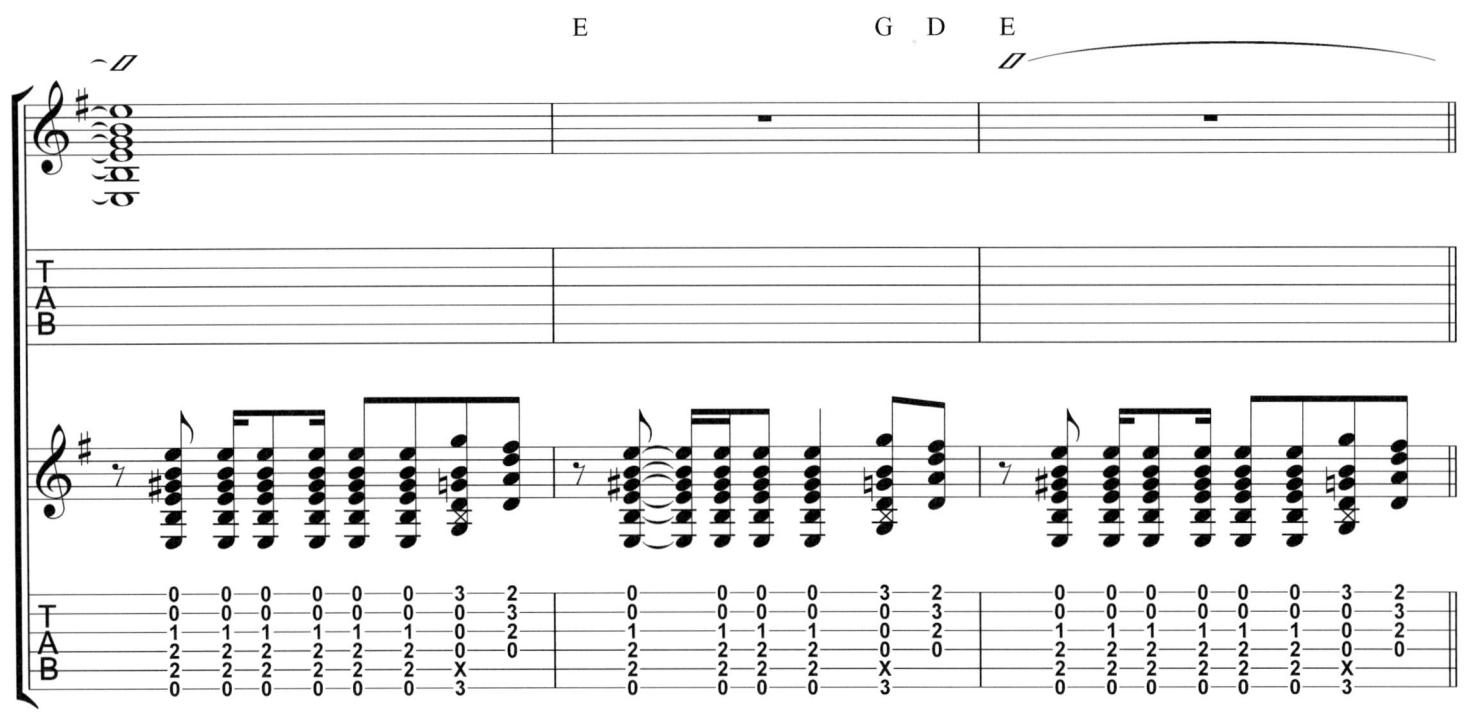

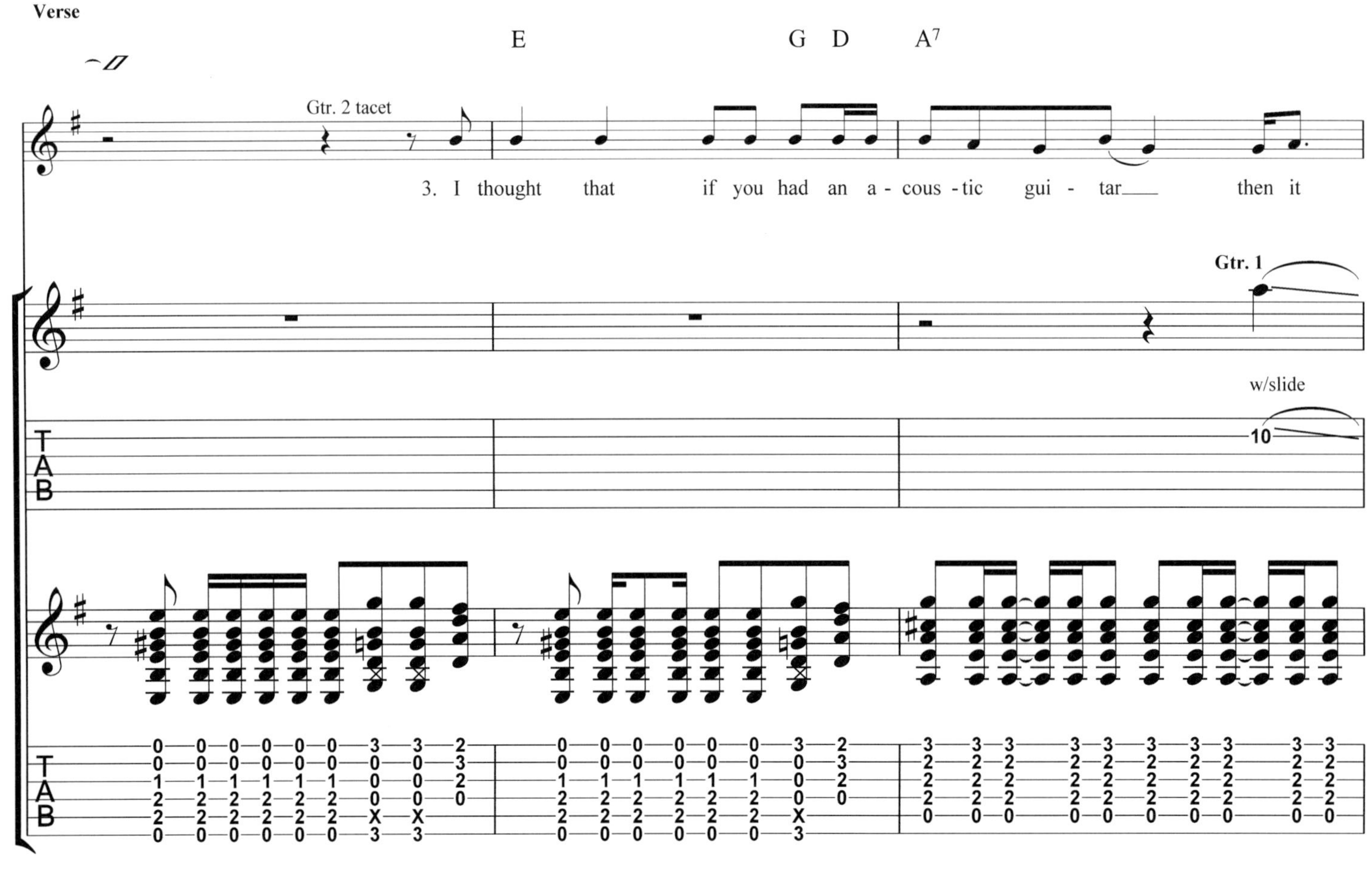

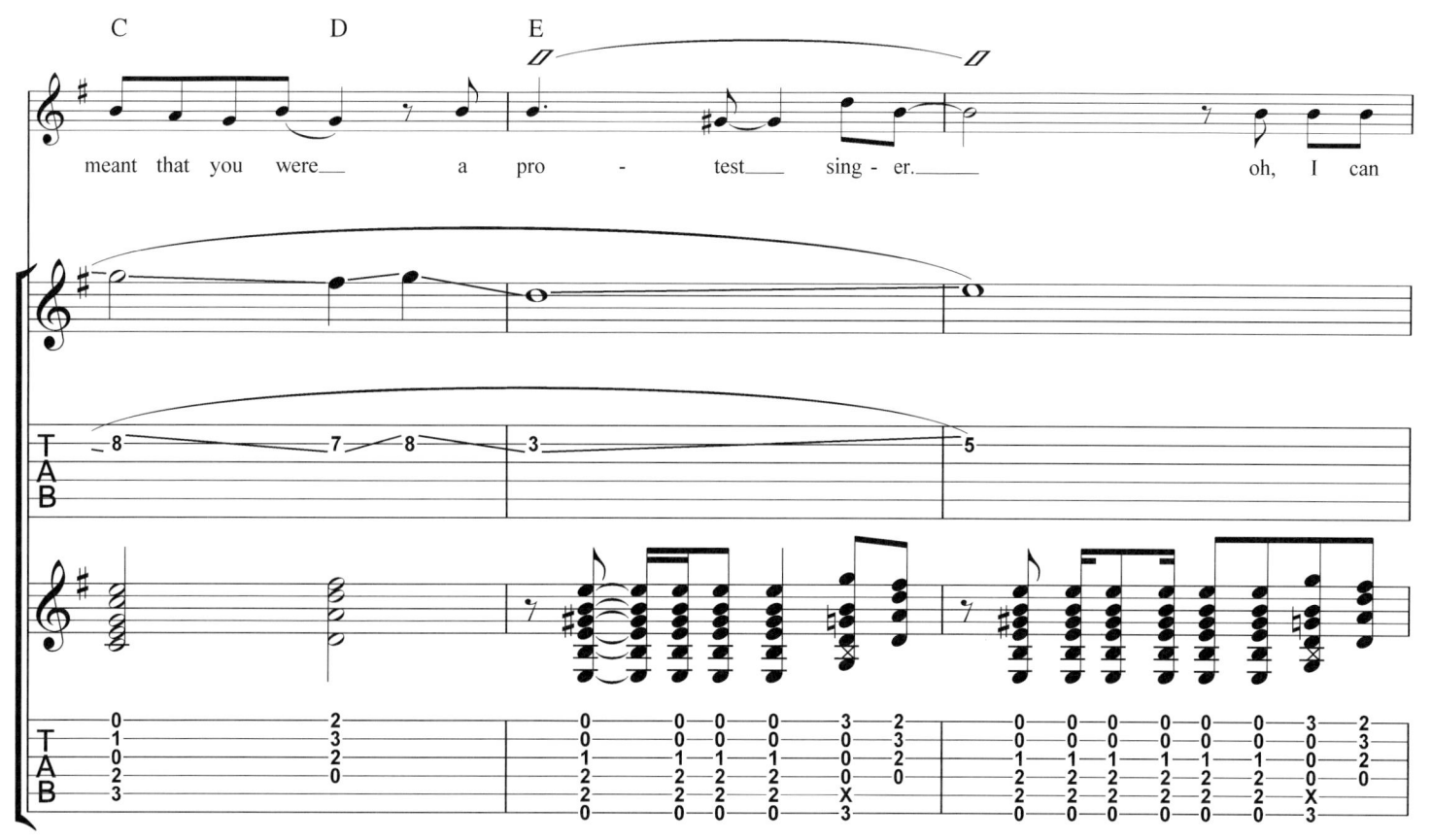
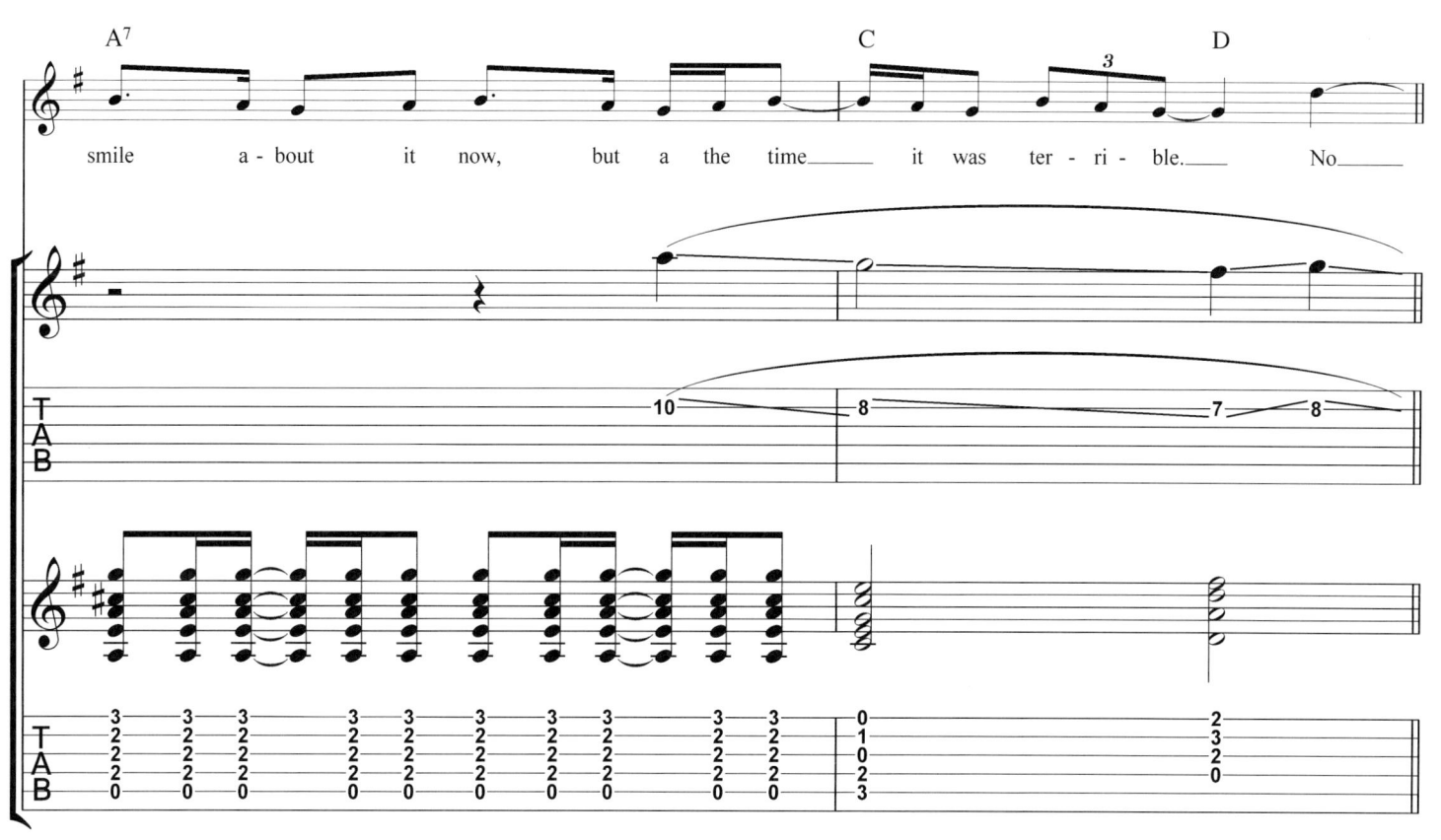

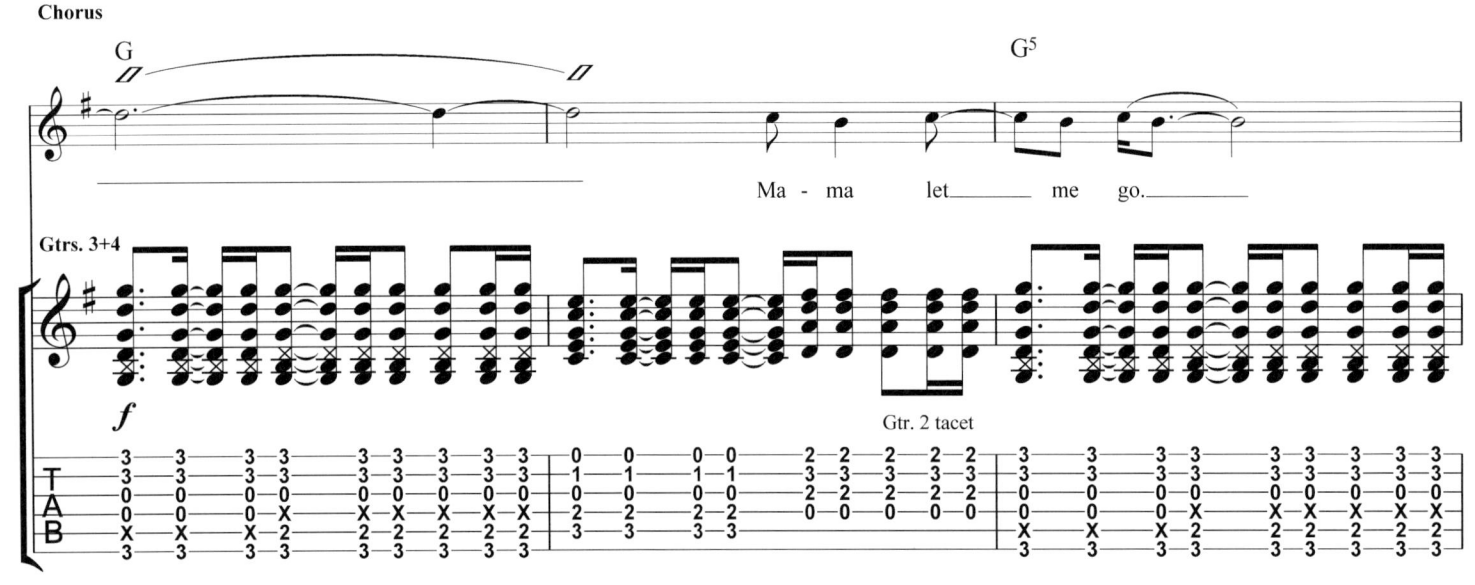
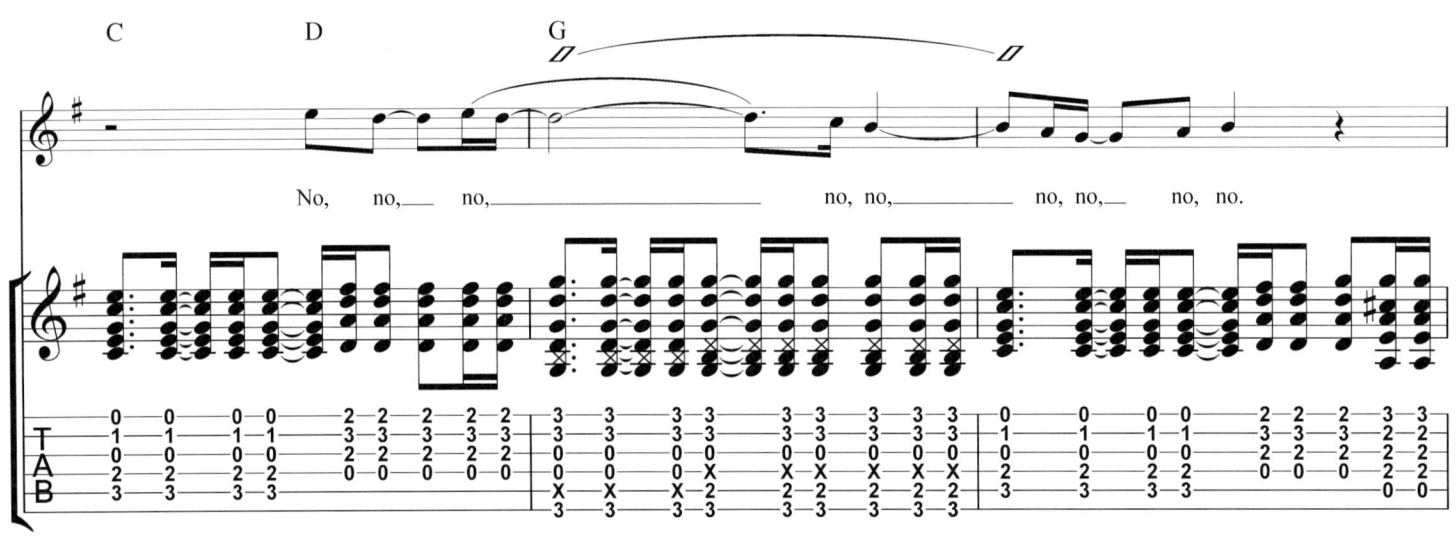
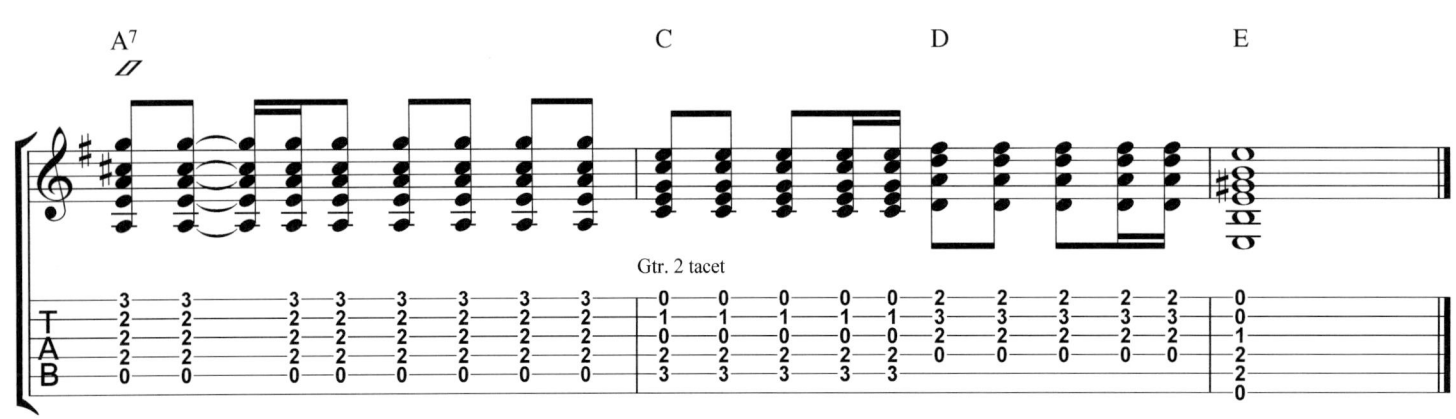

Stop Me If You Think You've Heard This One Before

Words & Music by
Morrissey & Johnny Marr

All Gtrs. capo 3rd fret.

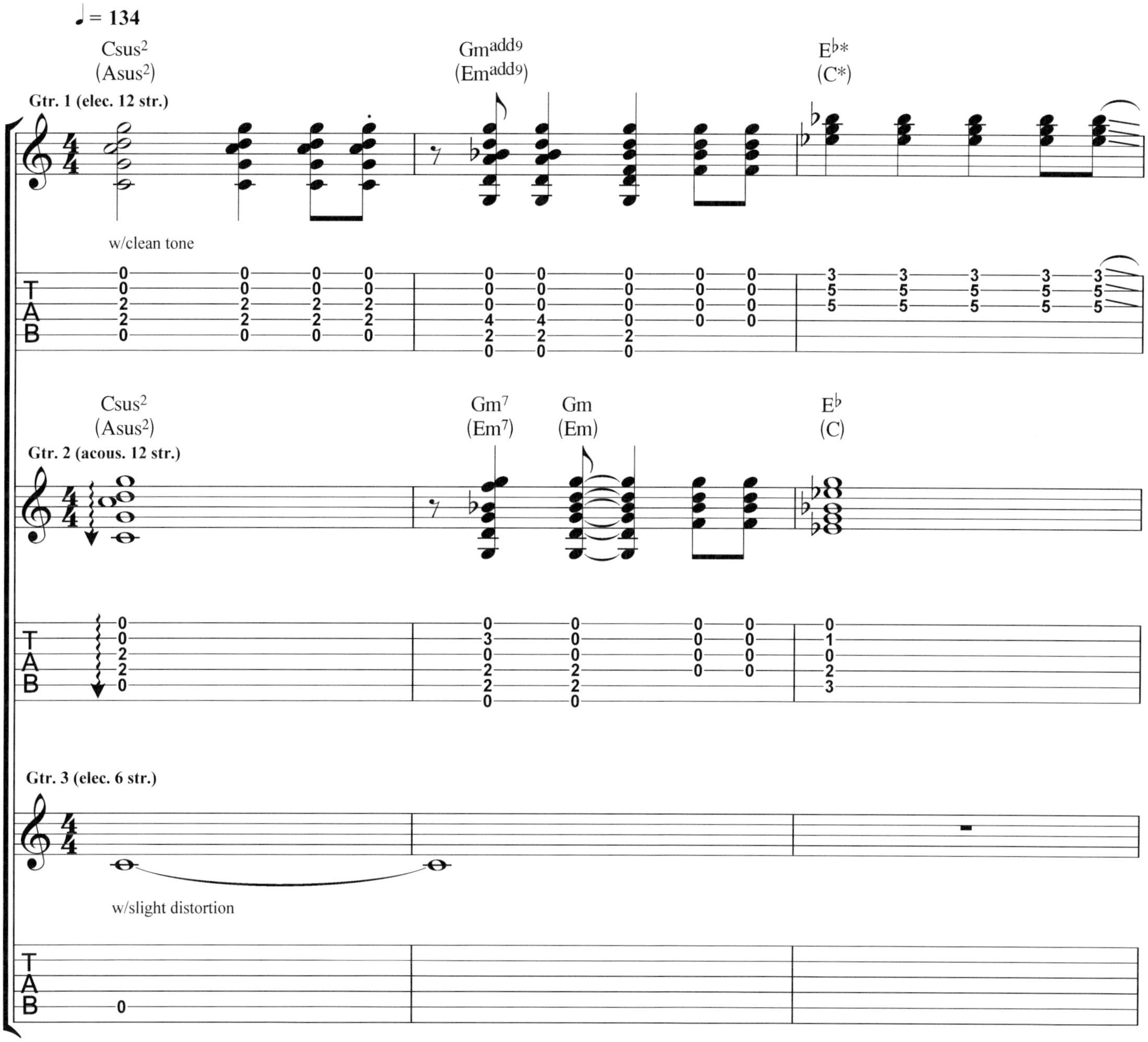

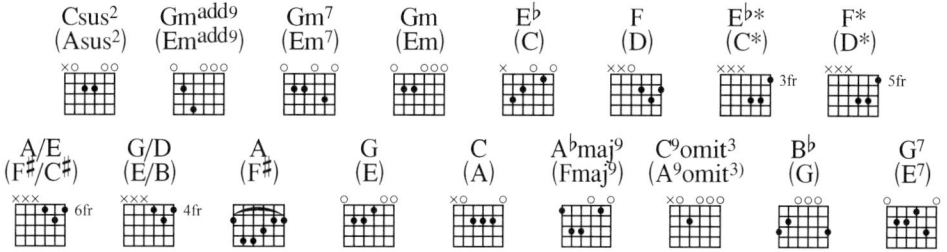

F* (D*)
A/E (F♯/C♯)
G/D (E/B)
F (D)
A (F♯)
G (E)

Verse
C (A)
Gm7 (Em7)
Gm (Em)
E♭ (C)
1. Stop me, oh, oh, oh, stop me, stop me if you think that you've
2. I was de - layed, I was way - laid, an e - mer - gen - cy stop: I smelt the
3. I was de - tained, I was re - strained, and broke my spleen and broke my knee and then he
Gtrs. 1+2
* combined part

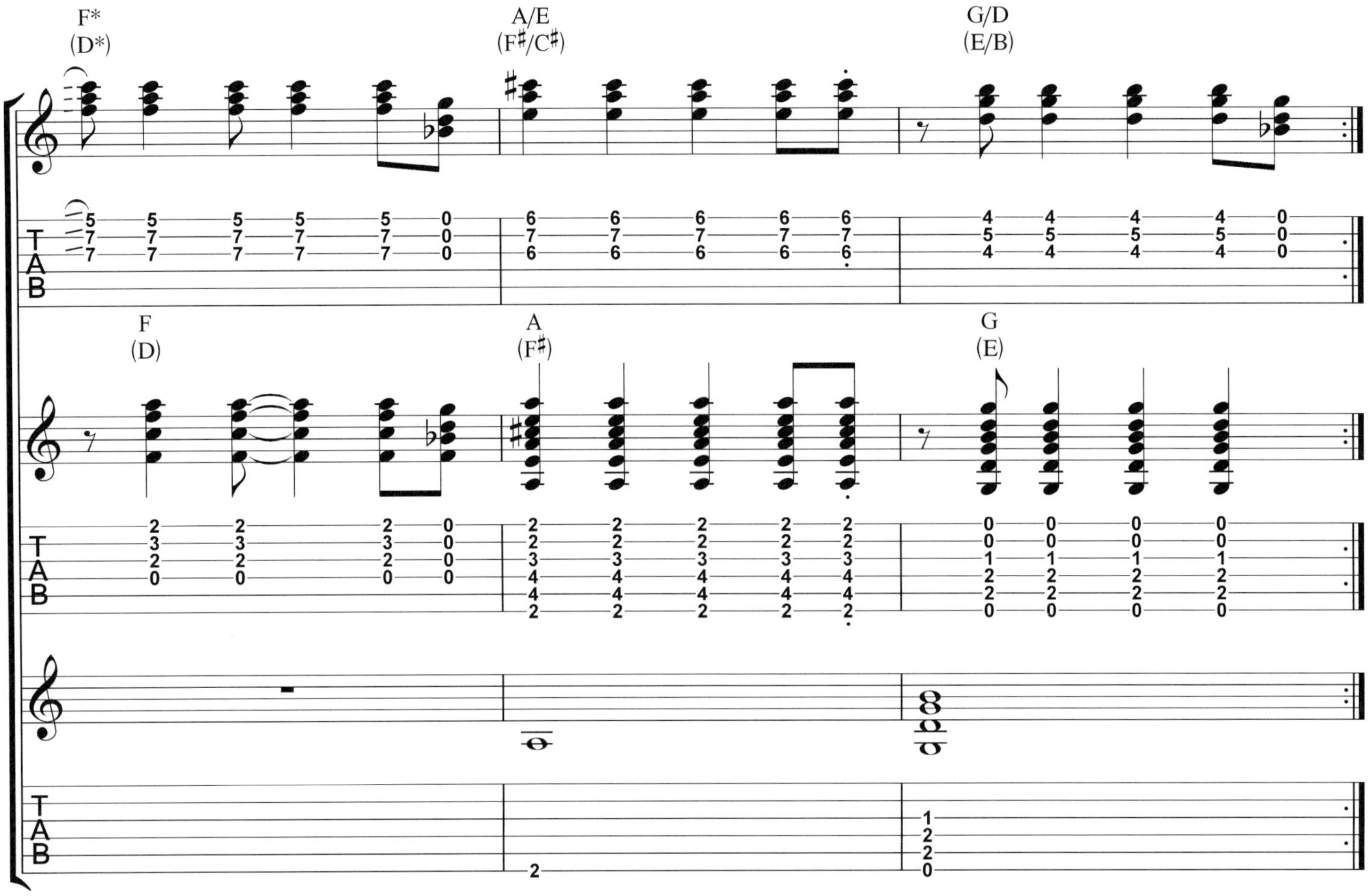

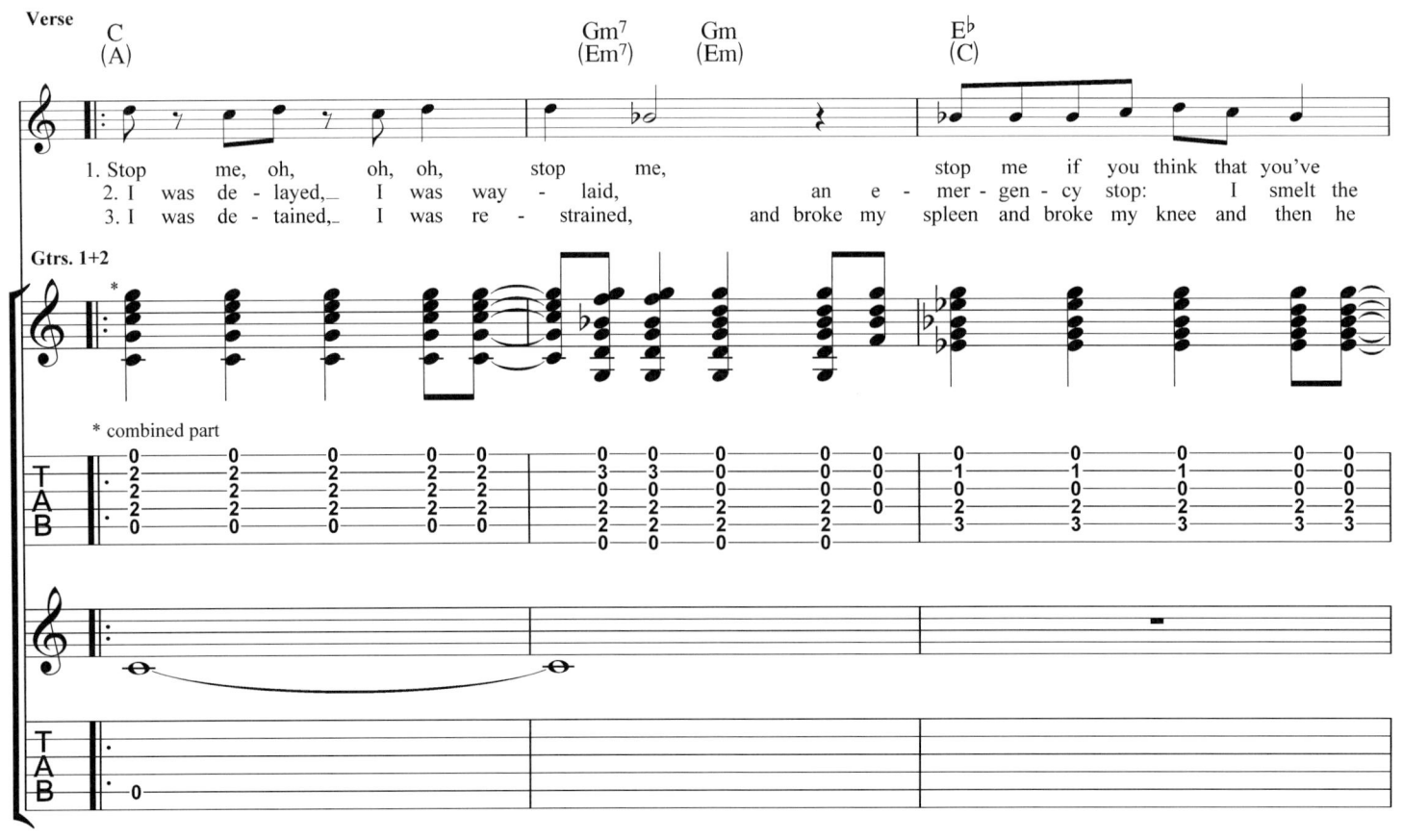

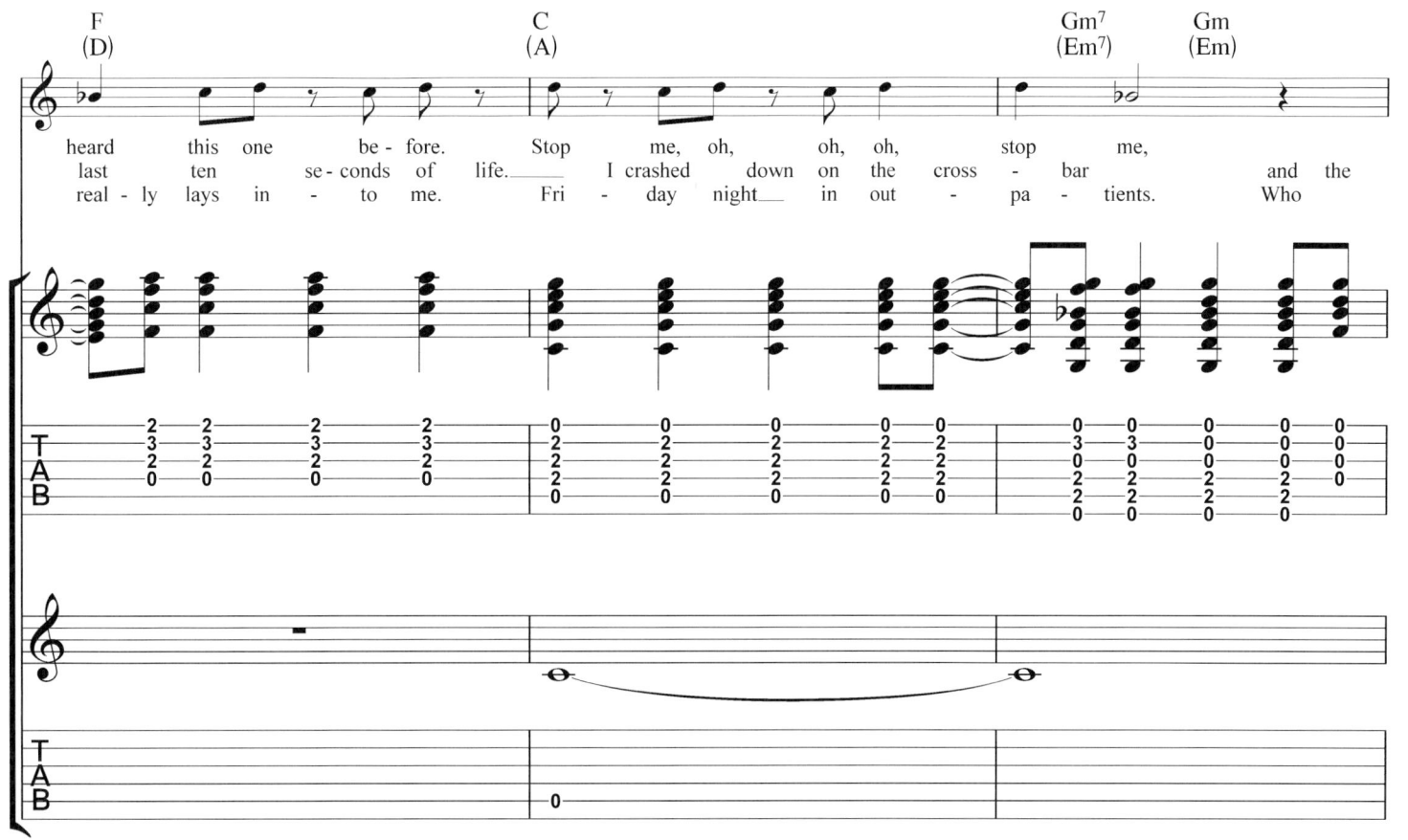
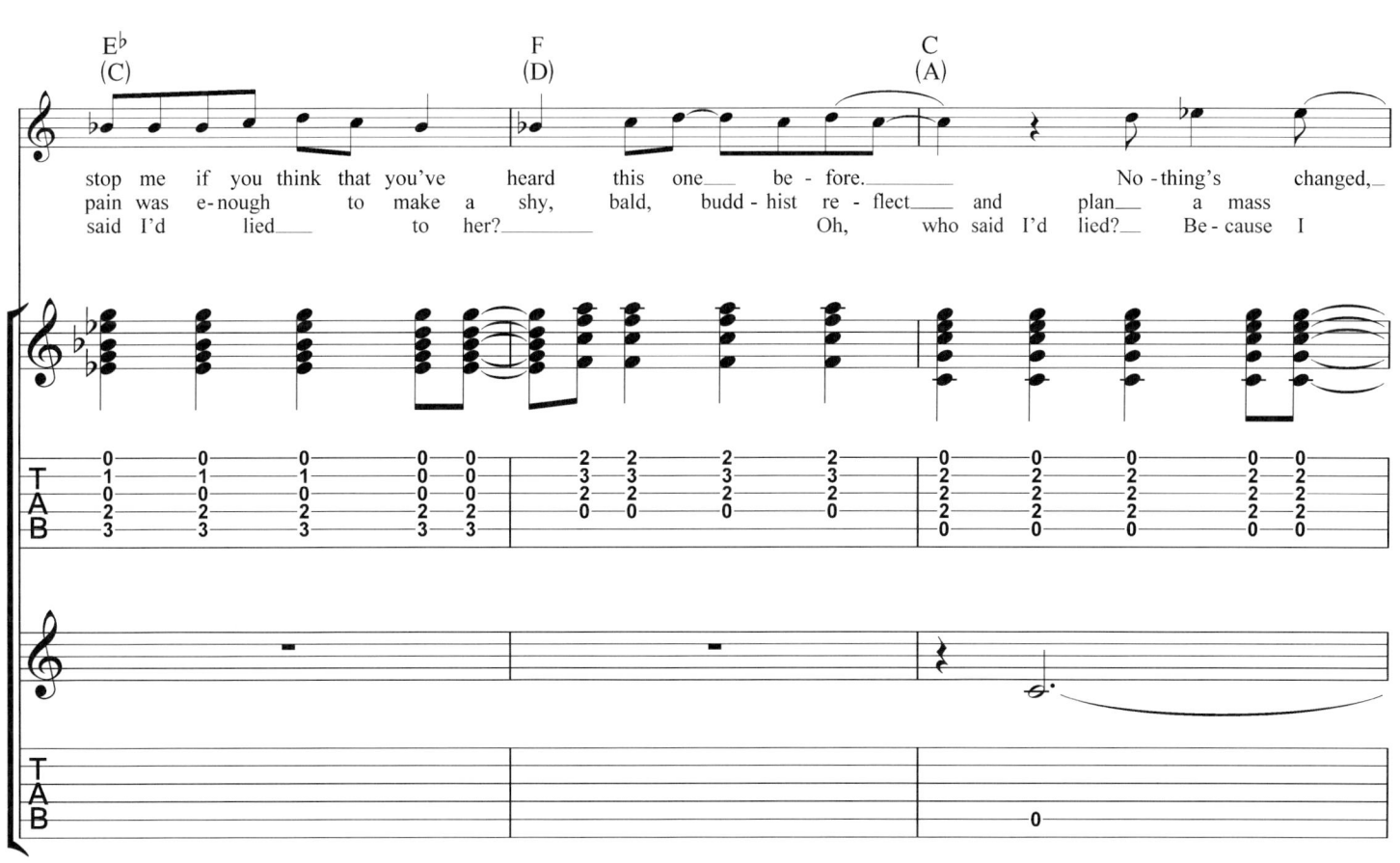

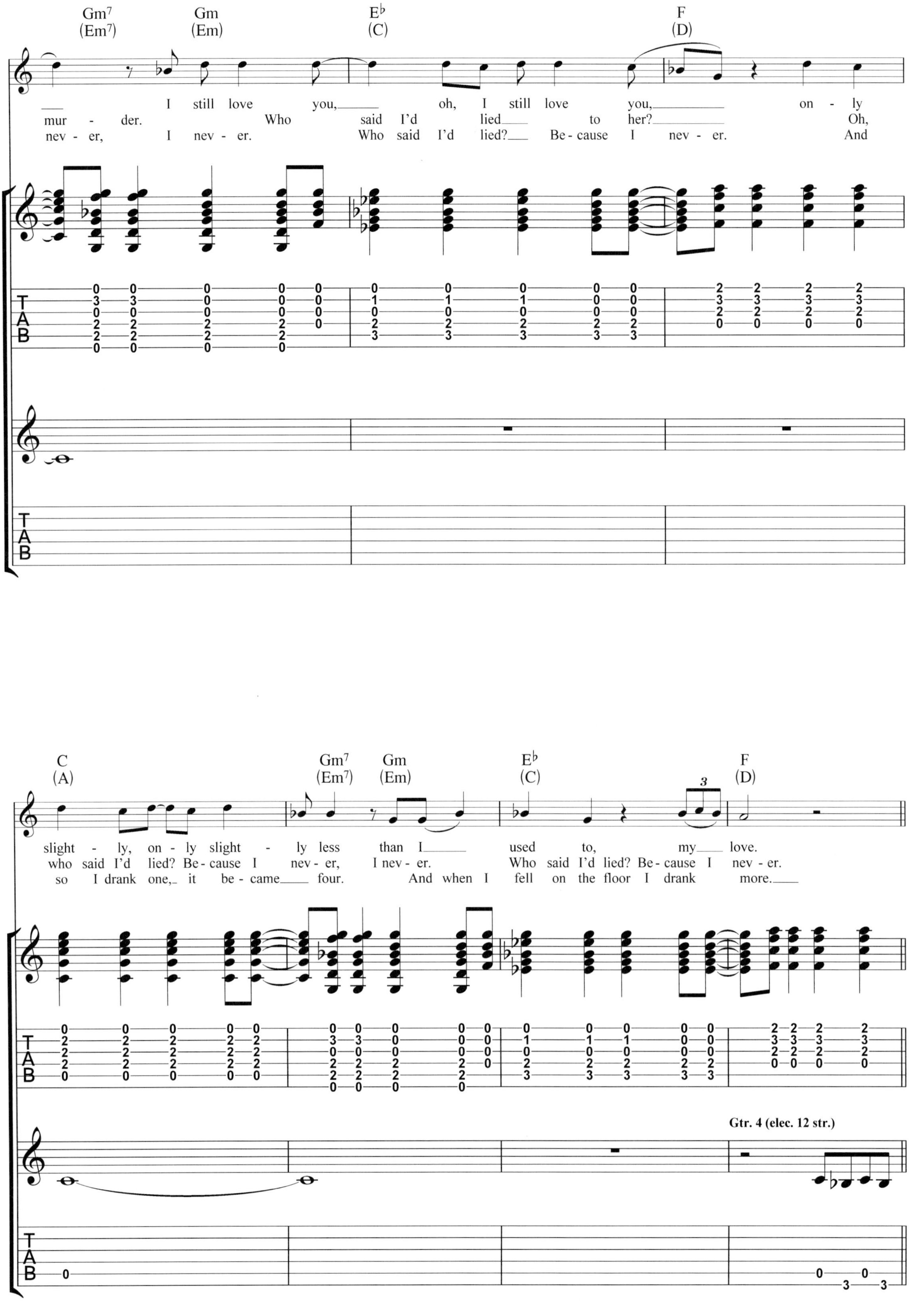
Gm7 (Em7) Gm (Em) E♭ (C) F (D)
I still love you, oh, I still love you, on - ly
mur - der. Who said I'd lied to her? Oh,
nev - er, I nev - er. Who said I'd lied? Be - cause I nev - er. And
C (A) Gm7 (Em7) Gm (Em) E♭ (C) F (D)
slight - ly, on - ly slight - ly less than I used to, my love.
who said I'd lied? Be - cause I nev - er, I nev - er. Who said I'd lied? Be - cause I nev - er.
so I drank one, it be - came four. And when I fell on the floor I drank more.
Gtr. 4 (elec. 12 str.)

3.
Verse
G (E)
C (A)
Gm7 (Em7) Gm (Em)
E♭ (C)
(1, 2, 3.) Stop me, oh, oh, oh, stop me, stop me if you think that you've
Gtrs. 1+2
* combined part
F (D)
C (A)
Gm7 (Em7) Gm (Em)
E♭ (C)
heard this one be- fore. Stop me, oh, oh, oh, stop me, stop me if you think that you've

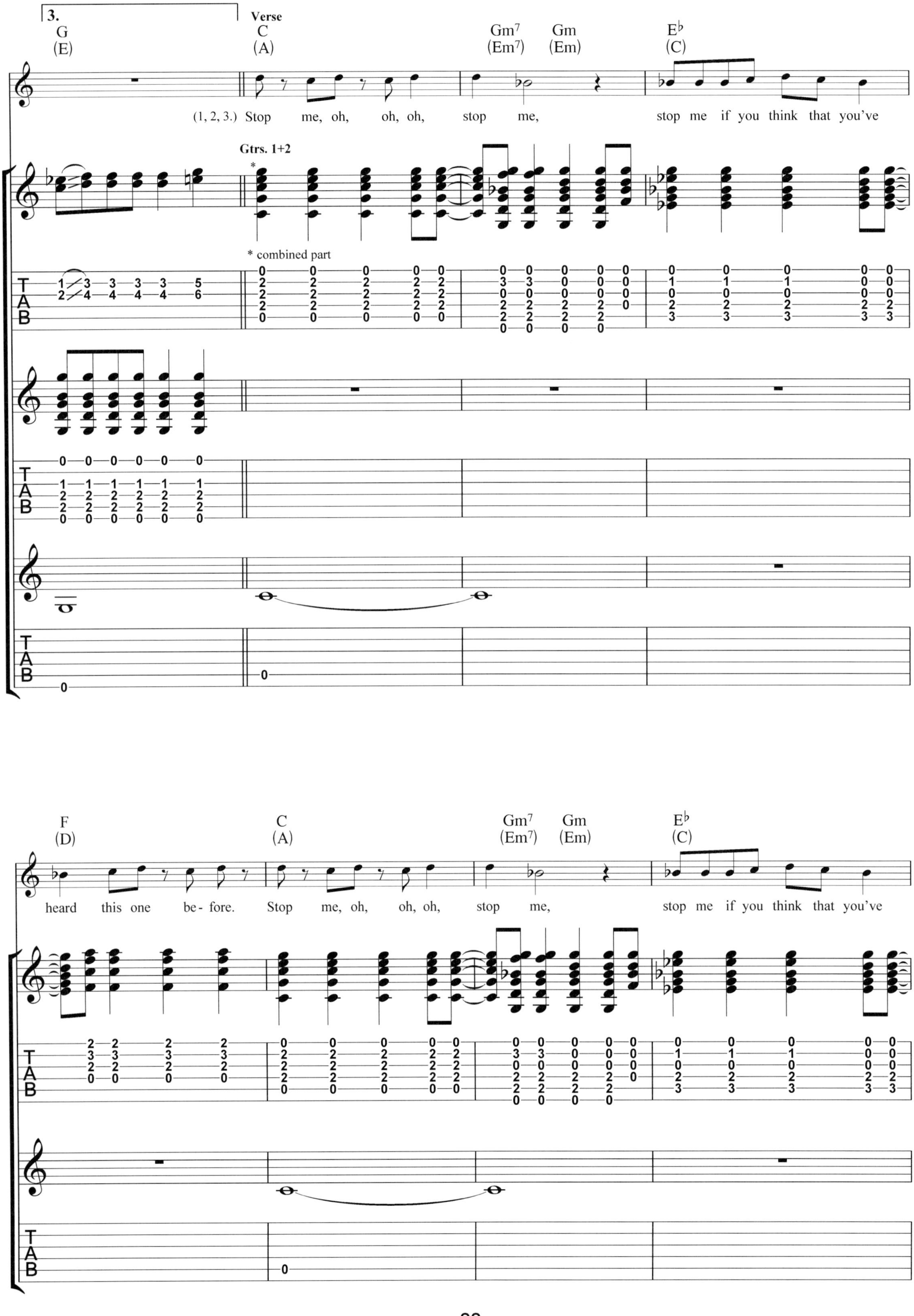

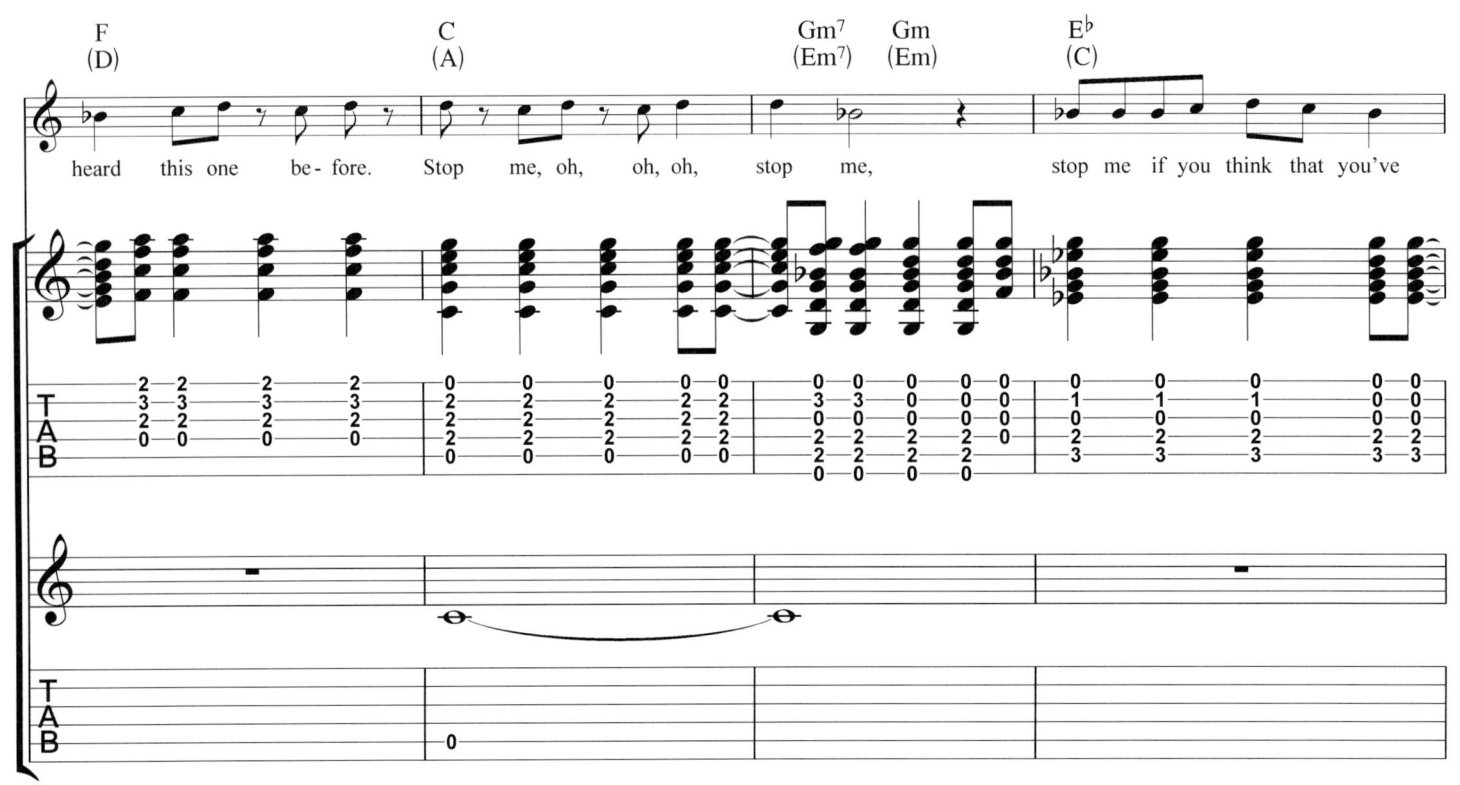

F (D) C (A) Gm7 (Em7) Gm (Em) E♭ (C)
heard this one be - fore. No - thing's changed, I still love you, oh, I still love you,
F (D) C (A) Gm7 (Em7) Gm (Em) E♭ (C) F (D)
on - ly slight - ly, on - ly slight - ly less than I used to, my love.
Gtr. 5 (elec. 6 str.)
w/distortion

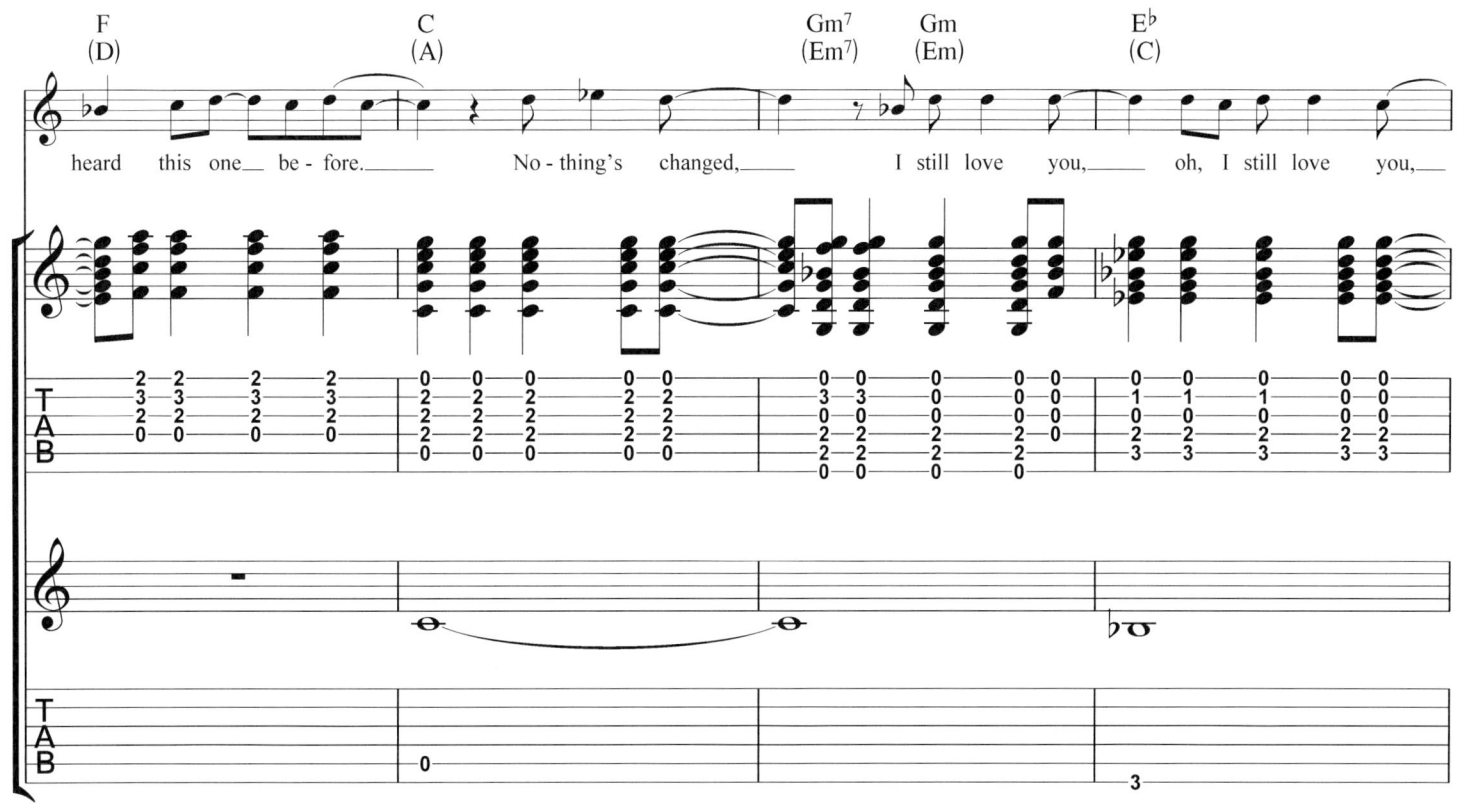

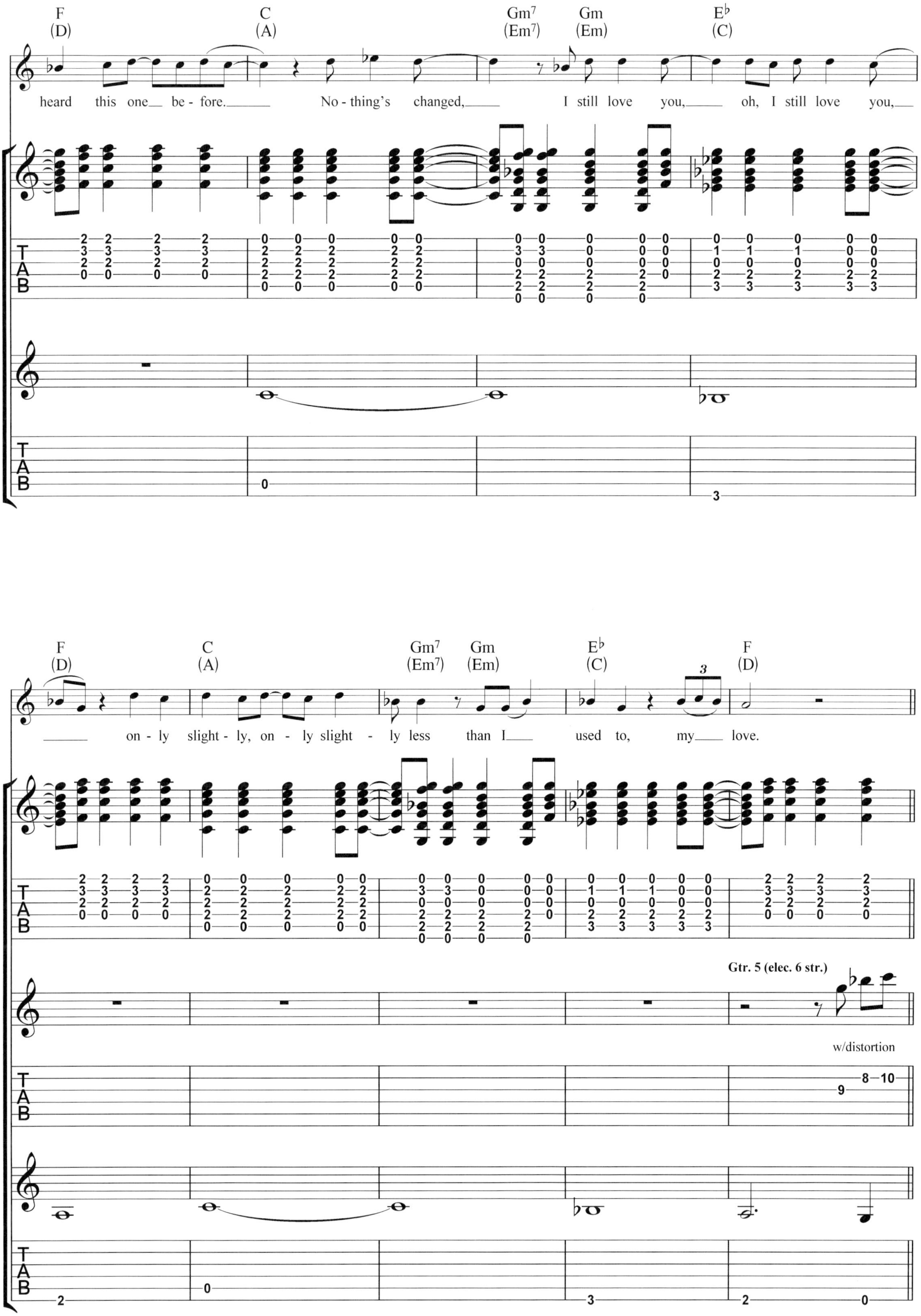

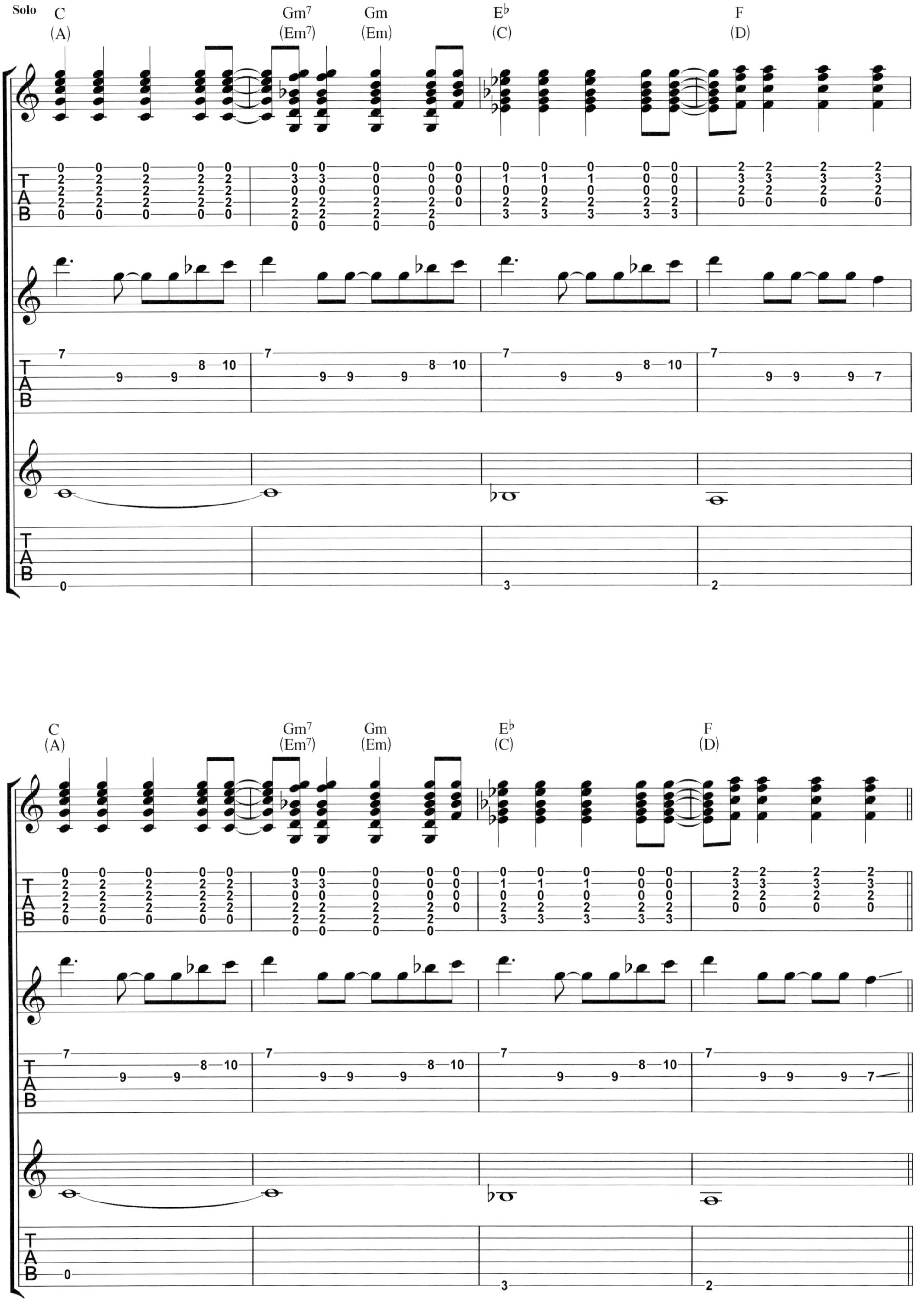

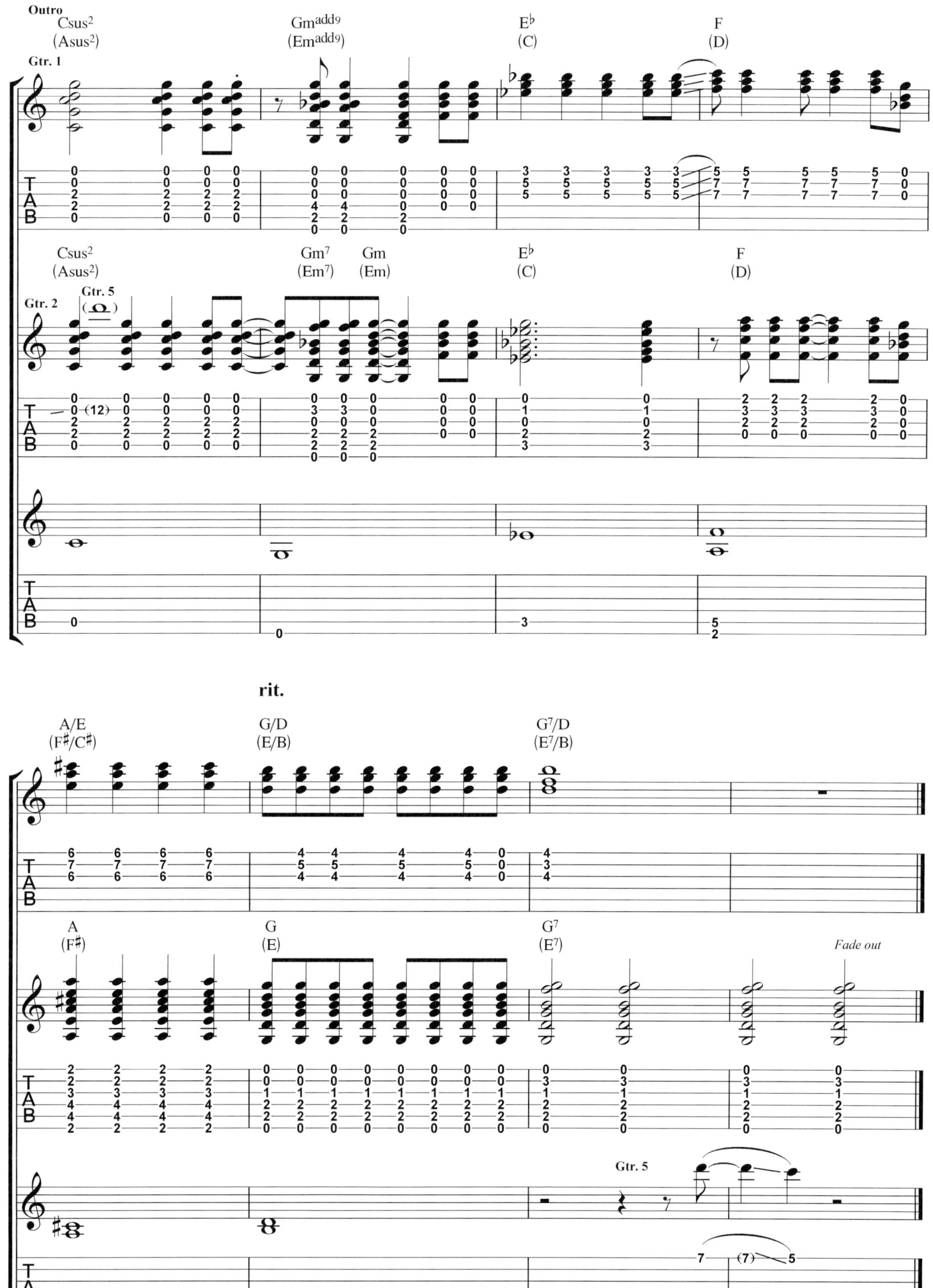

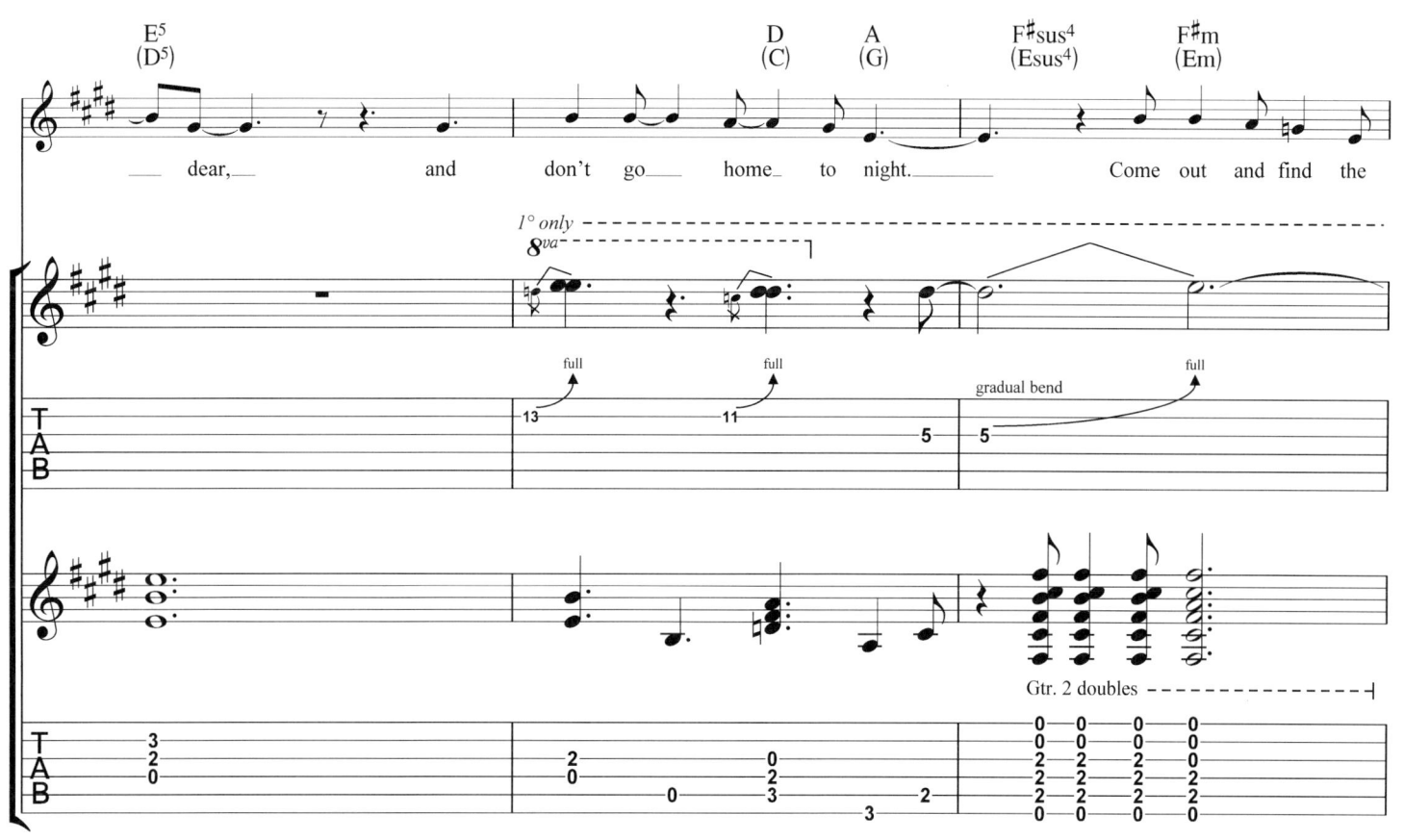

1.
C5 (B♭5)
D5 (C5)
E5 D5 C5 (D5) (C5) (B♭5)
D5 (C5)
E5 (D5)
one that you love and who loves you,
One that you love and who loves you.
Gtr. 4 (elec.)
mf w/dist.
1/2
full

B (A)
Gtr. 2
Gtrs. 3+4 tacet
Gtr. 2 tacet
2. Is it wrong
1/4

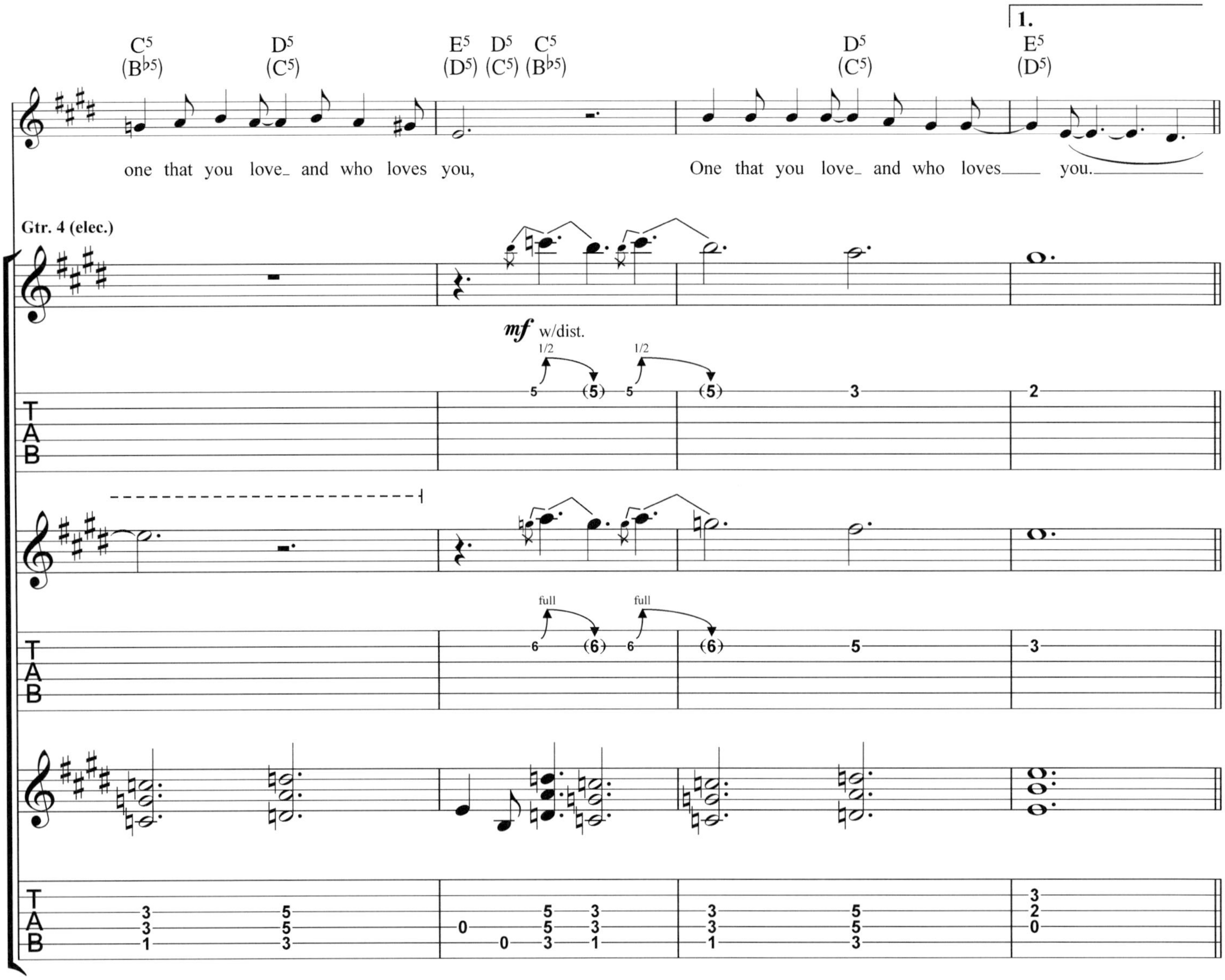

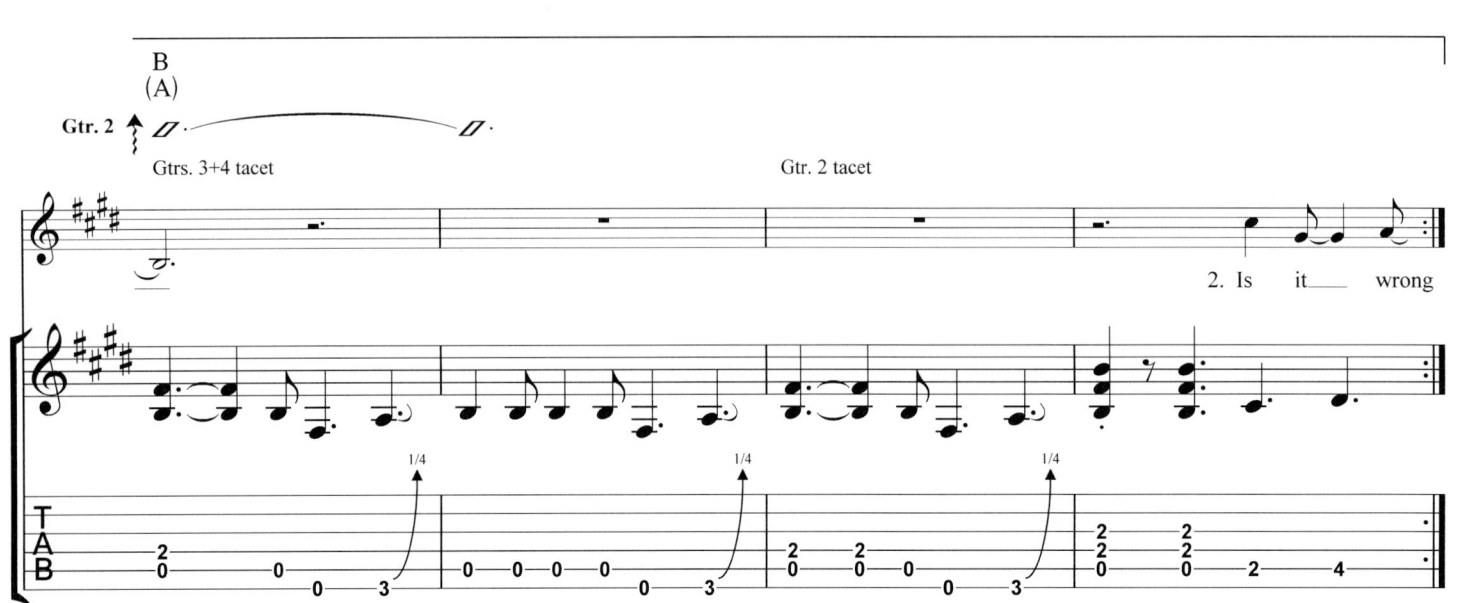

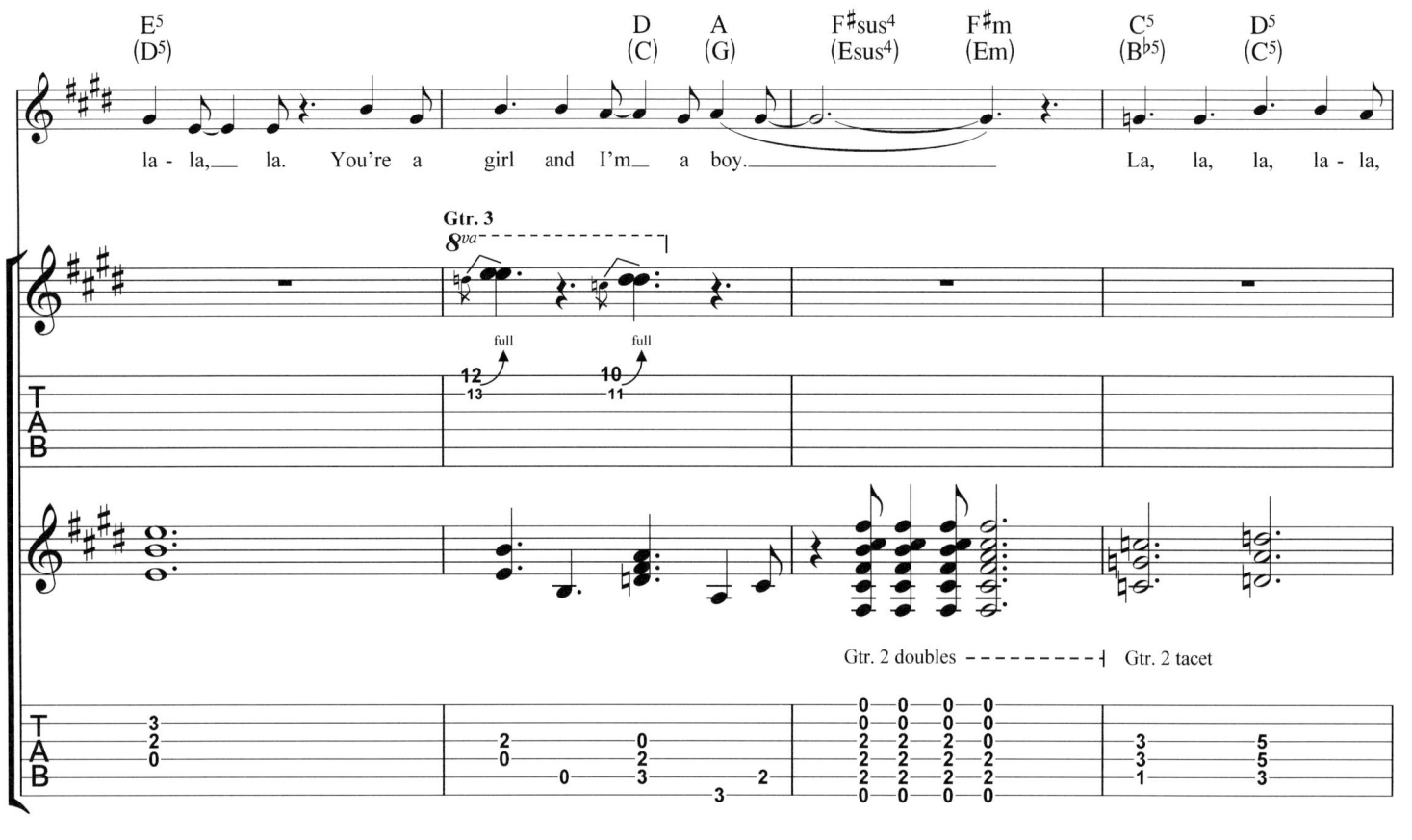

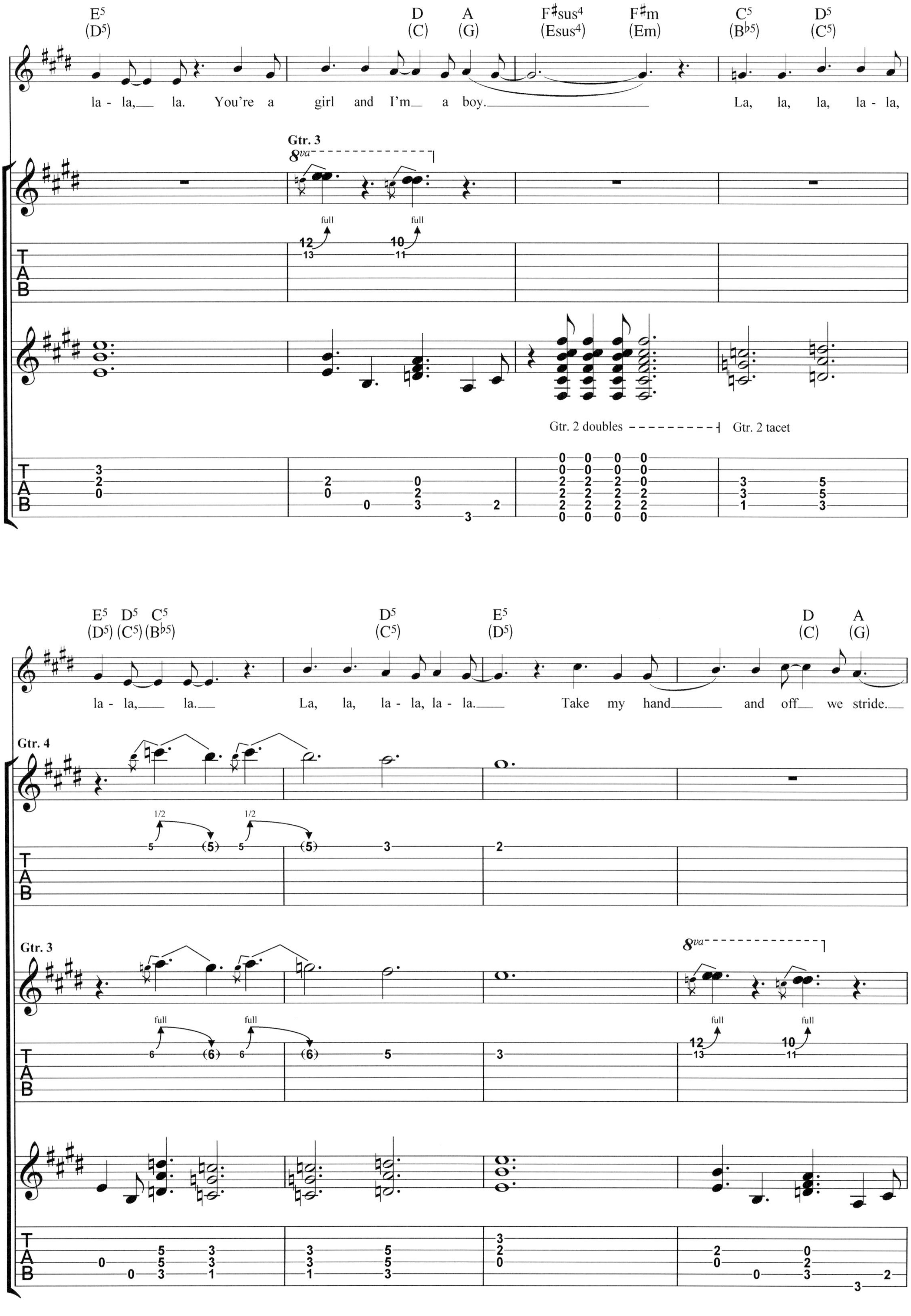
E5 (D5) D (C) A (G) F♯sus4 (Esus4) F♯m (Em) C5 (B♭5) D5 (C5)
la - la, la. You're a girl and I'm a boy. La, la, la, la - la,
Gtr. 3
8va
full
Gtr. 2 doubles
Gtr. 2 tacet
E5 (D5) D5 (C5) C5 (B♭5) D5 (C5) E5 (D5) D (C) A (G)
la - la, la. La, la, la - la, la - la. Take my hand and off we stride.
Gtr. 4
1/2
Gtr. 3
full
8va

Chorus
E5 (D5)
E5 (D5)
D (C)
A (G)
F♯sus4 (Esus4)
F♯m (Em)
Shei - la take a, Shei - la take a bow.
Gtr. 3
8va
full
full
Gtr. 2 doubles
C5 (B♭5)
D5 (C5)
E5 (D5)
D (C)
A (G)
La, la, la, la - la, la - la, la. Throw your home - work on - to the fire,
Gtr. 2 tacet

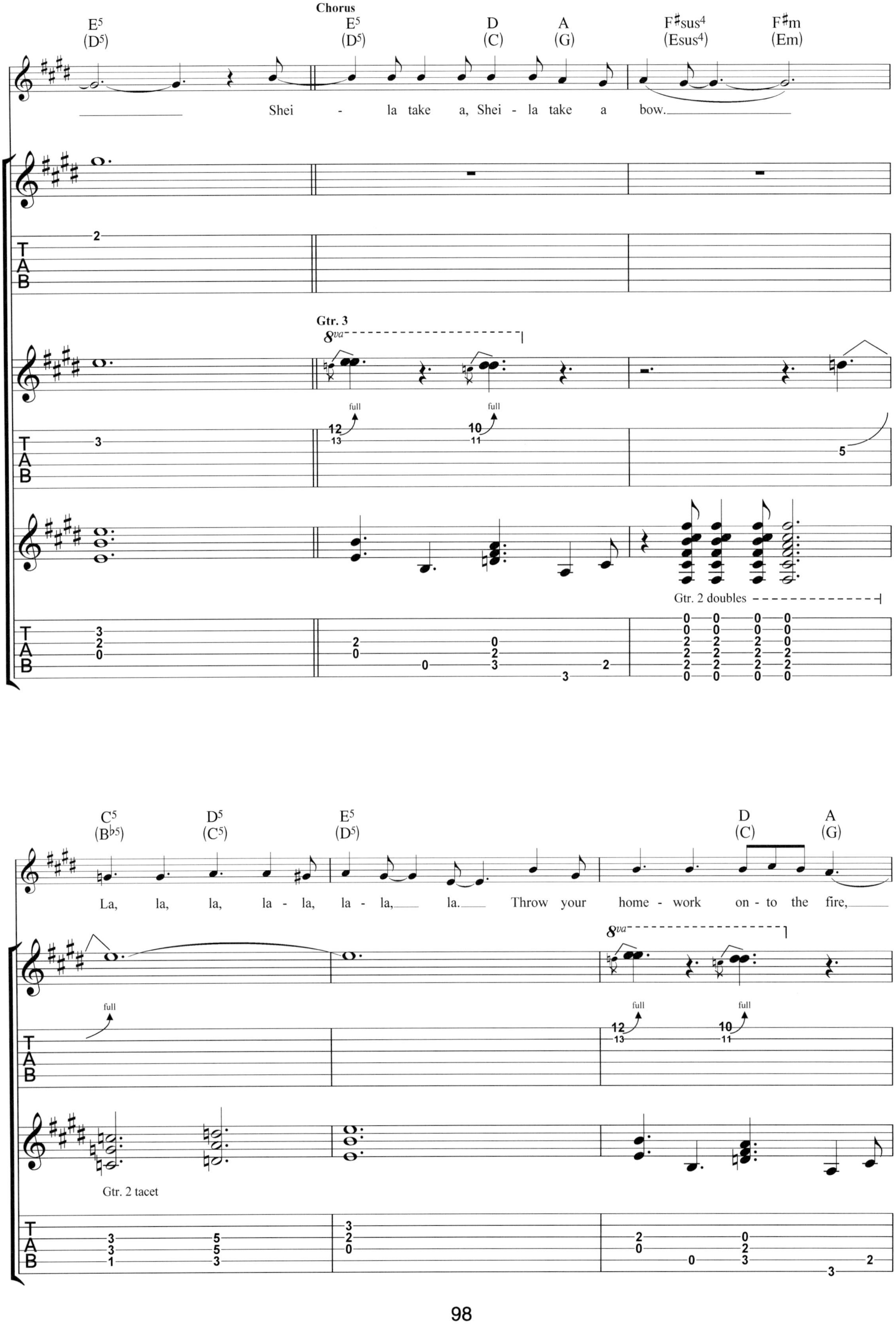

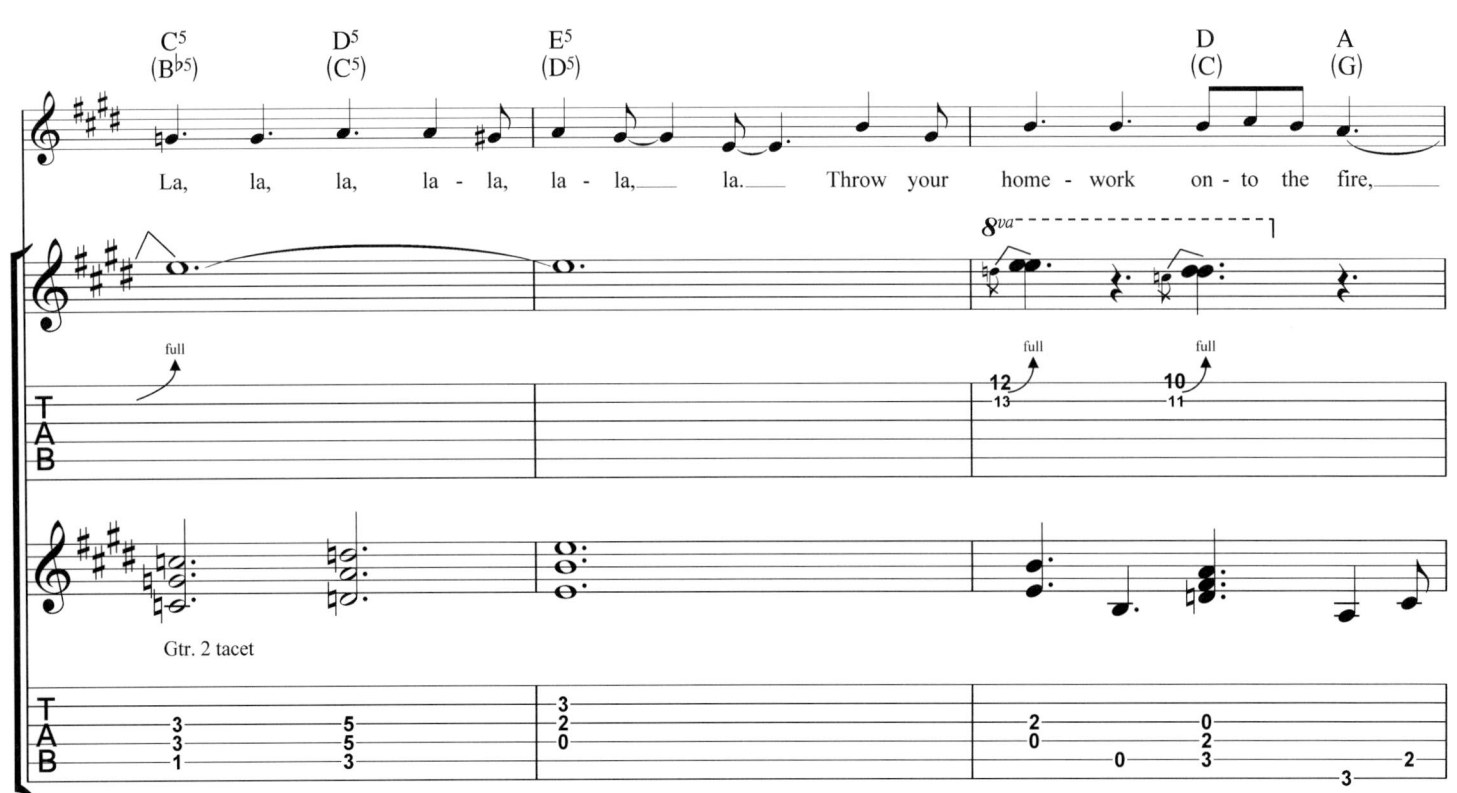

Shoplifters Of The World Unite

Words & Music by
Morrissey & Johnny Marr

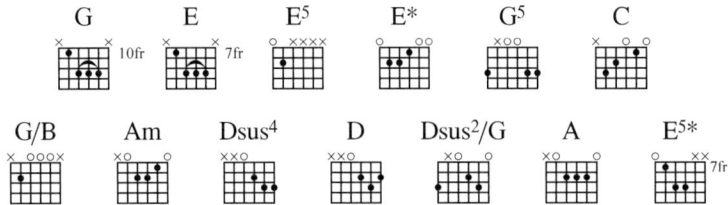

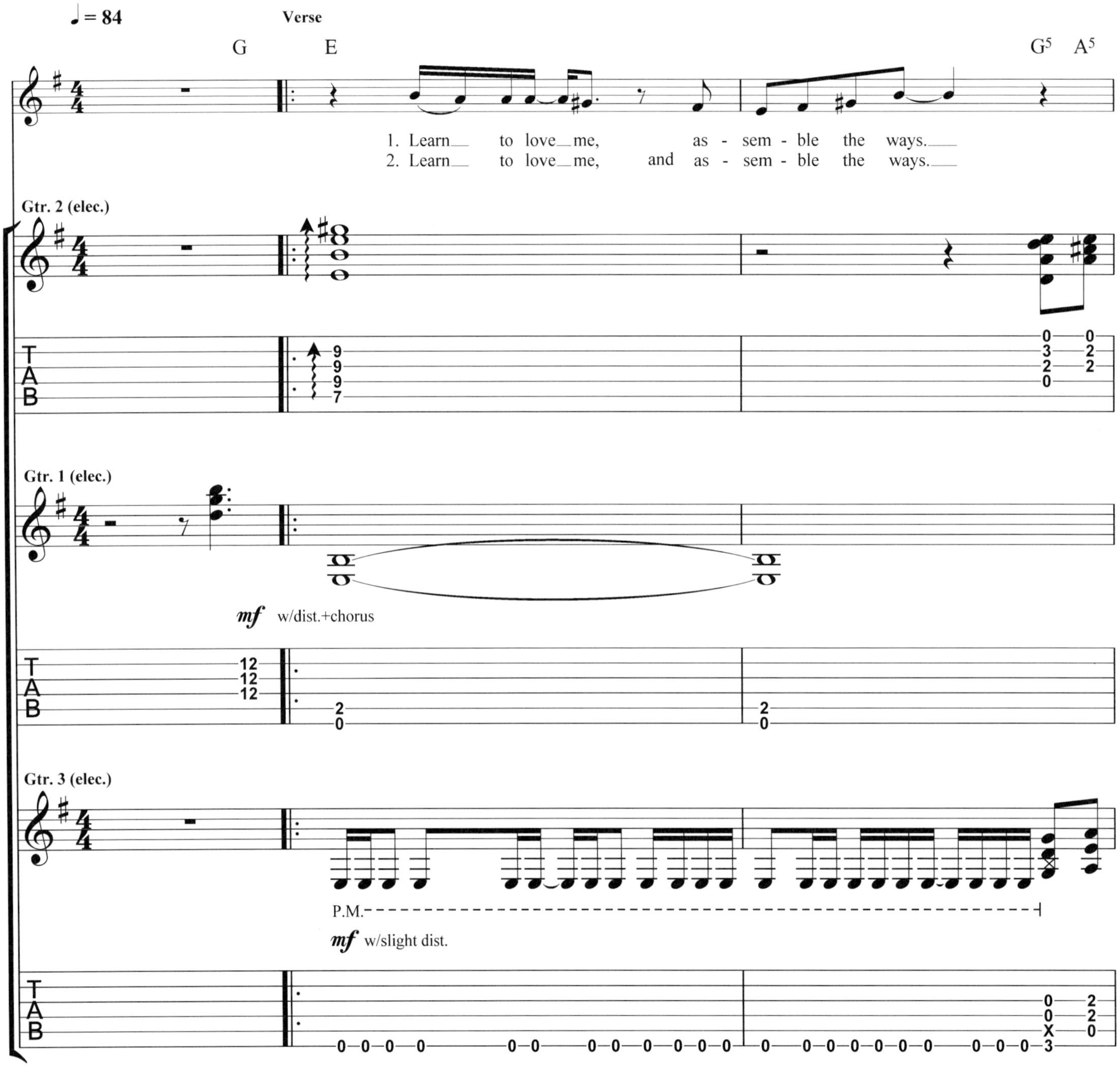

E5
G5 A5 E5
Gtr. 1
Now, to-day, to-mor-row and al - ways. My on-ly weak-ness is a
Now, to-day, to-mor-row and al - ways. My on-ly weak-ness is a
P.M.
P.M.

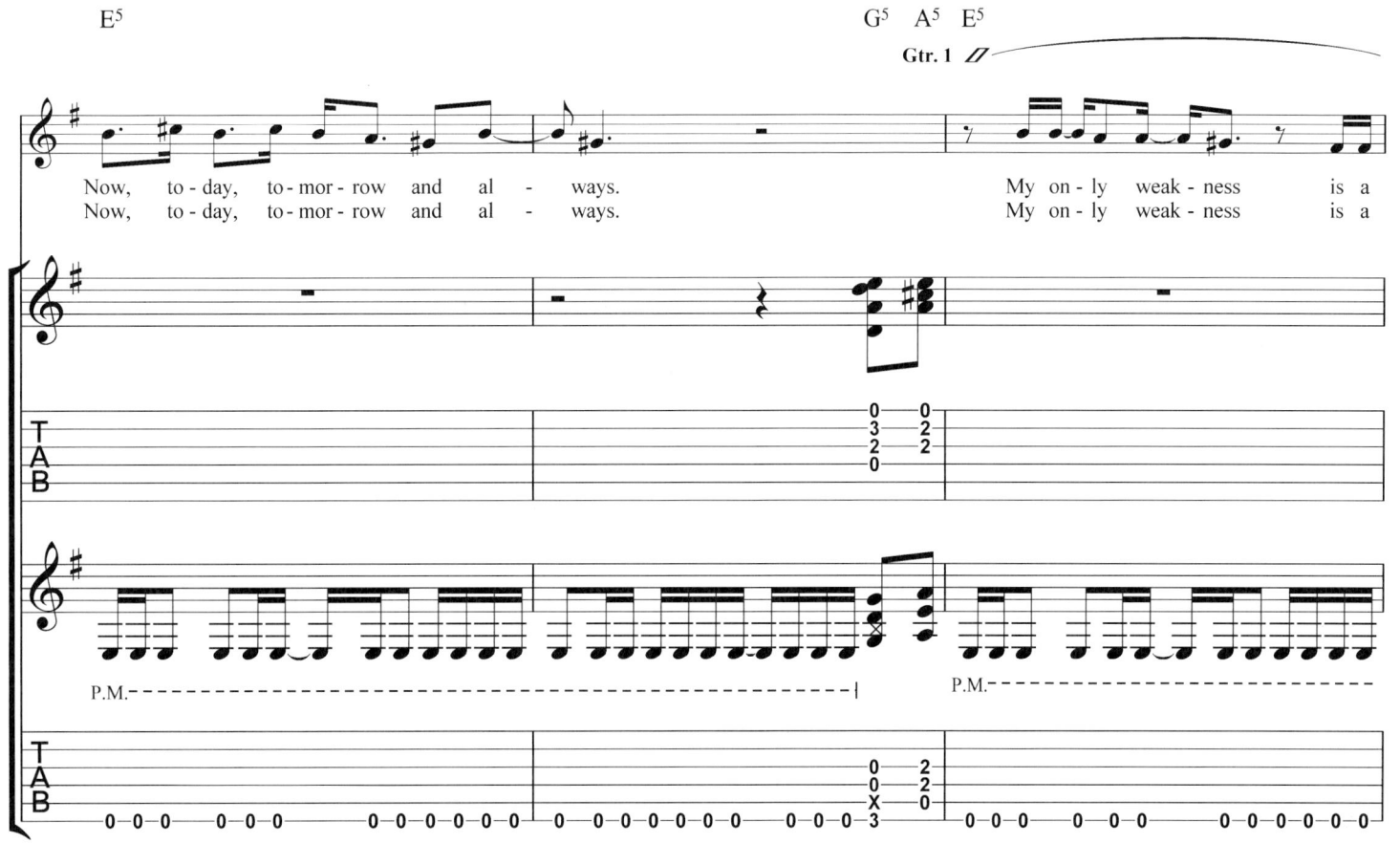

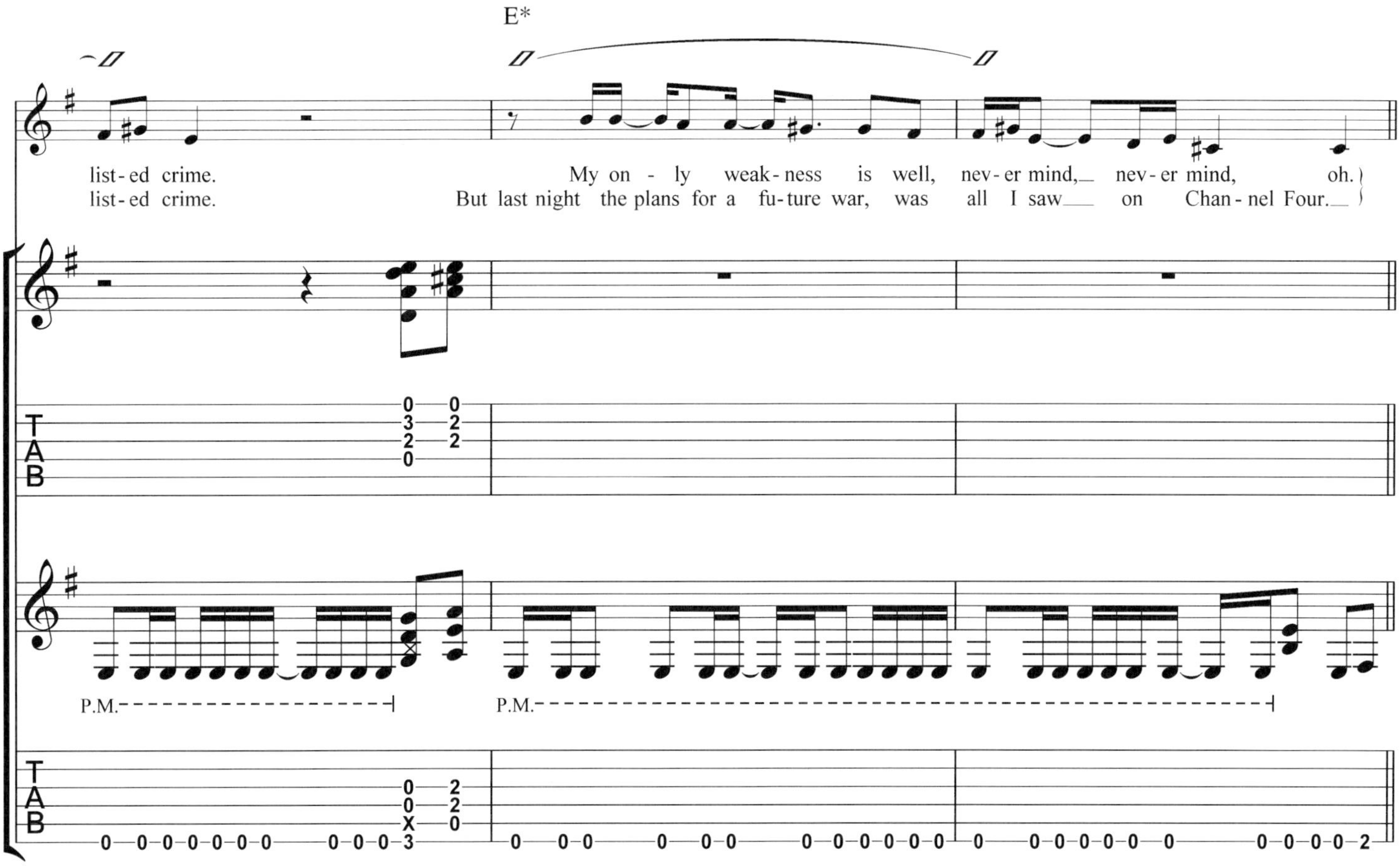
E*
list-ed crime. My on - ly weak-ness is well, nev-er mind, nev-er mind, oh.
list-ed crime. But last night the plans for a fu-ture war, was all I saw on Chan-nel Four.
P.M.
P.M.

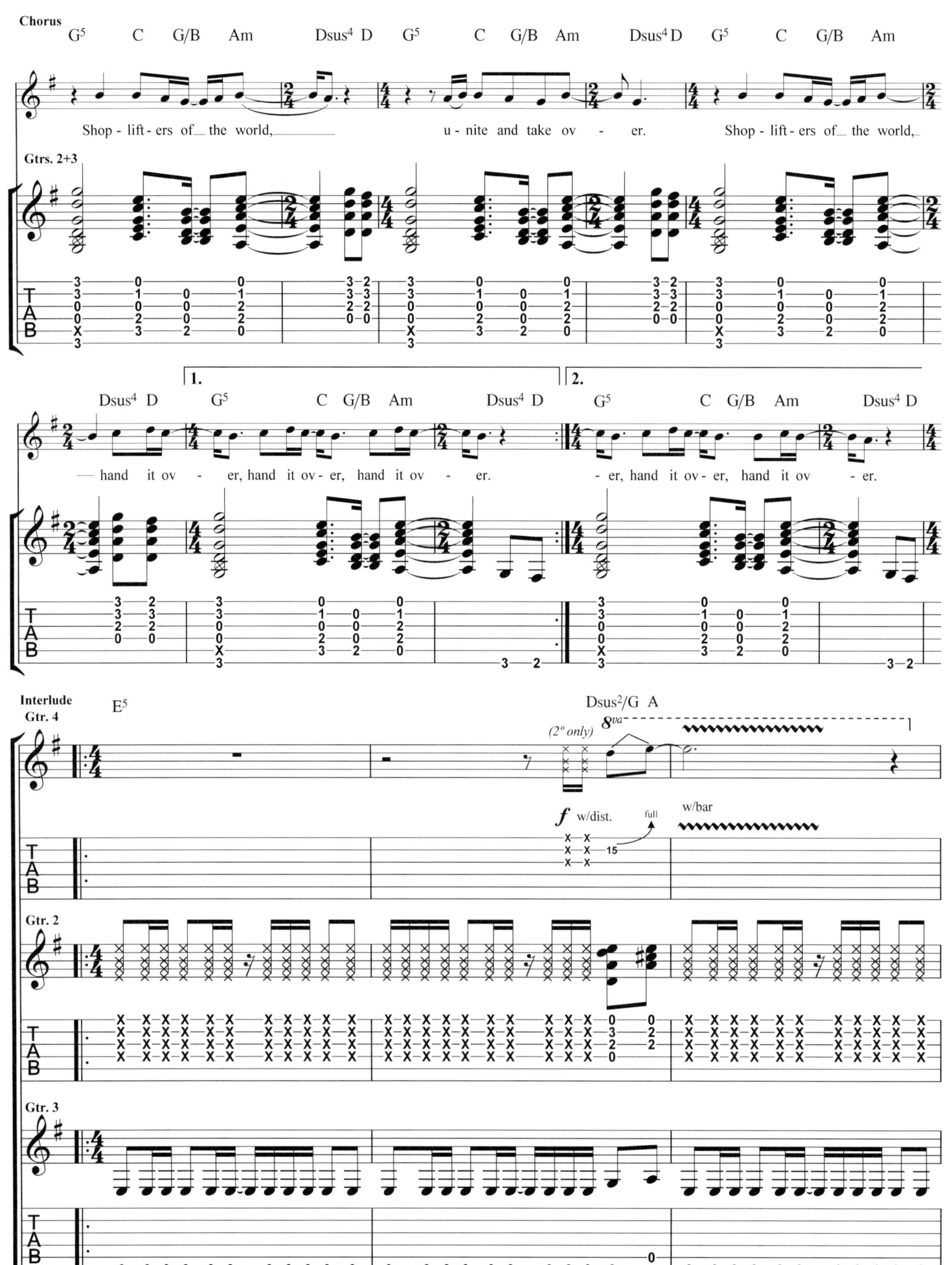

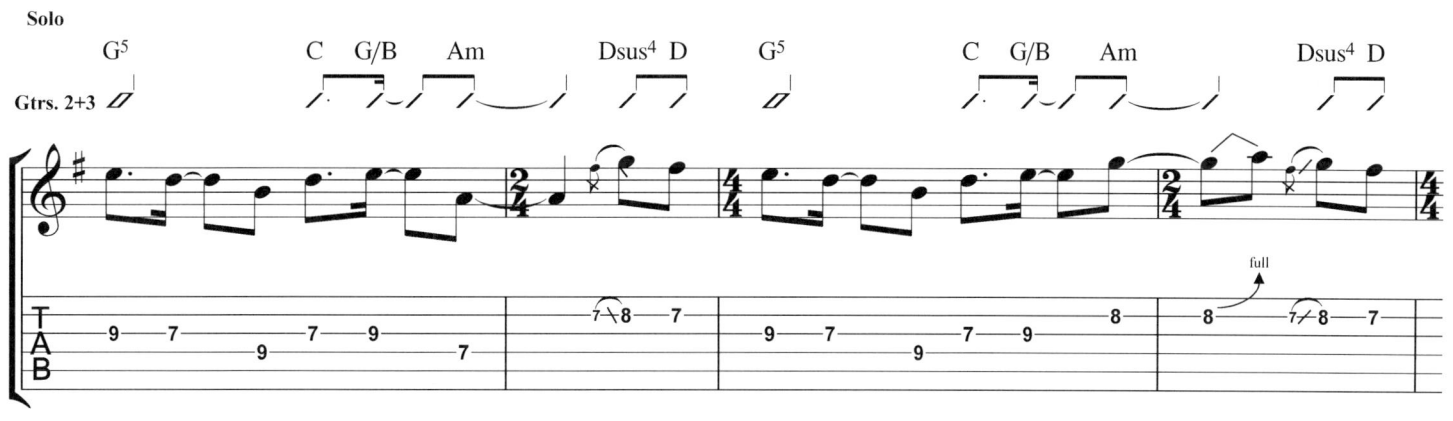

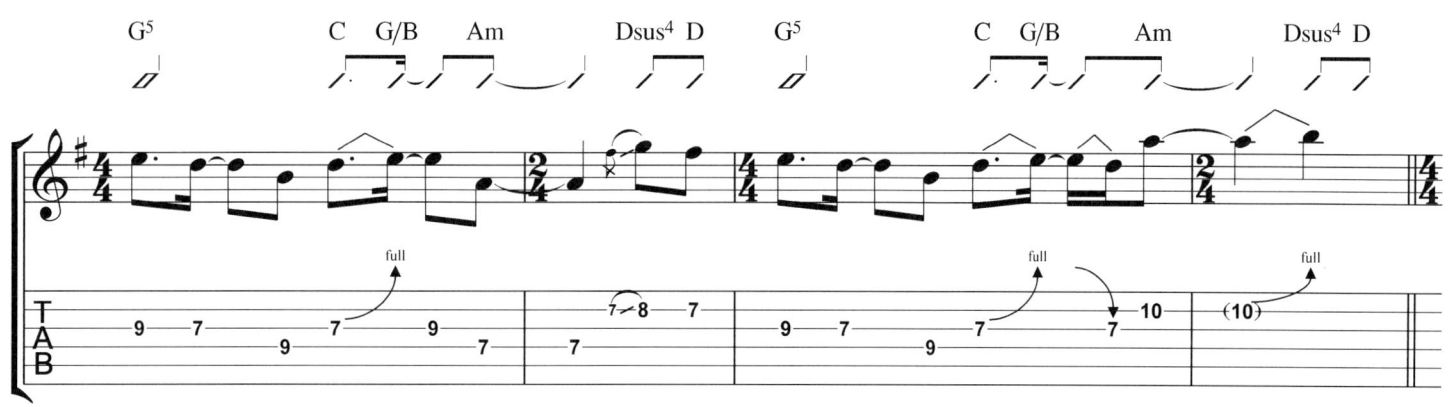

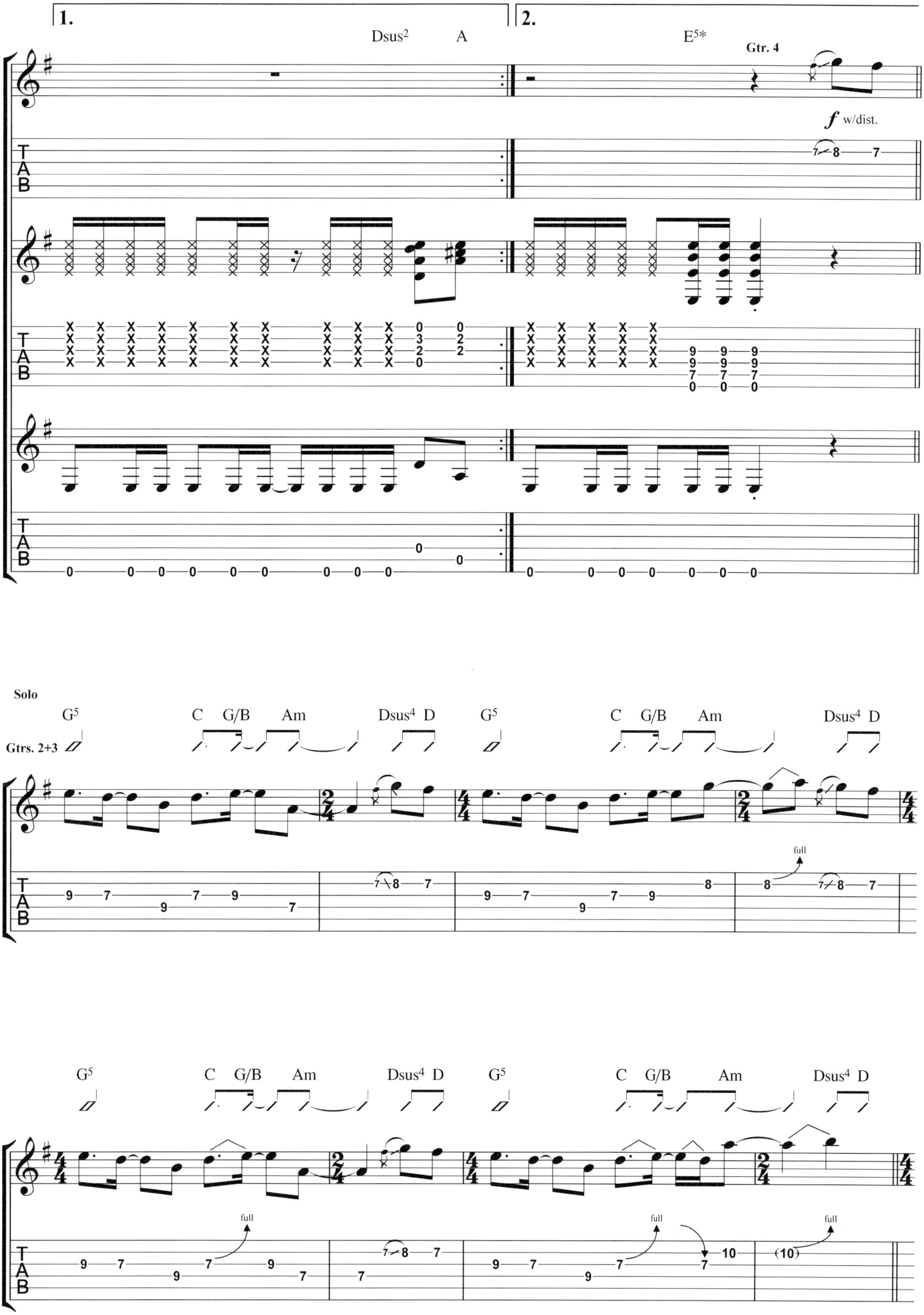
1.
Dsus2 A
2.
E5*
Gtr. 4
f w/dist.
Solo
Gtrs. 2+3
G5 C G/B Am Dsus4 D G5 C G/B Am Dsus4 D
full
G5 C G/B Am Dsus4 D G5 C G/B Am Dsus4 D
full
full
full

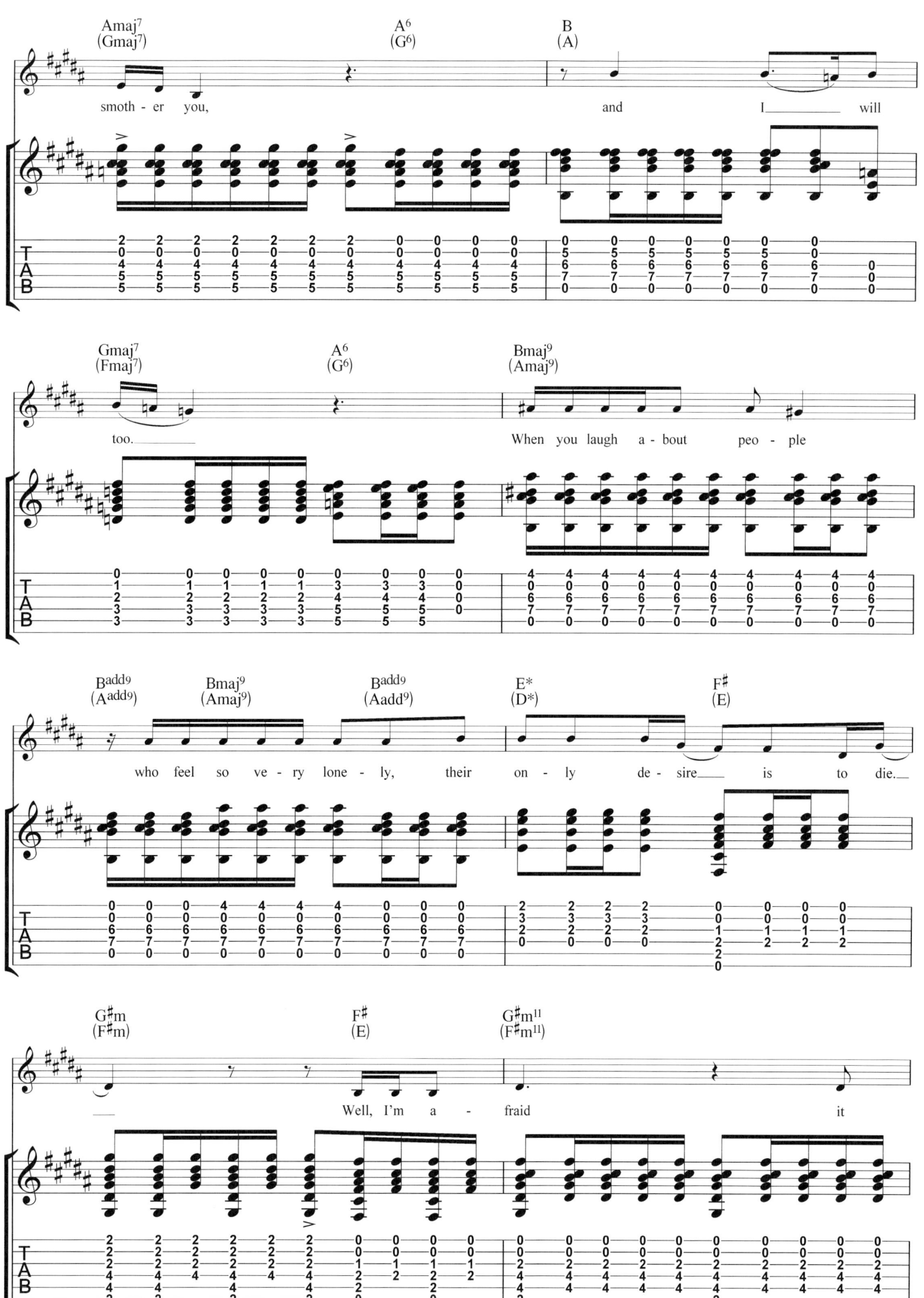

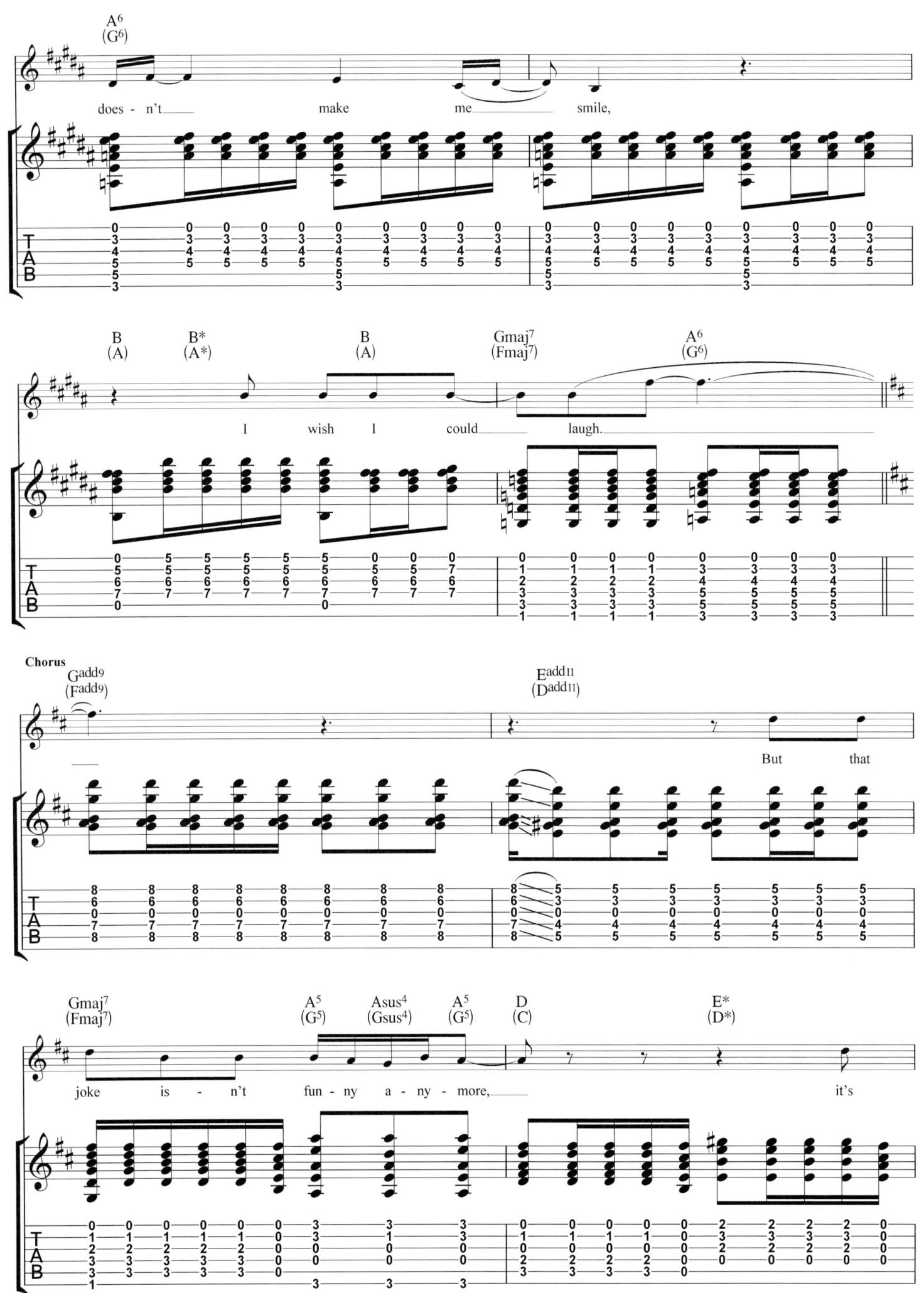

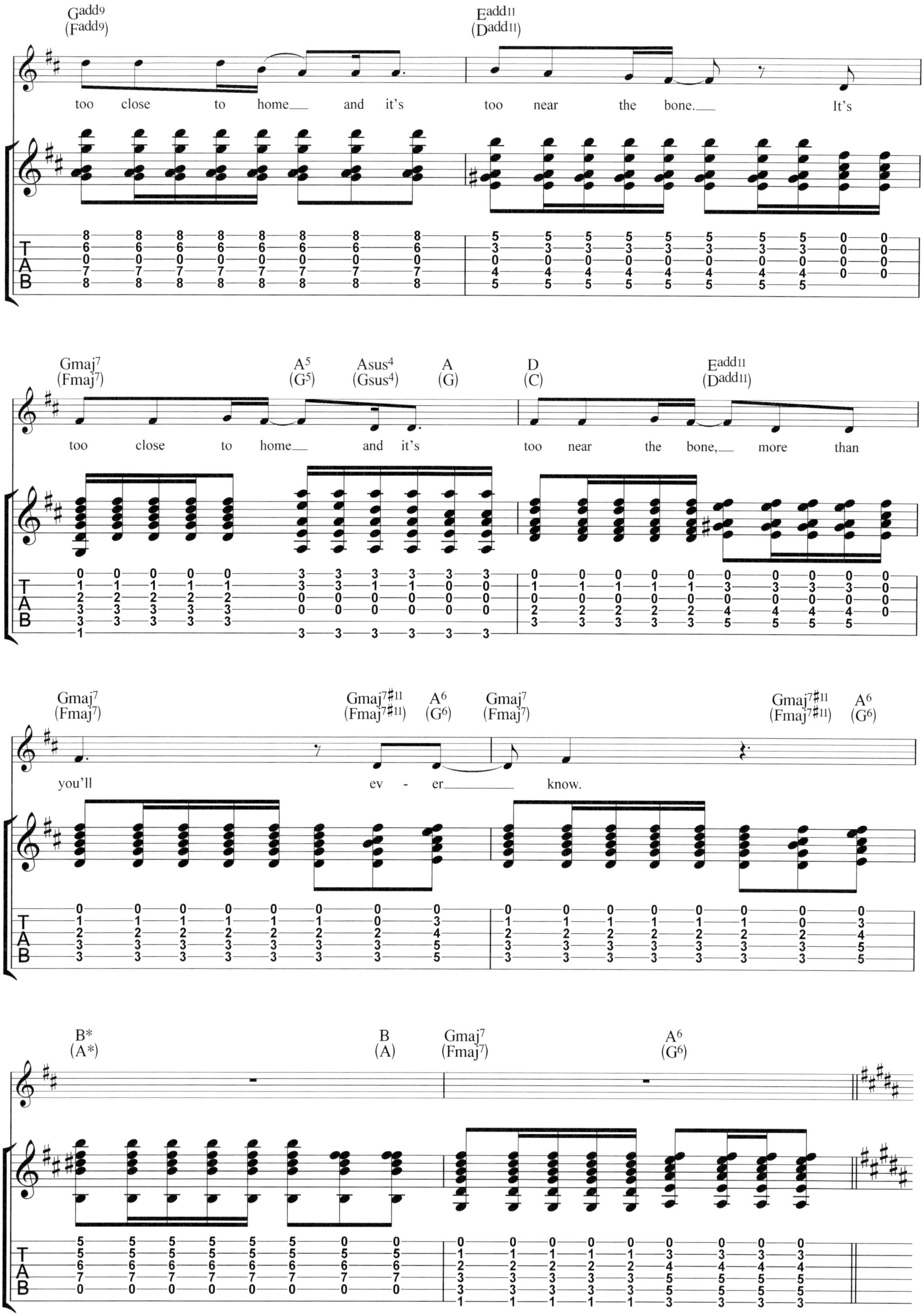
Gadd9 (Fadd9)
Eadd11 (Dadd11)
too close to home and it's too near the bone. It's
Gmaj7 (Fmaj7)
A5 (G5)
Asus4 (Gsus4)
A (G)
D (C)
Eadd11 (Dadd11)
too close to home and it's too near the bone, more than
Gmaj7 (Fmaj7)
Gmaj7♯11 (Fmaj7♯11)
A6 (G6)
Gmaj7 (Fmaj7)
Gmaj7♯11 (Fmaj7♯11)
A6 (G6)
you'll ev - er know.
B* (A*)
B (A)
Gmaj7 (Fmaj7)
A6 (G6)
TAB

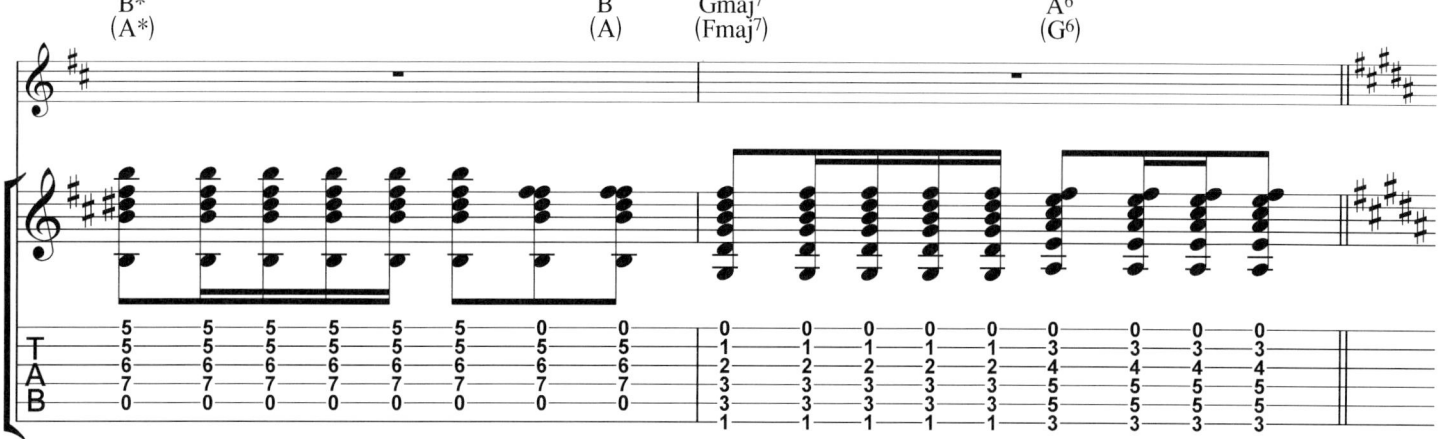

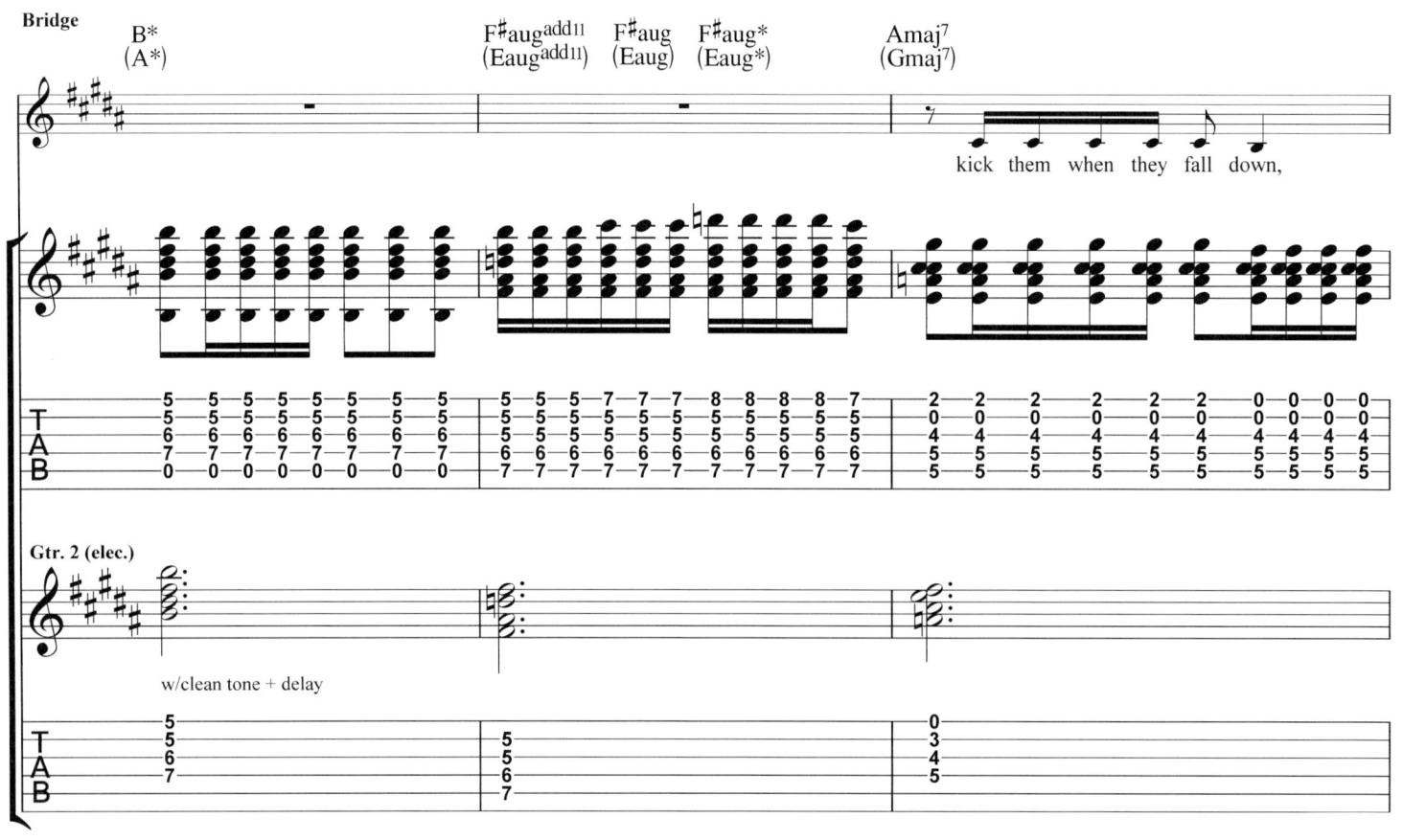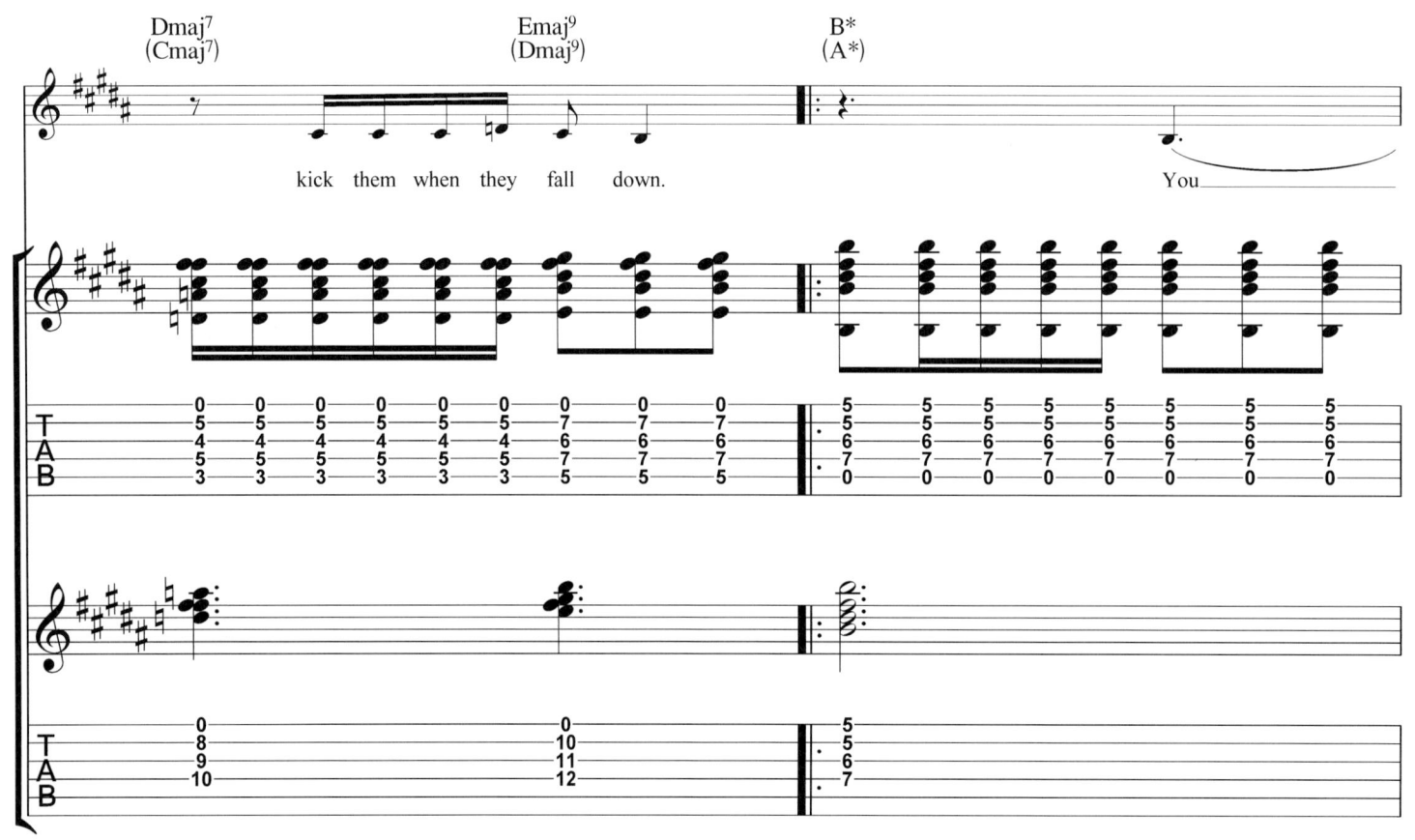

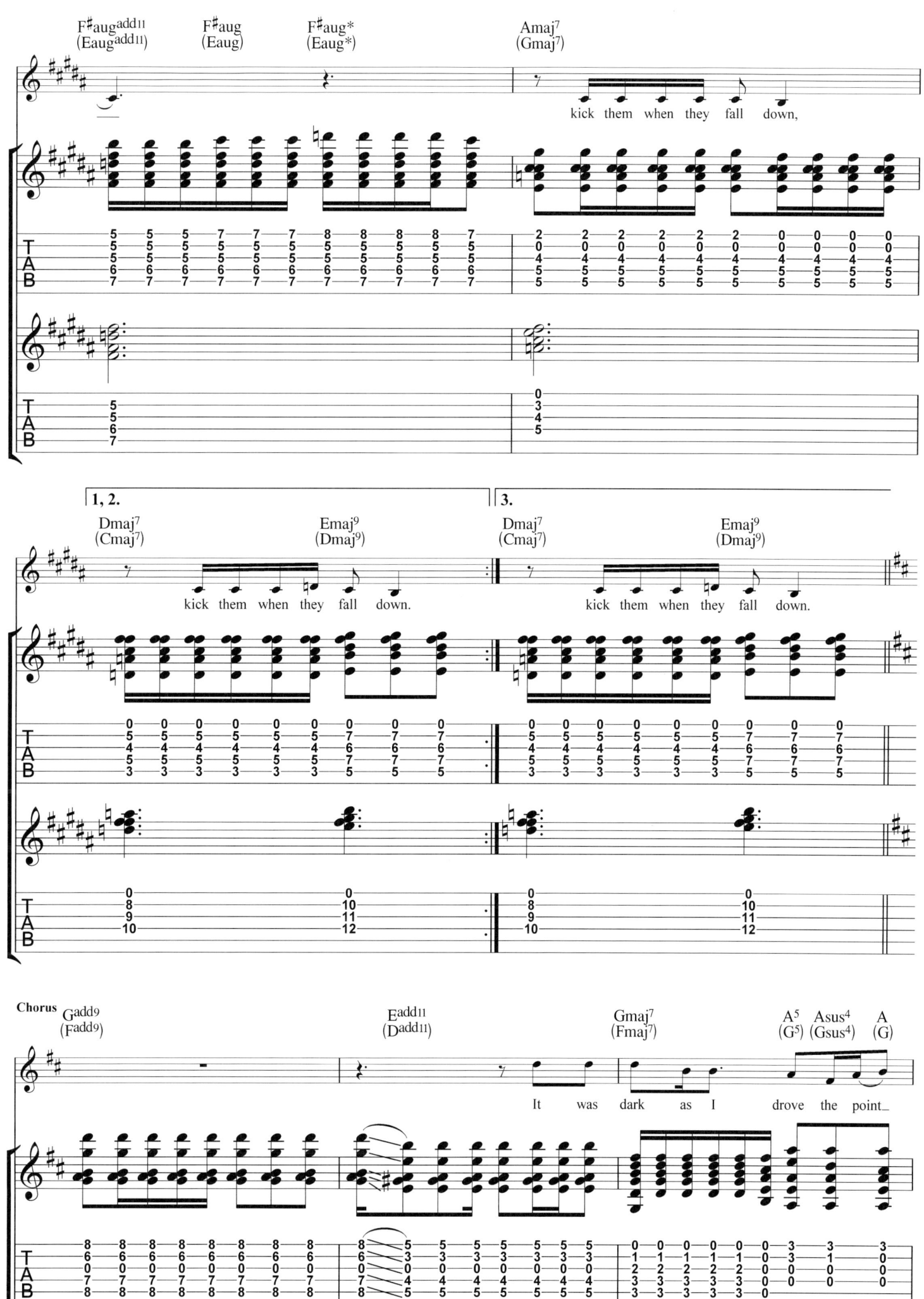

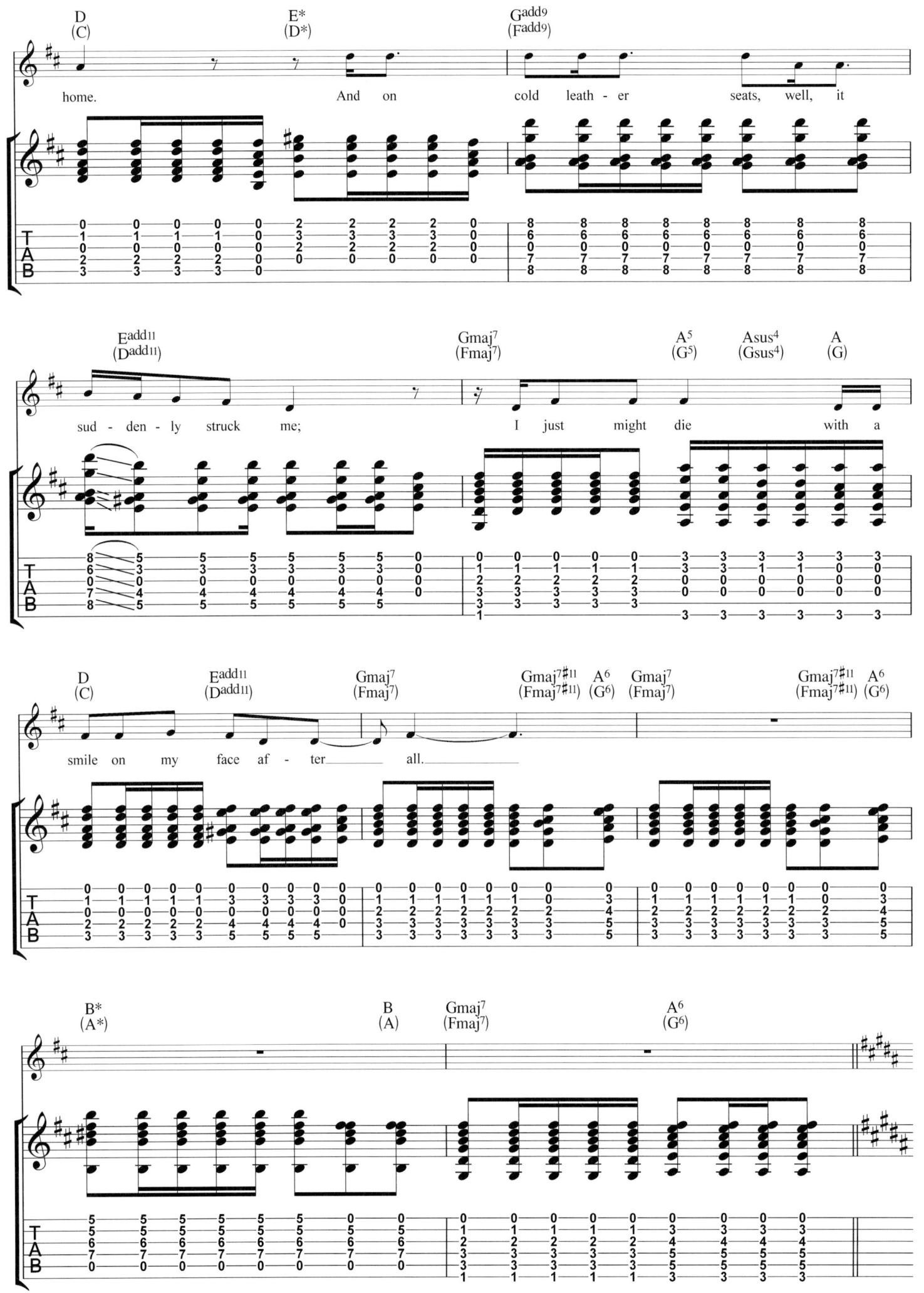

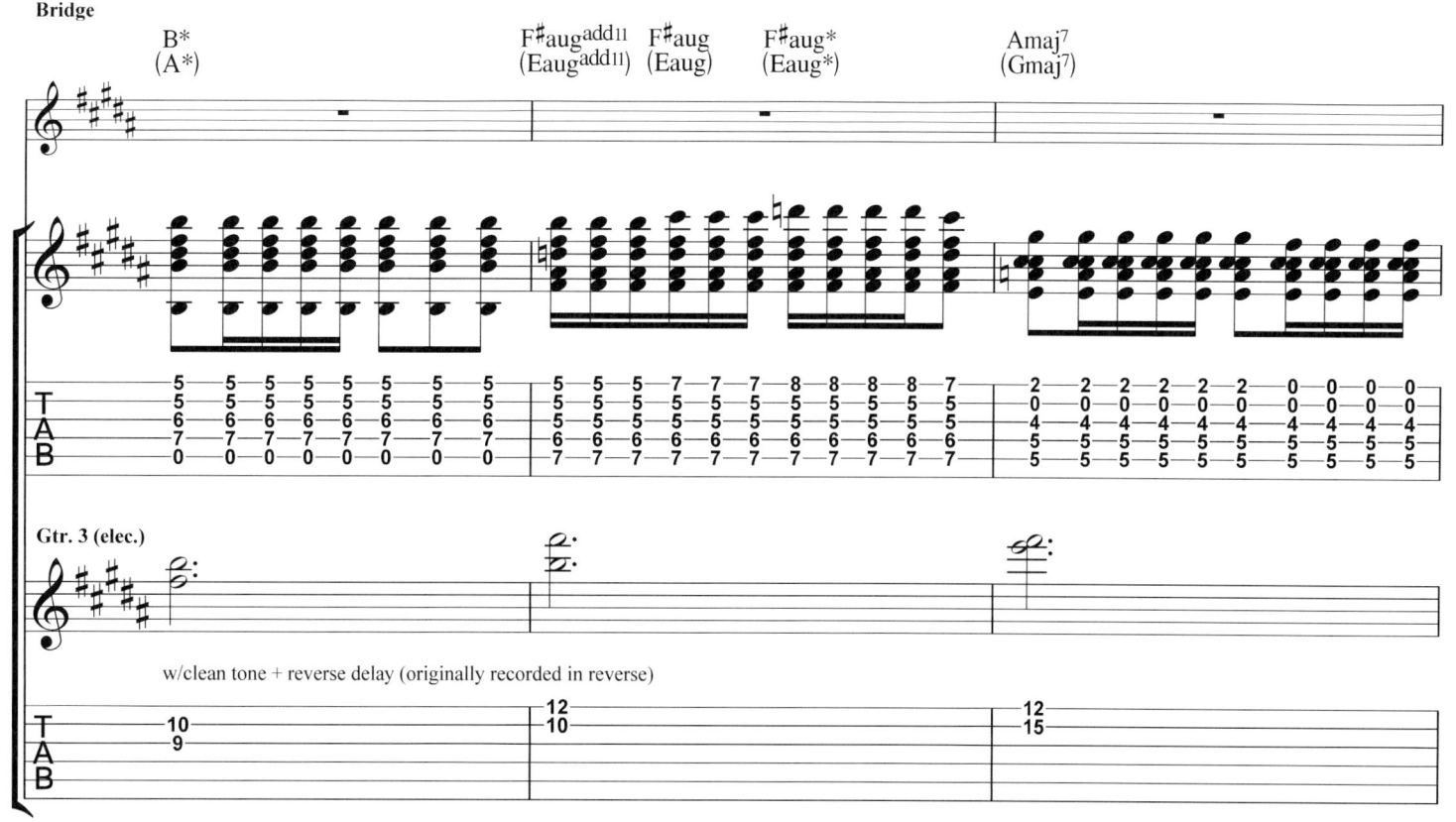
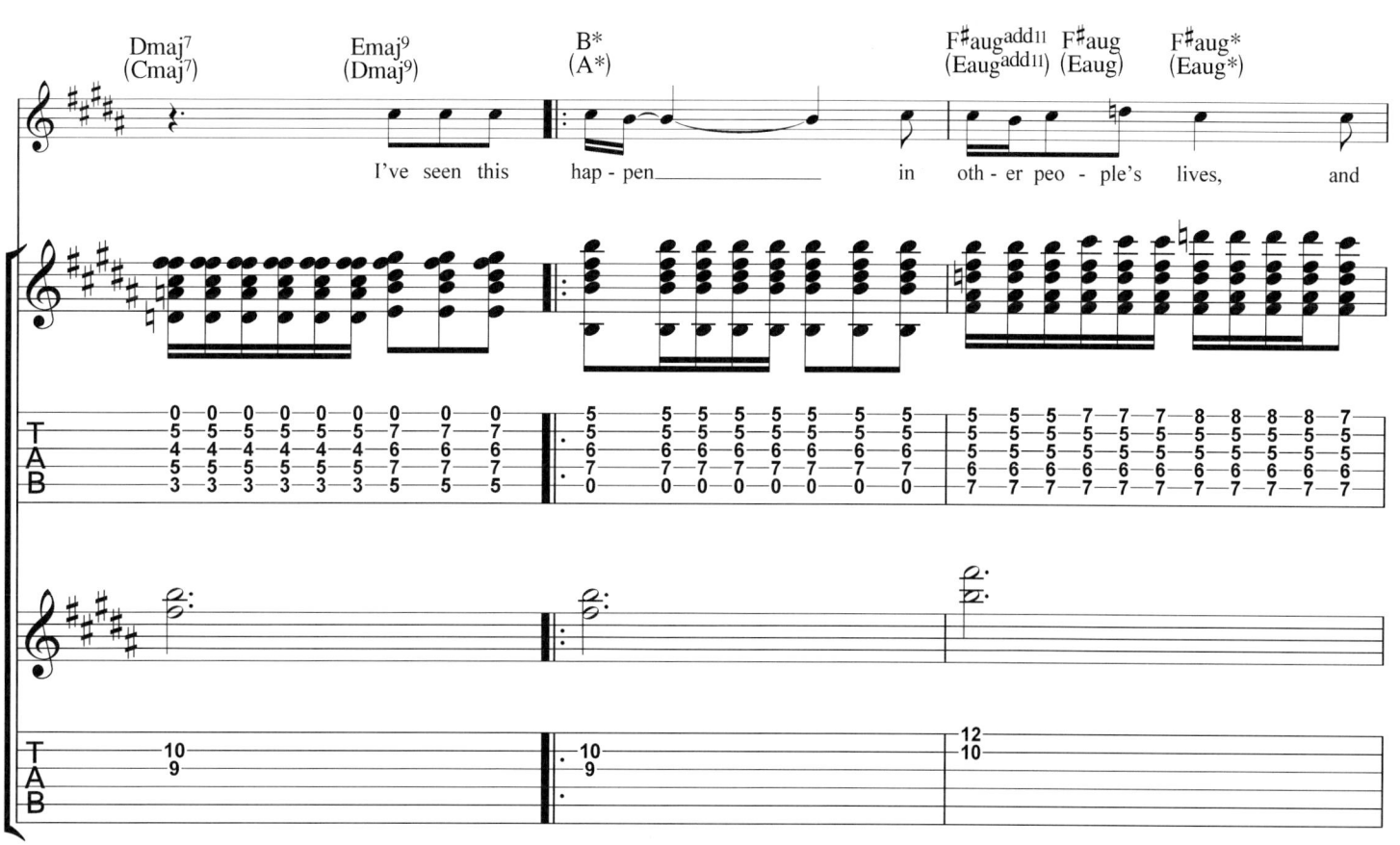

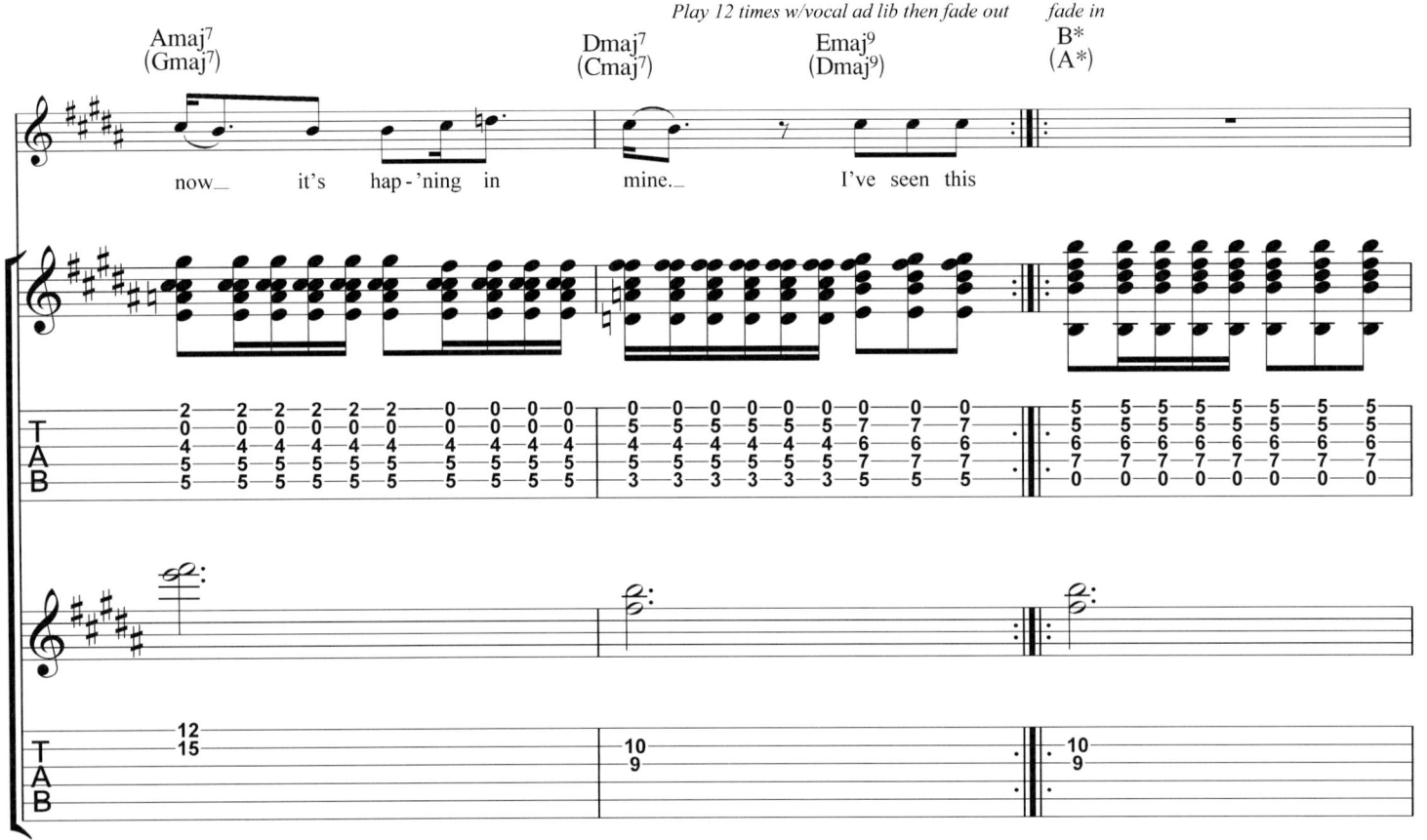
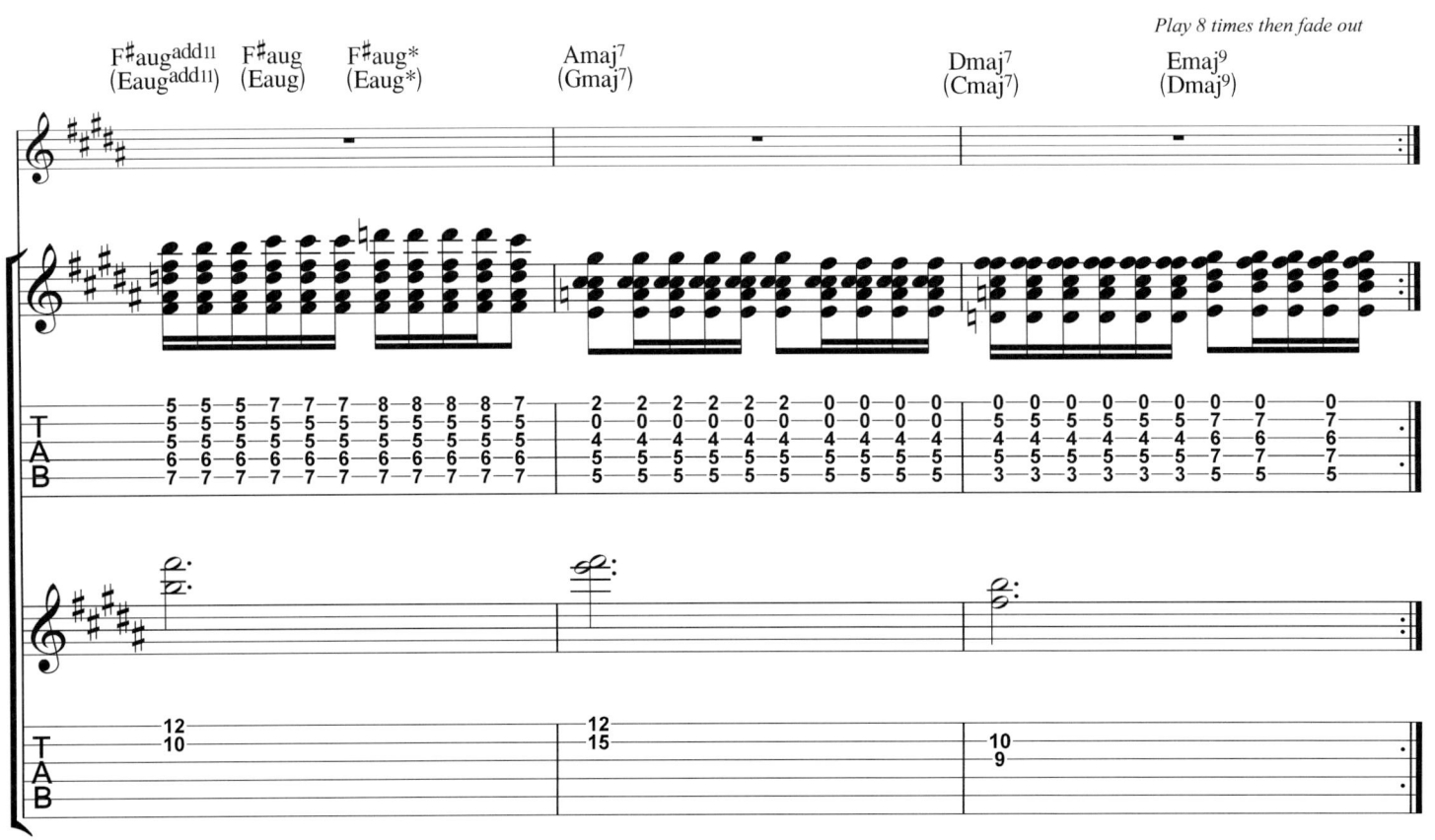

There Is A Light That Never Goes Out

Words by Morrissey
Music by Johnny Marr

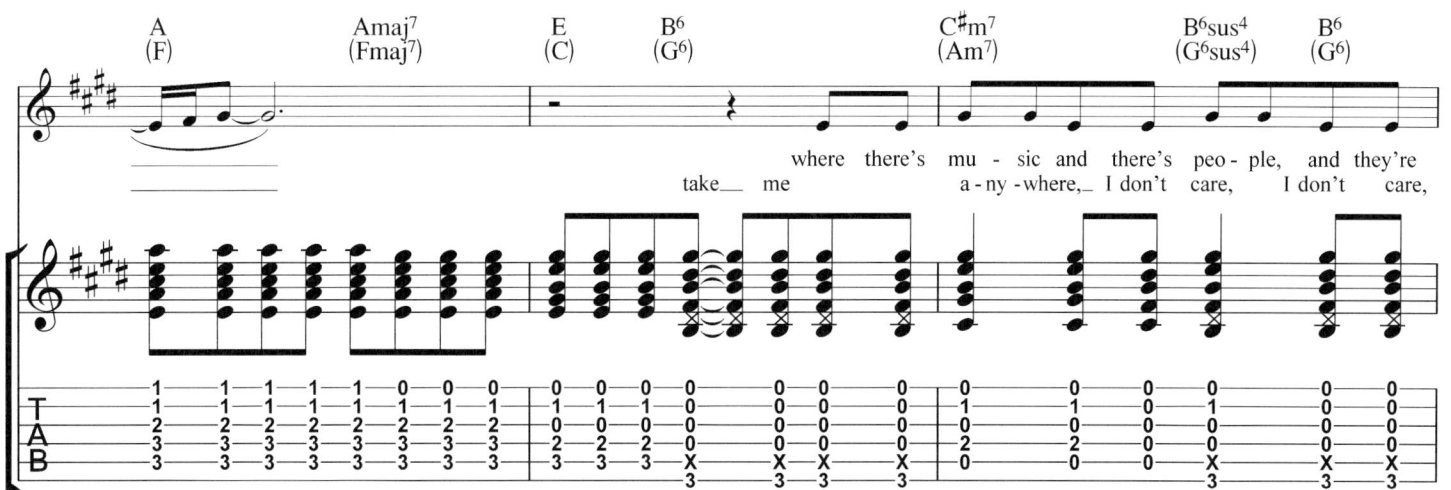

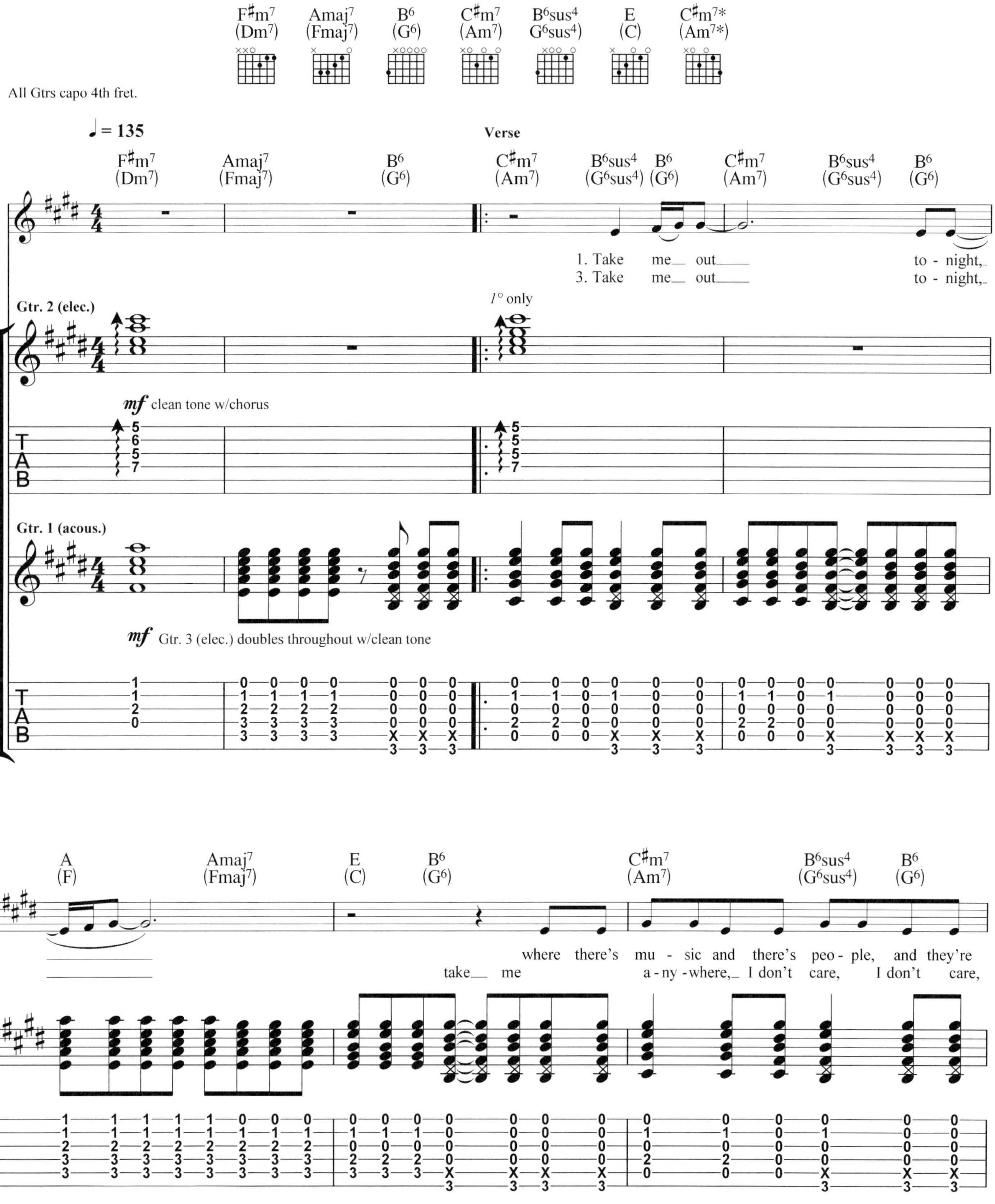

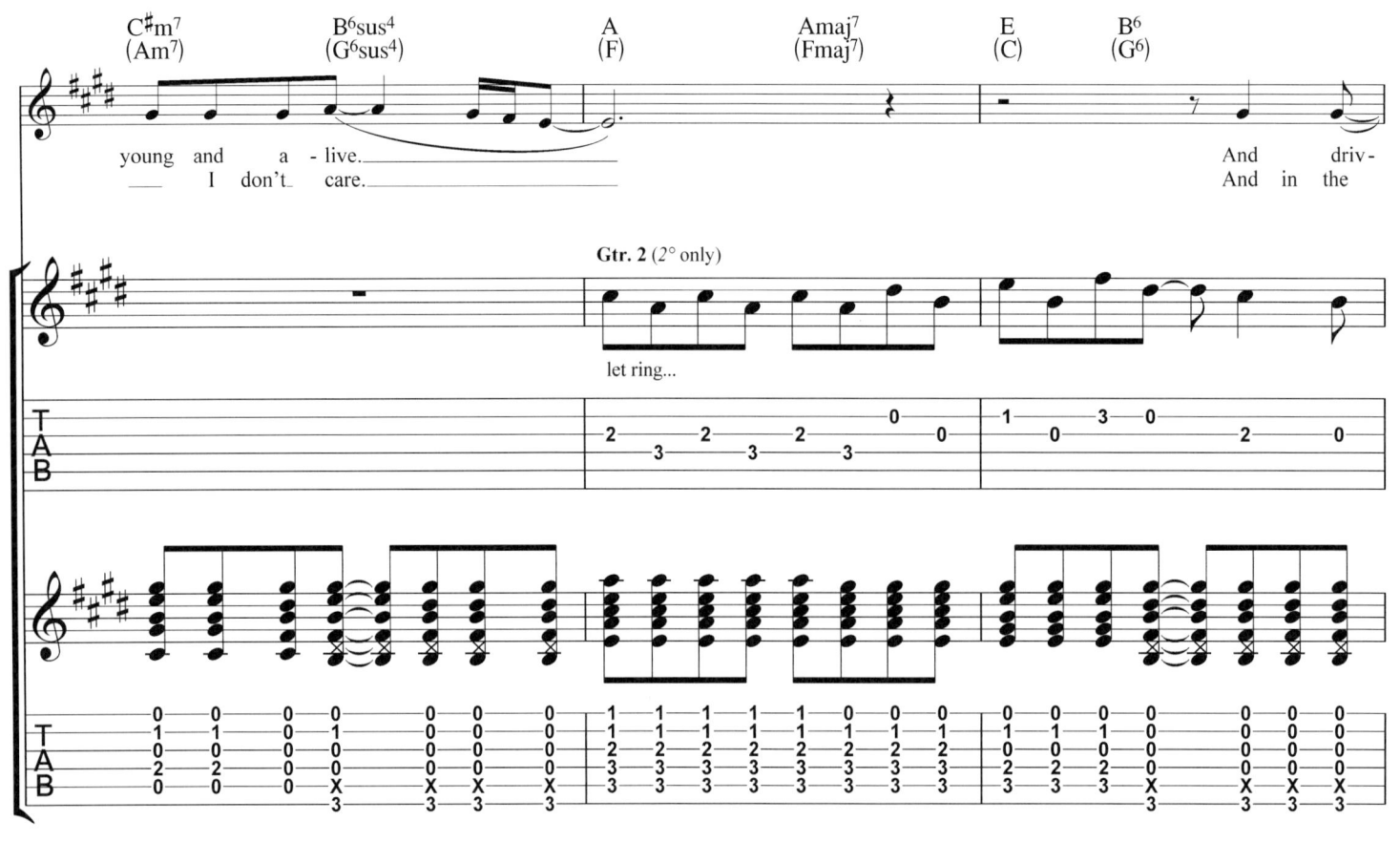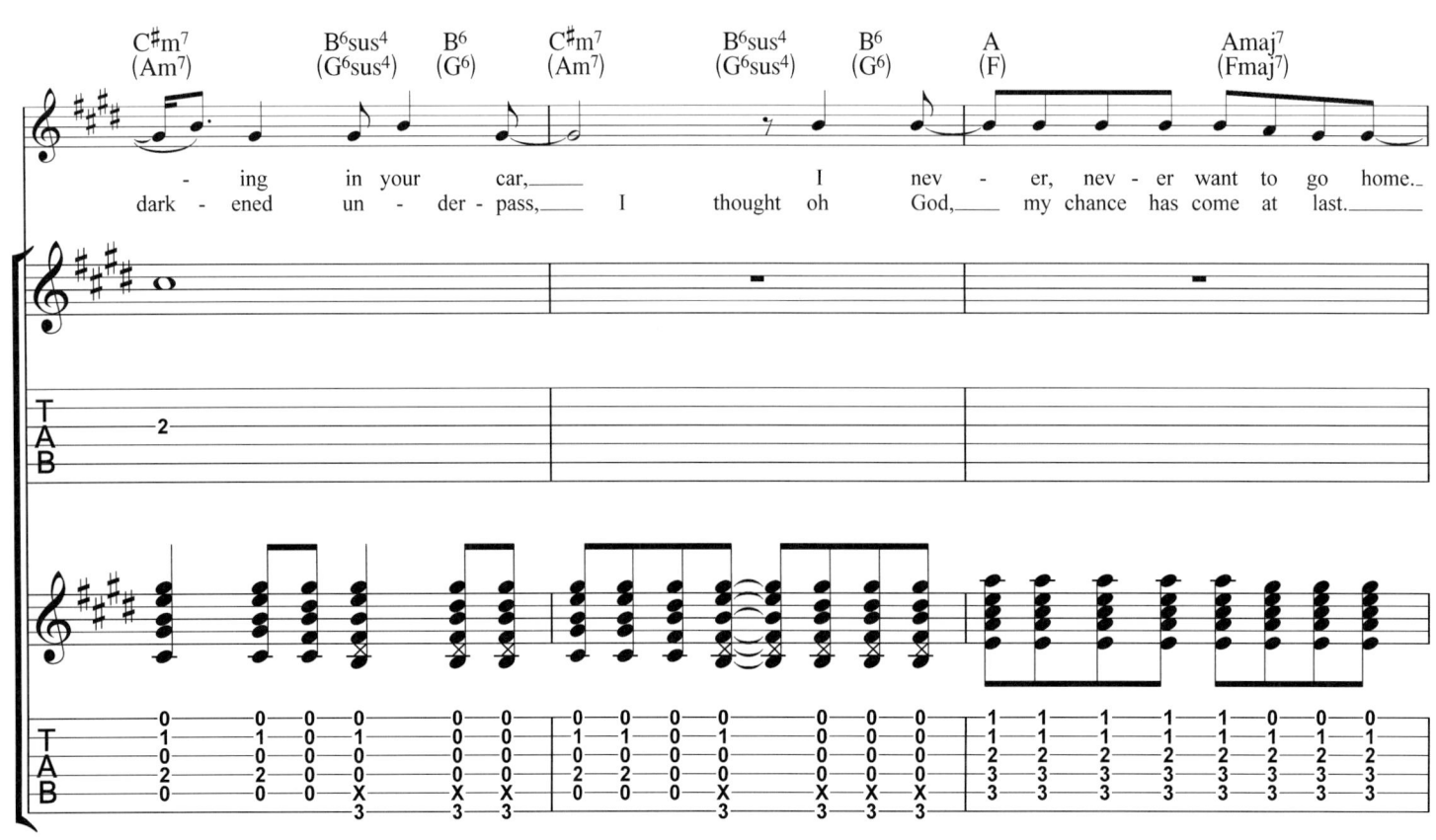

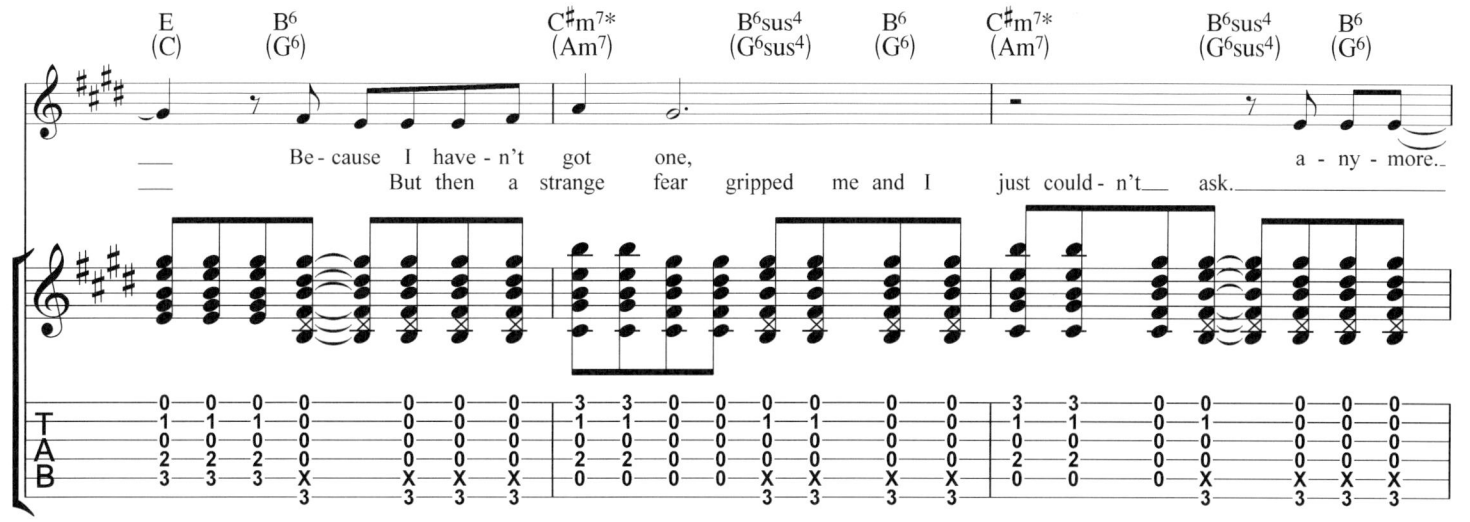
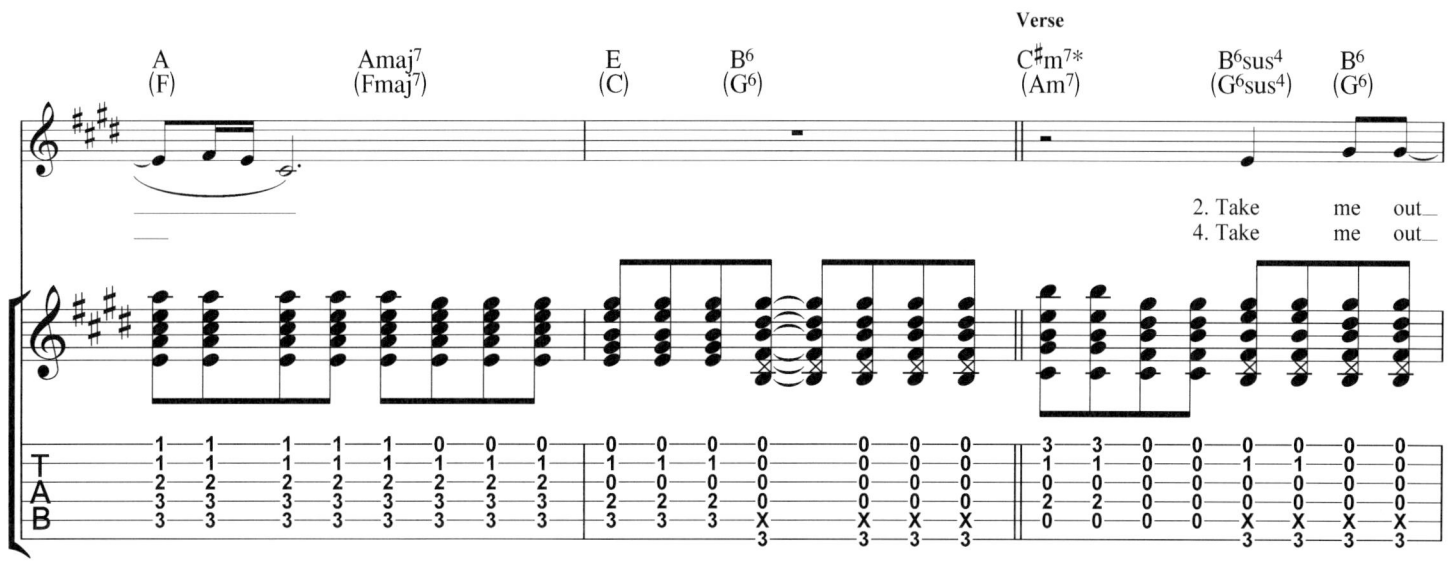
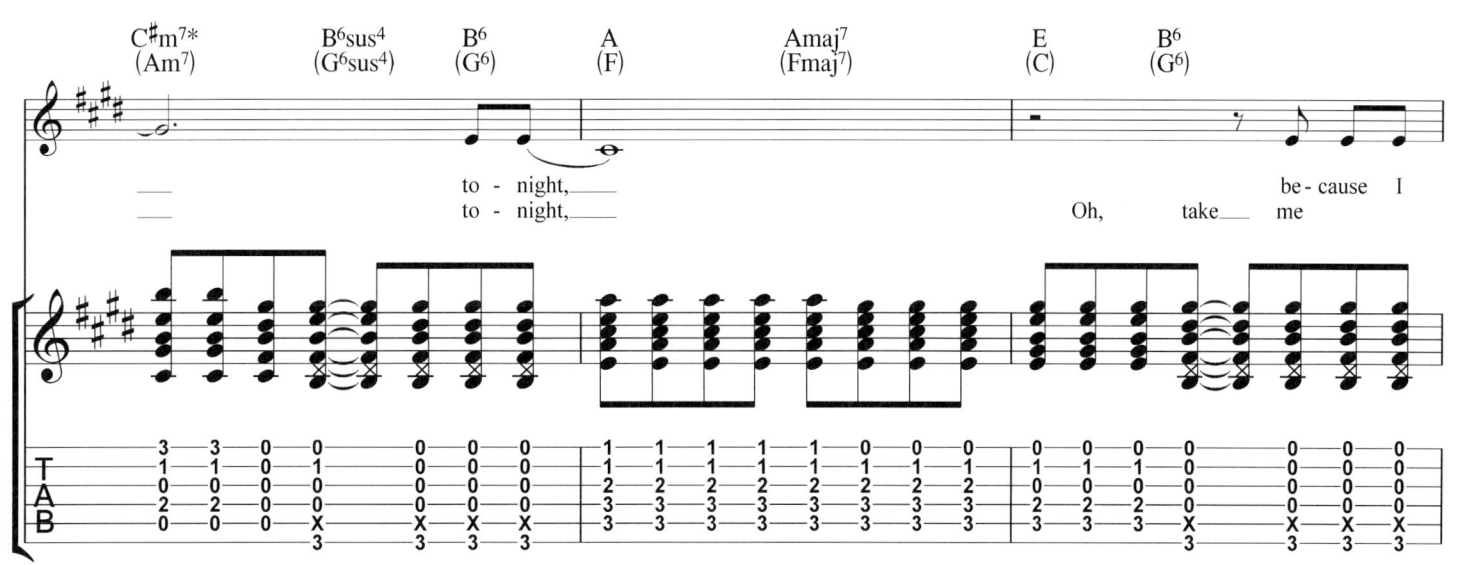

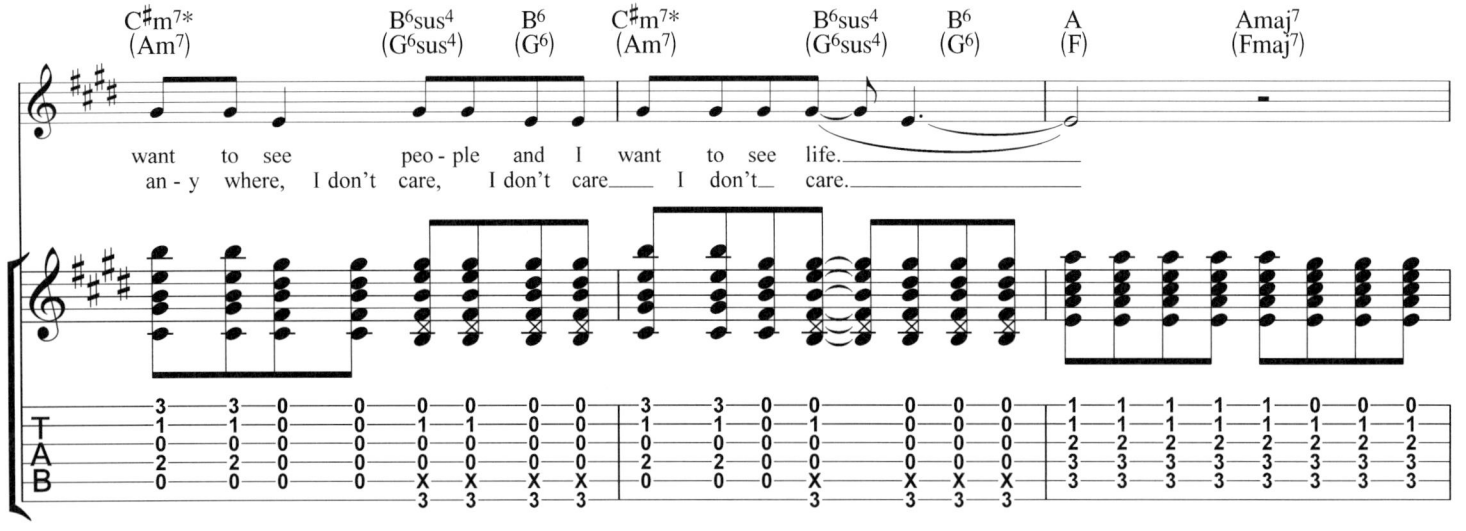
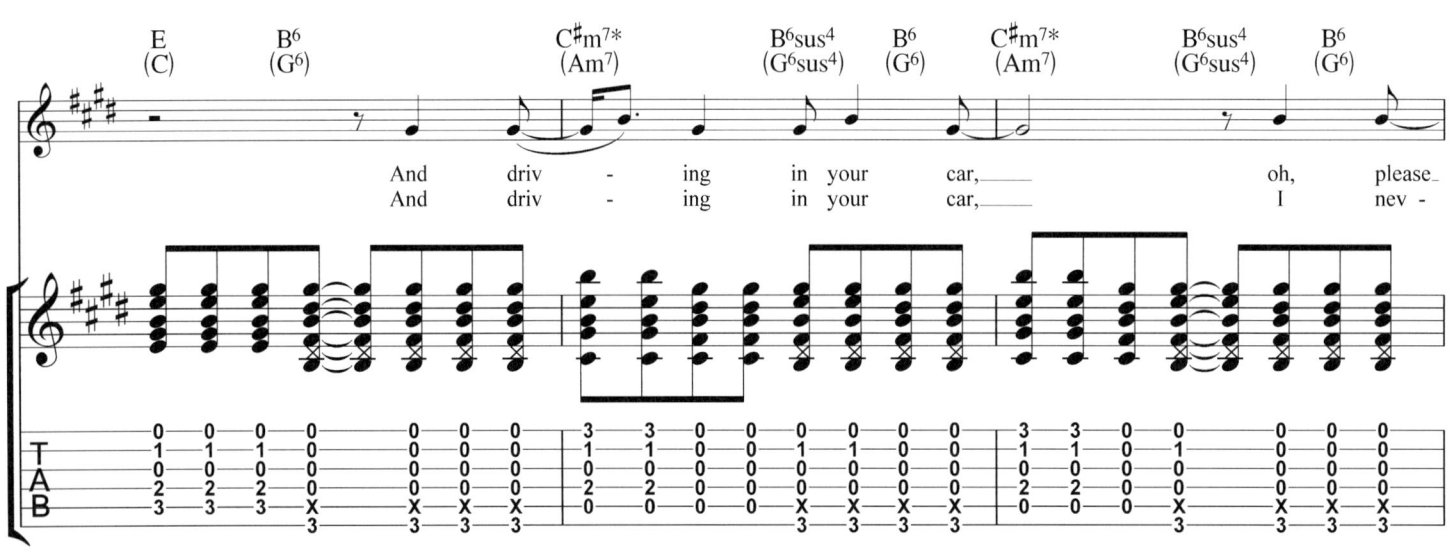
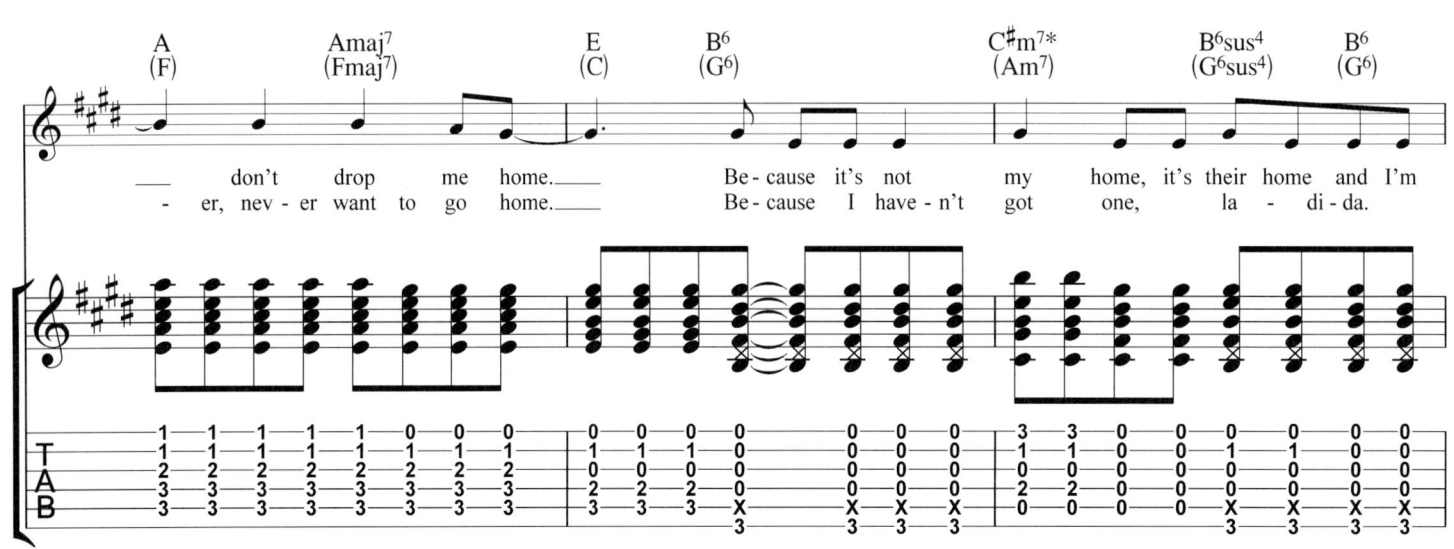

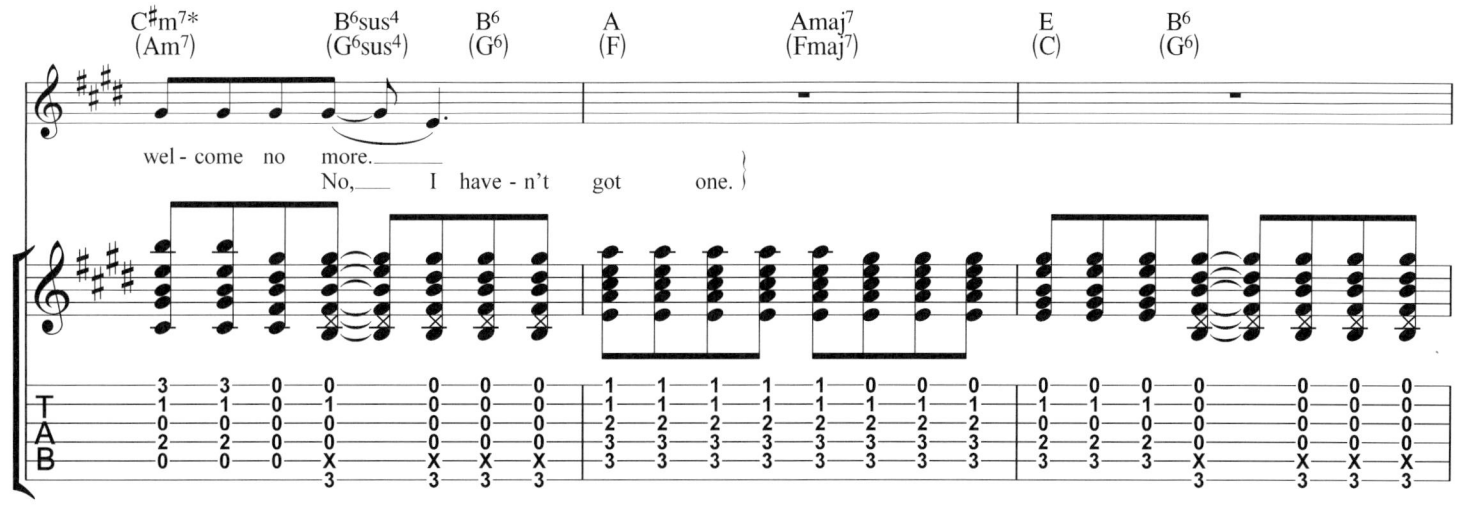
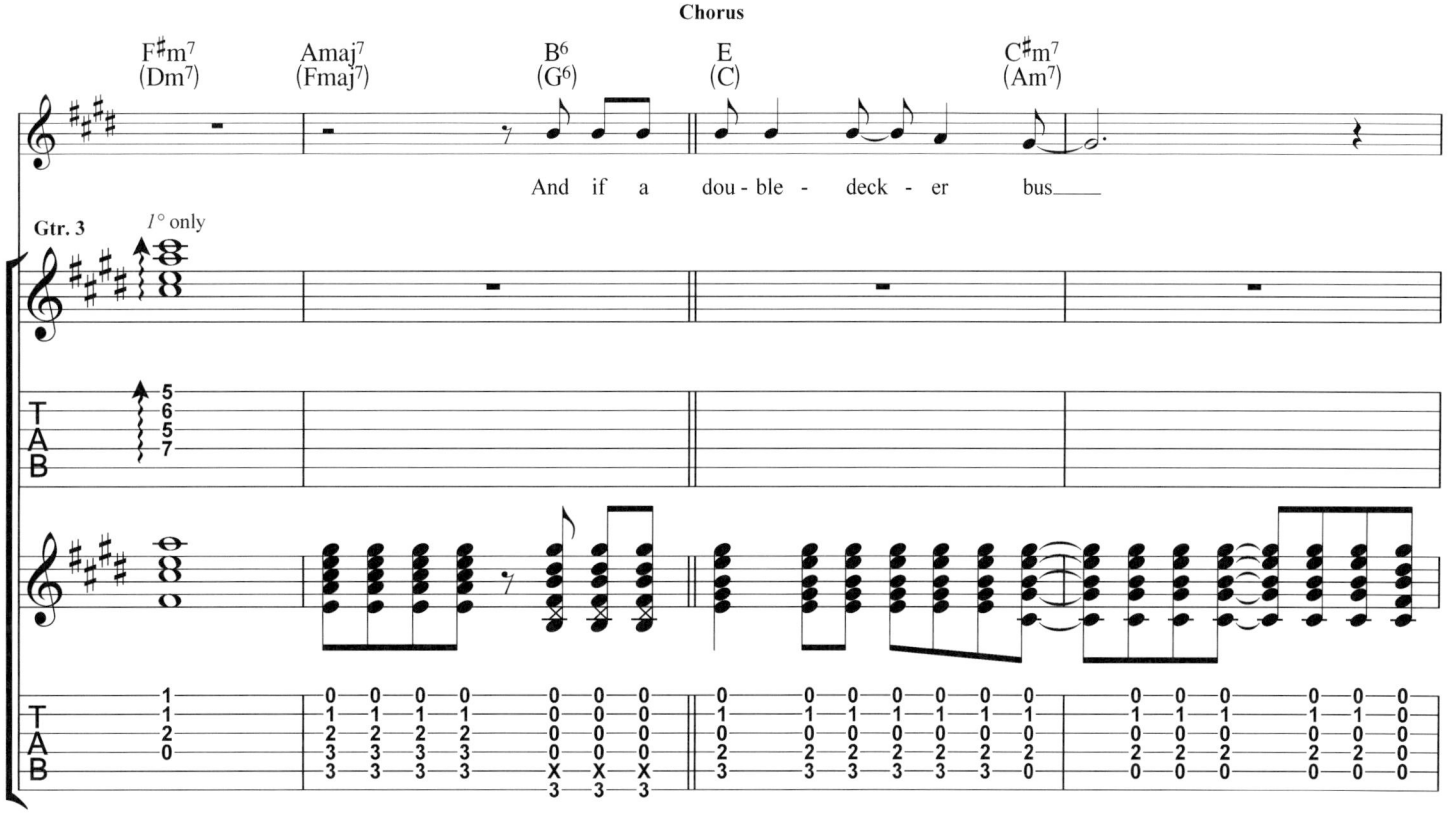
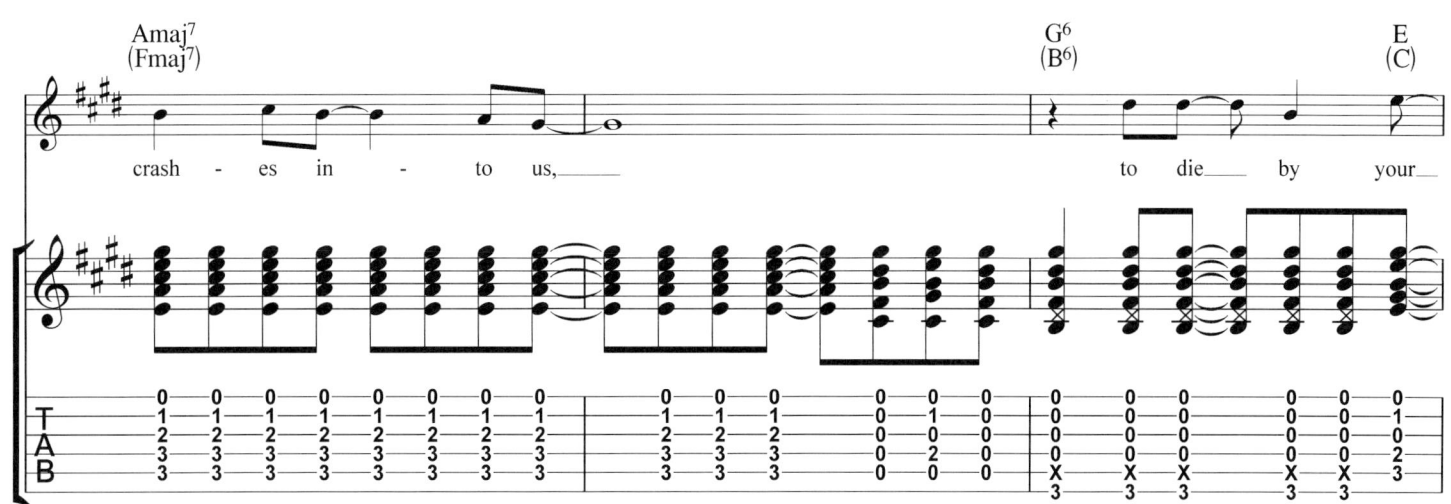

119

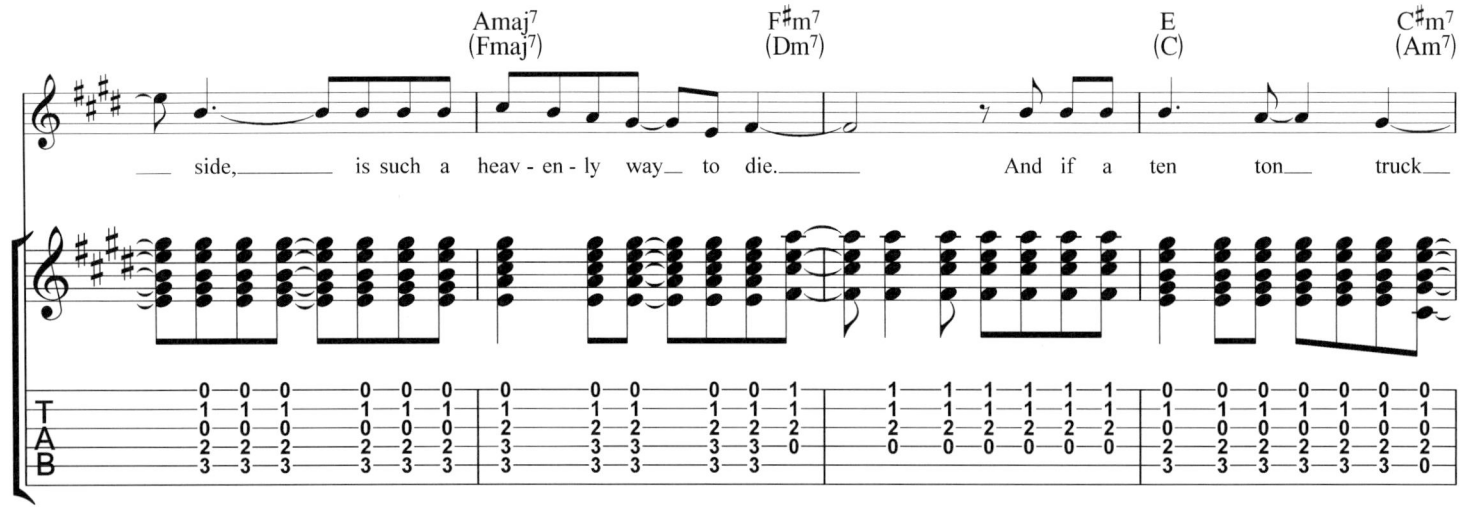
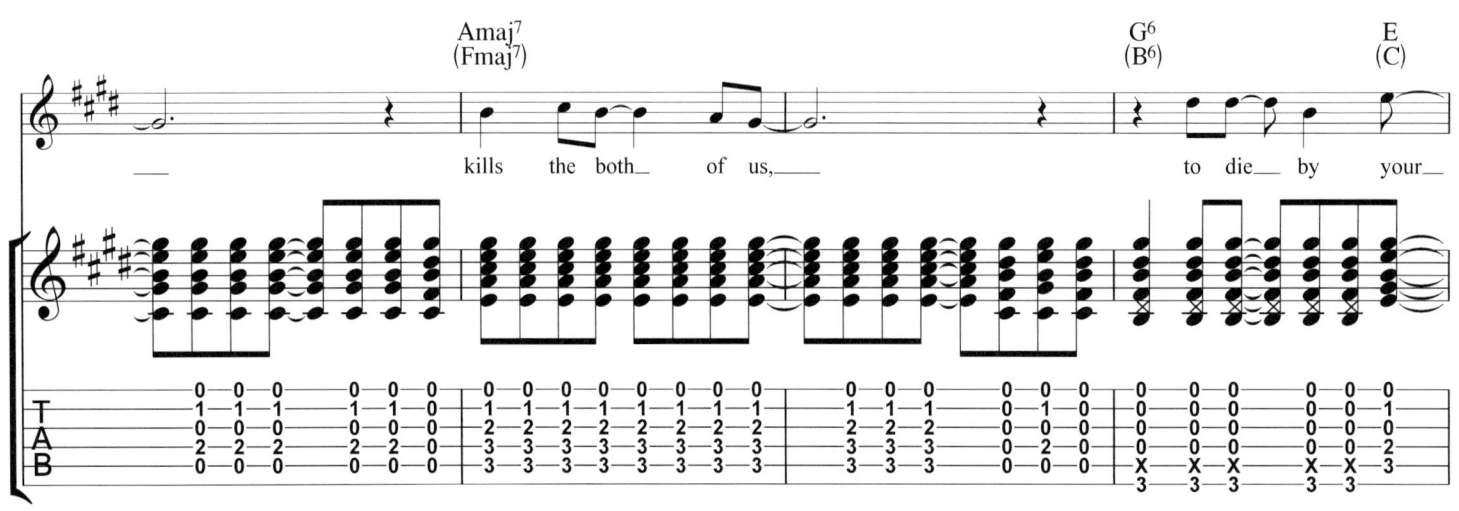
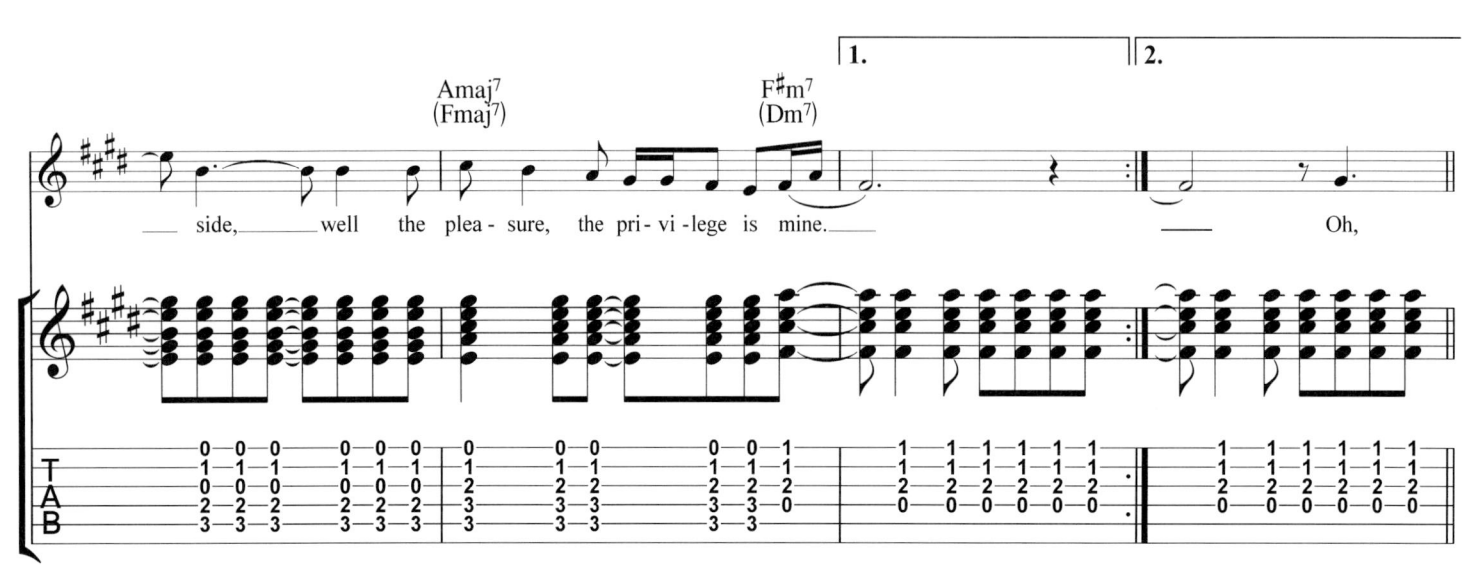

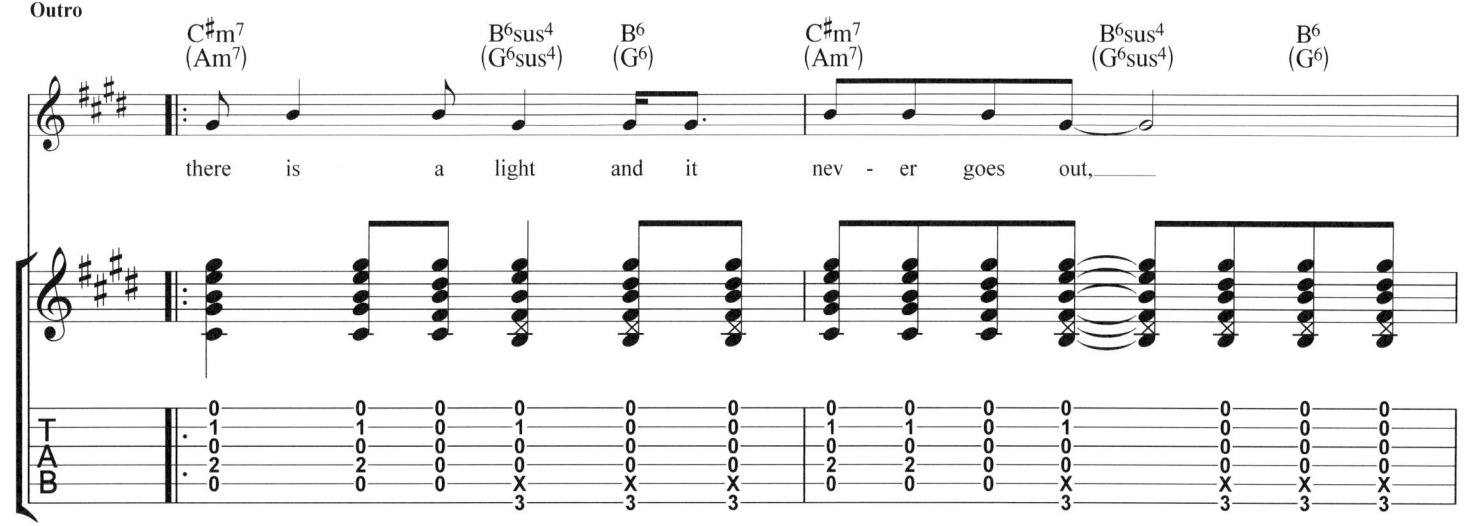
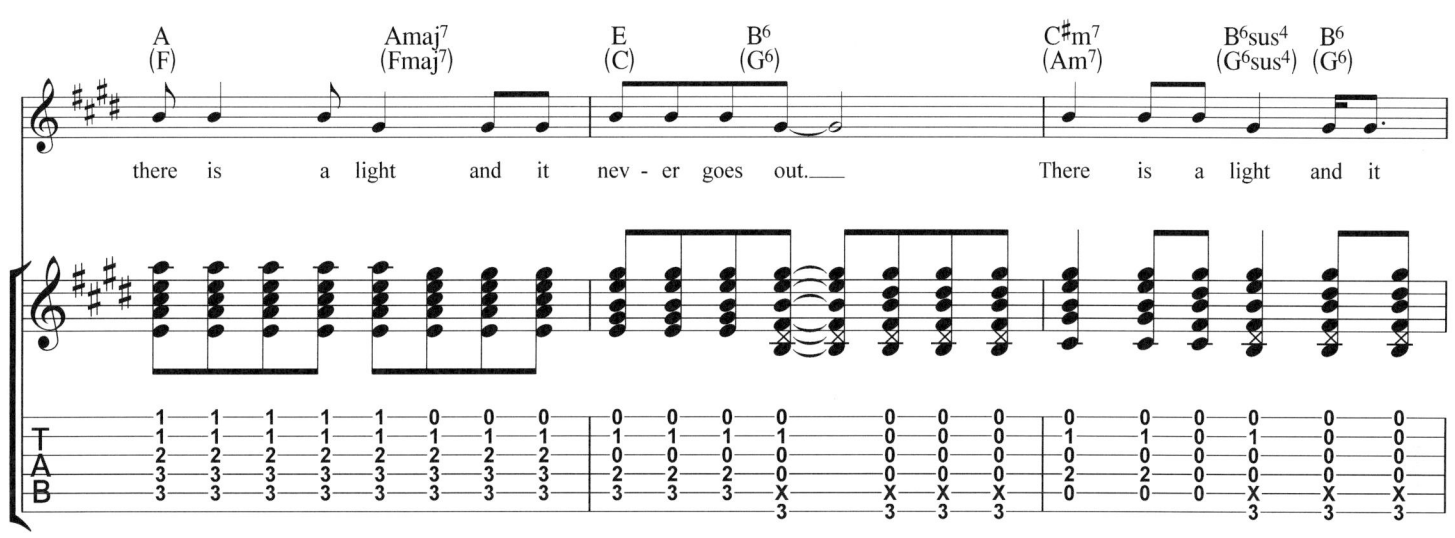
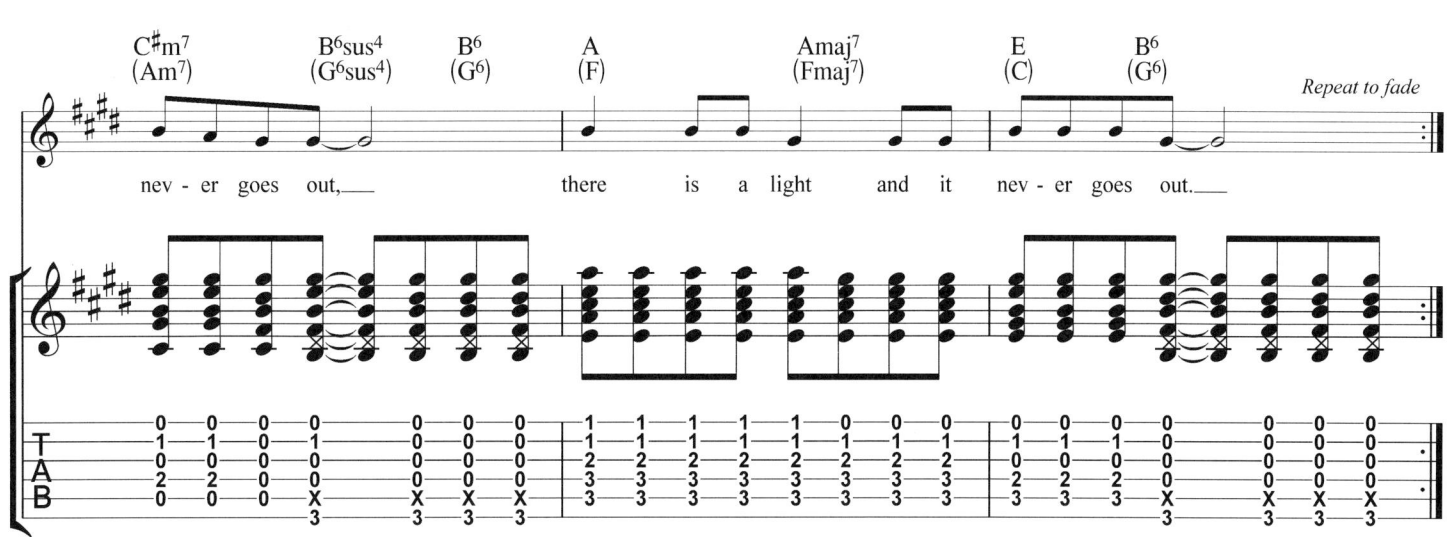

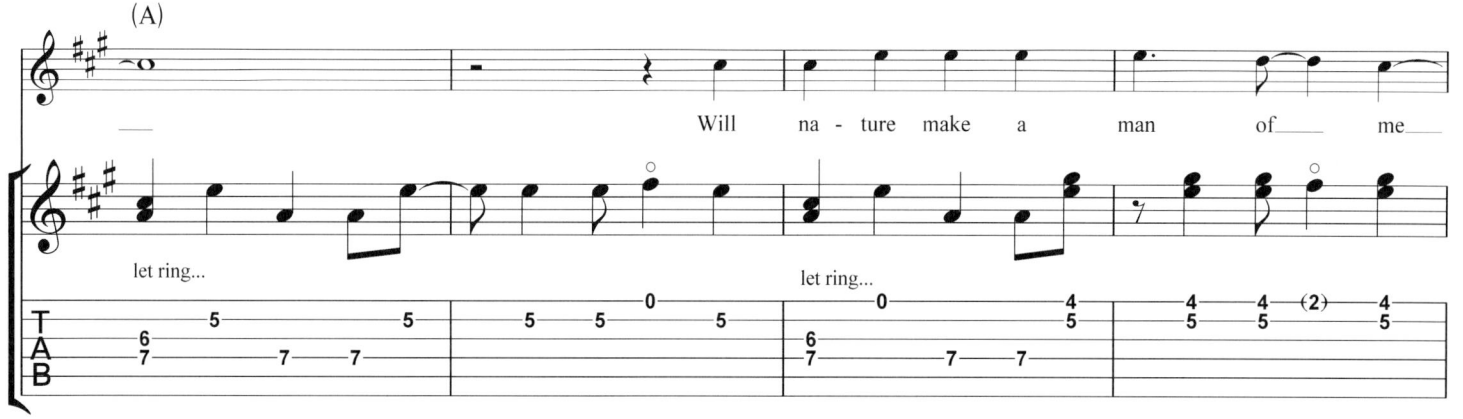
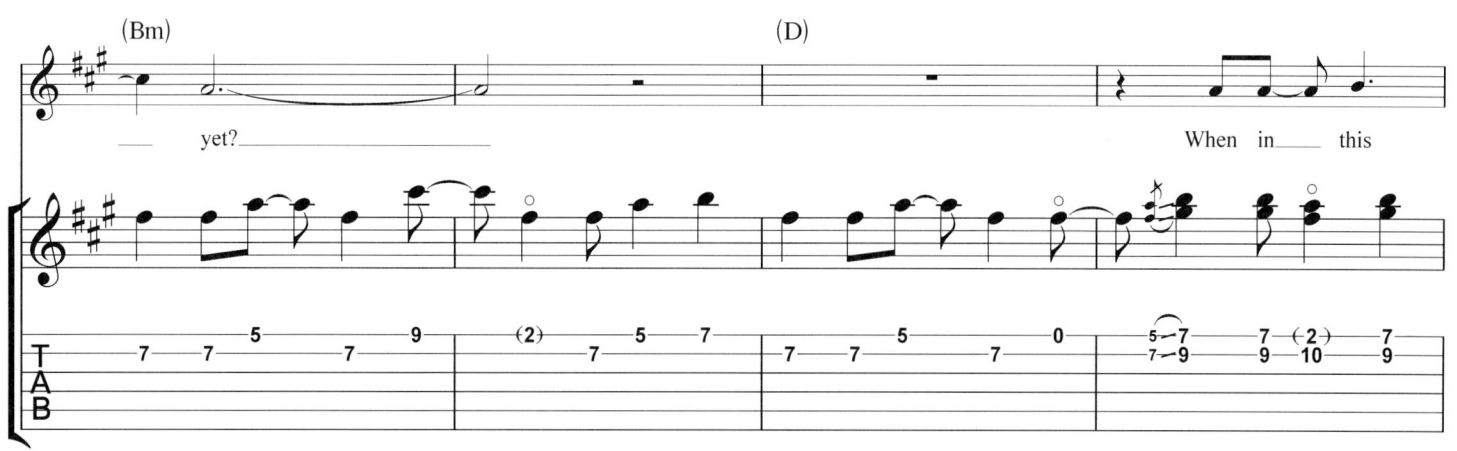

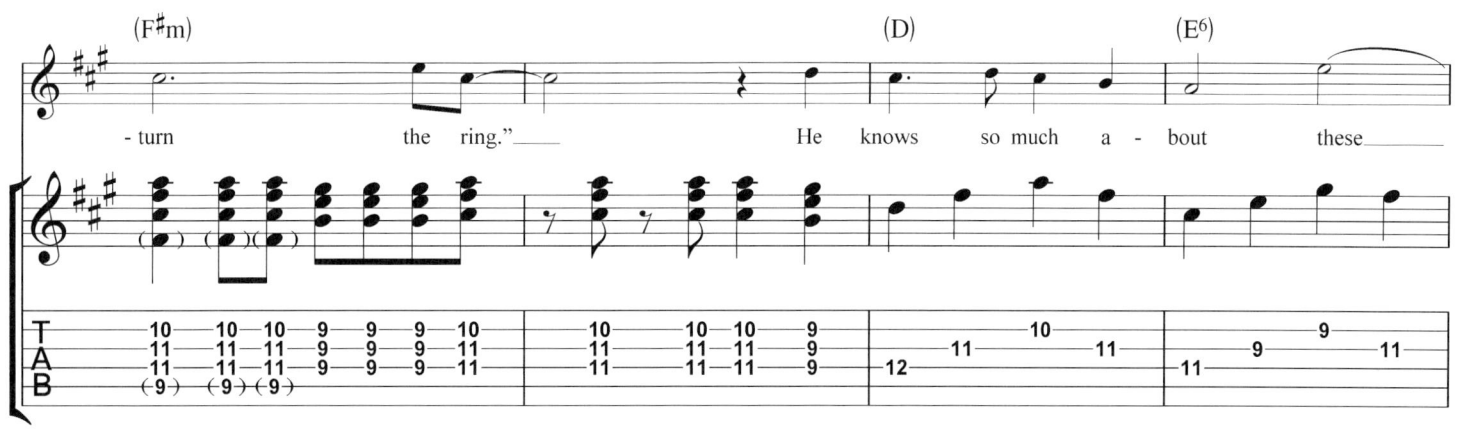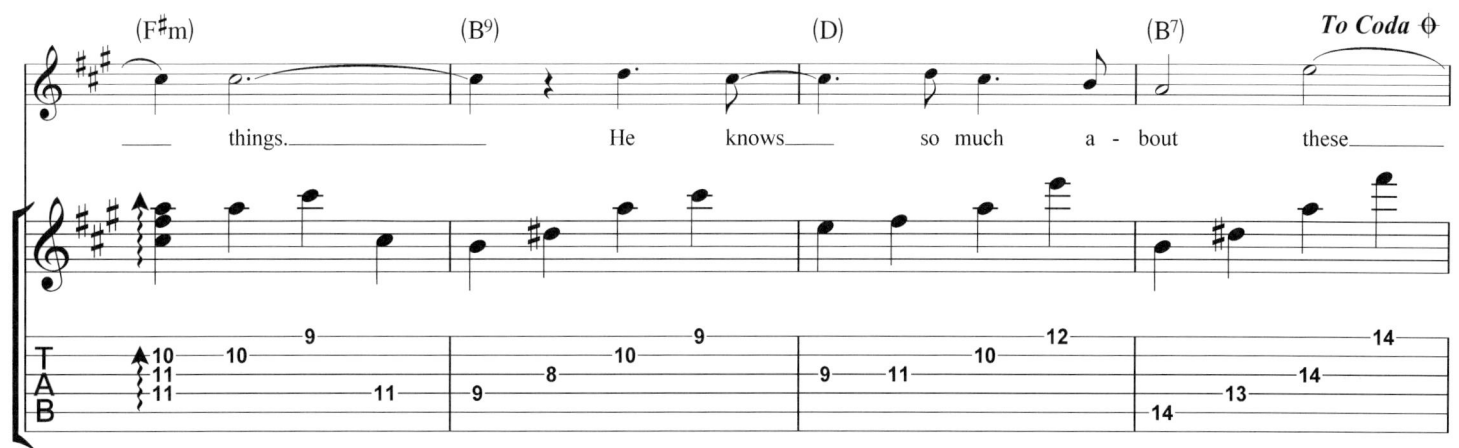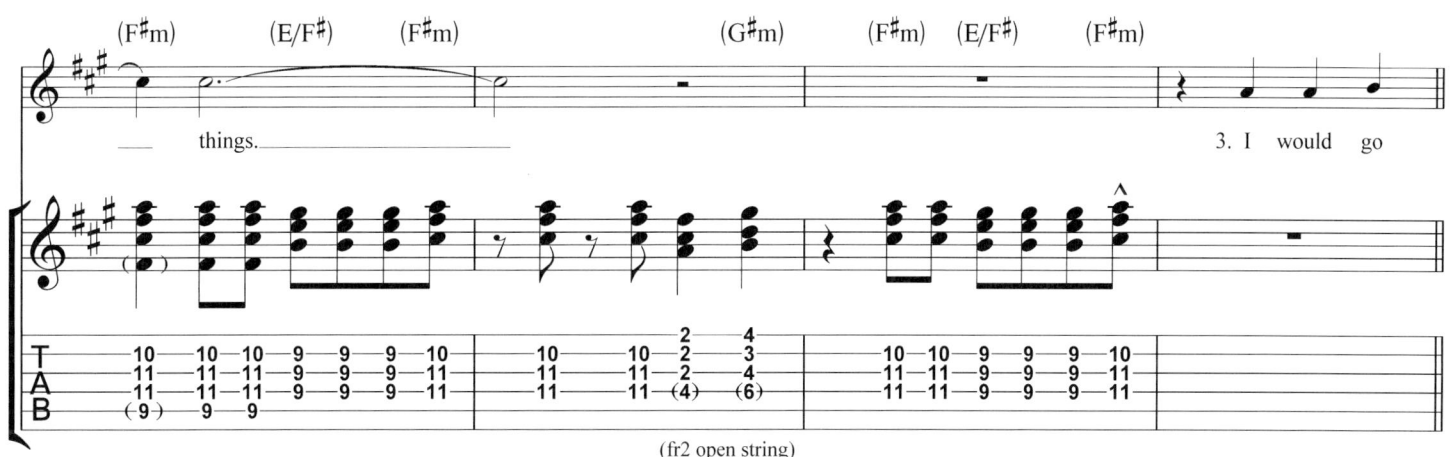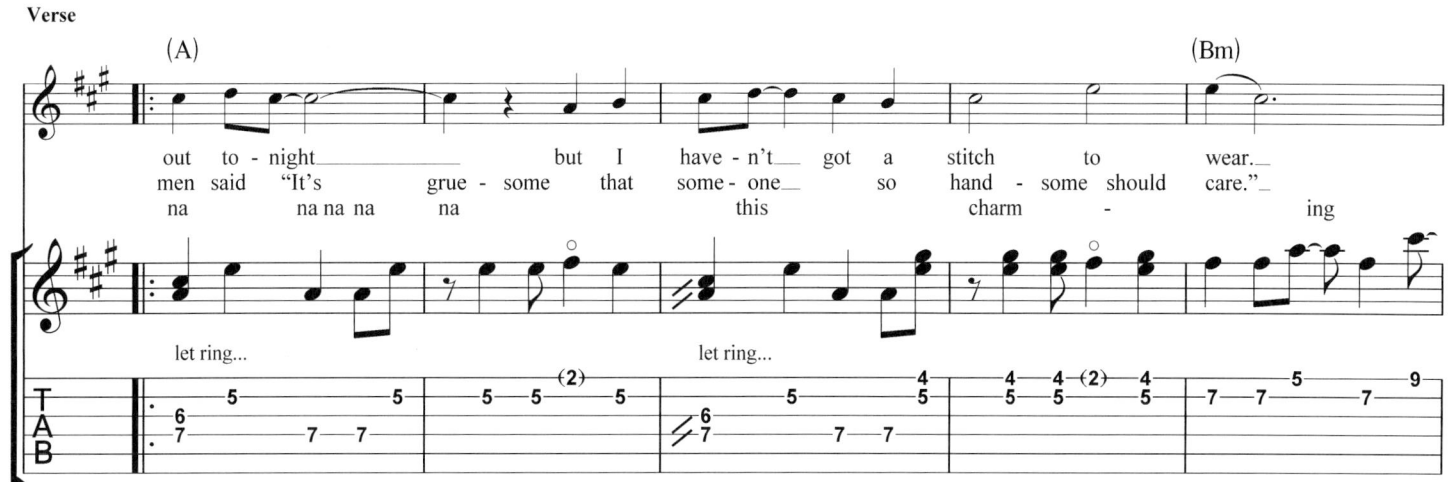

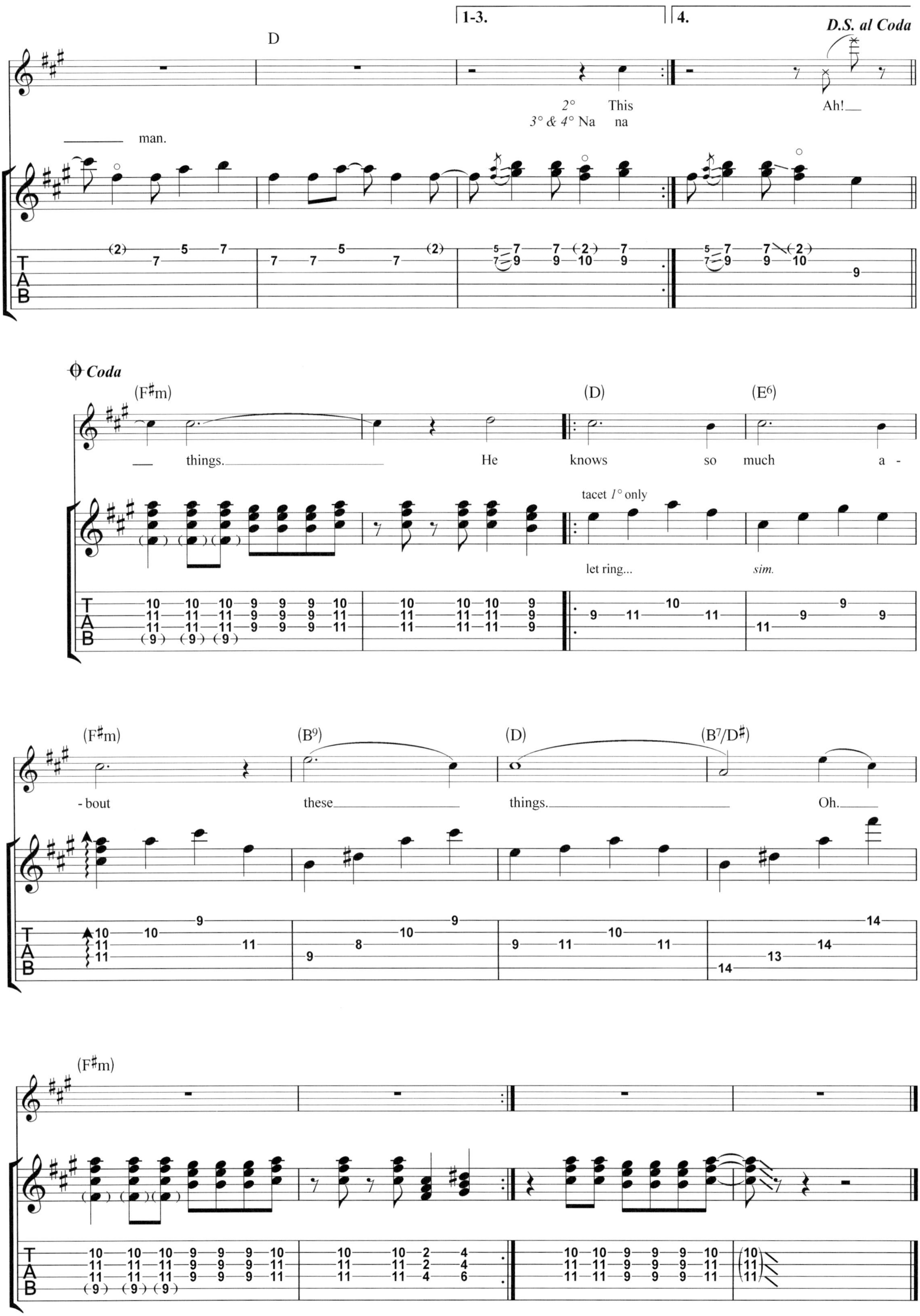
1-3.
4.
D.S. al Coda
D
2° This
3° & 4° Na na
Ah!
man.
Coda
(F♯m)
(D)
(E6)
things.
He
knows
so
much
a -
tacet 1° only
let ring...
sim.
(F♯m)
(B9)
(D)
(B7/D♯)
- bout
these
things.
Oh.
(F♯m)

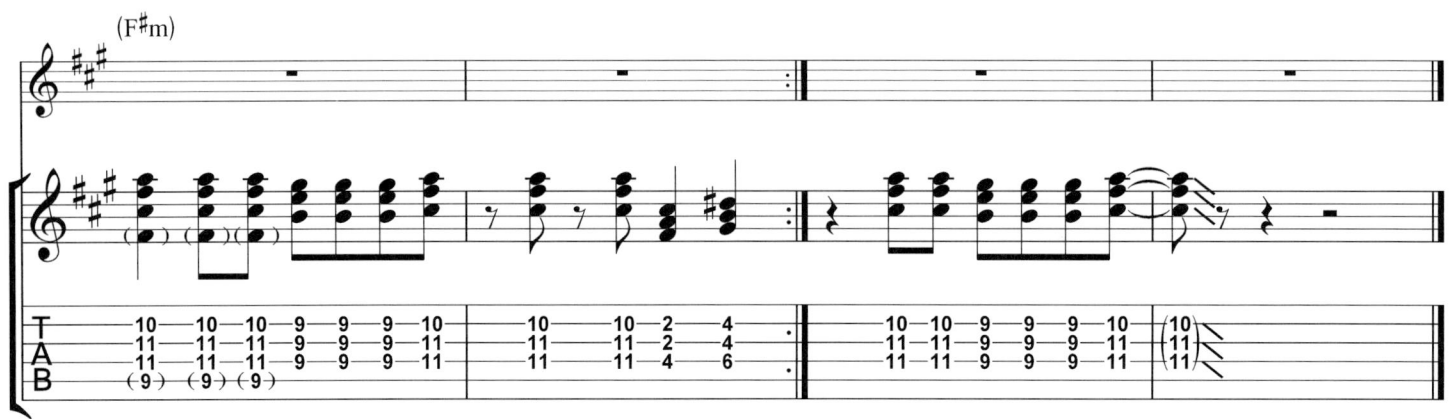

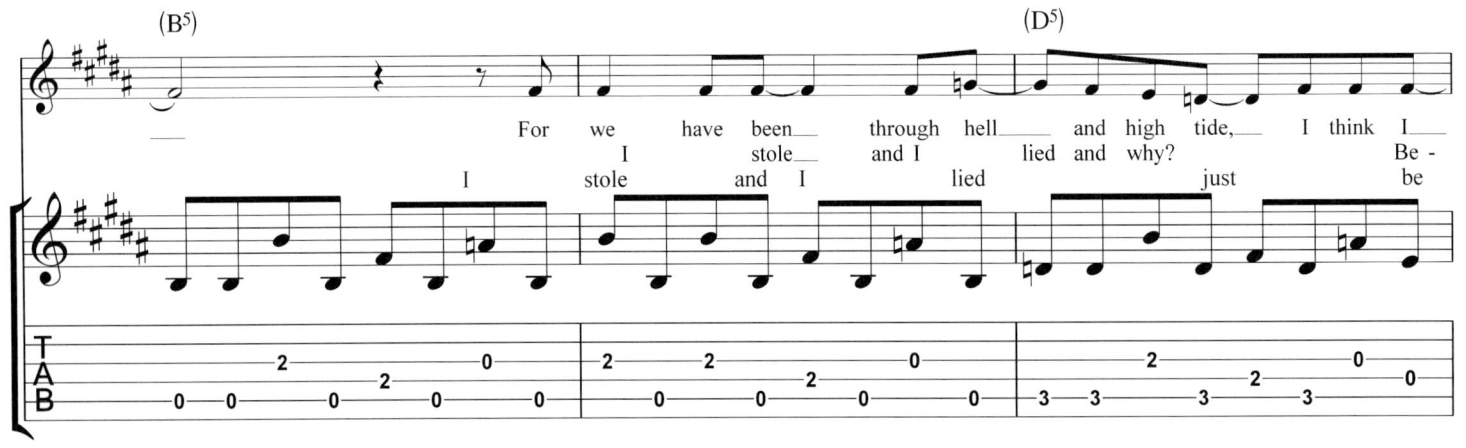
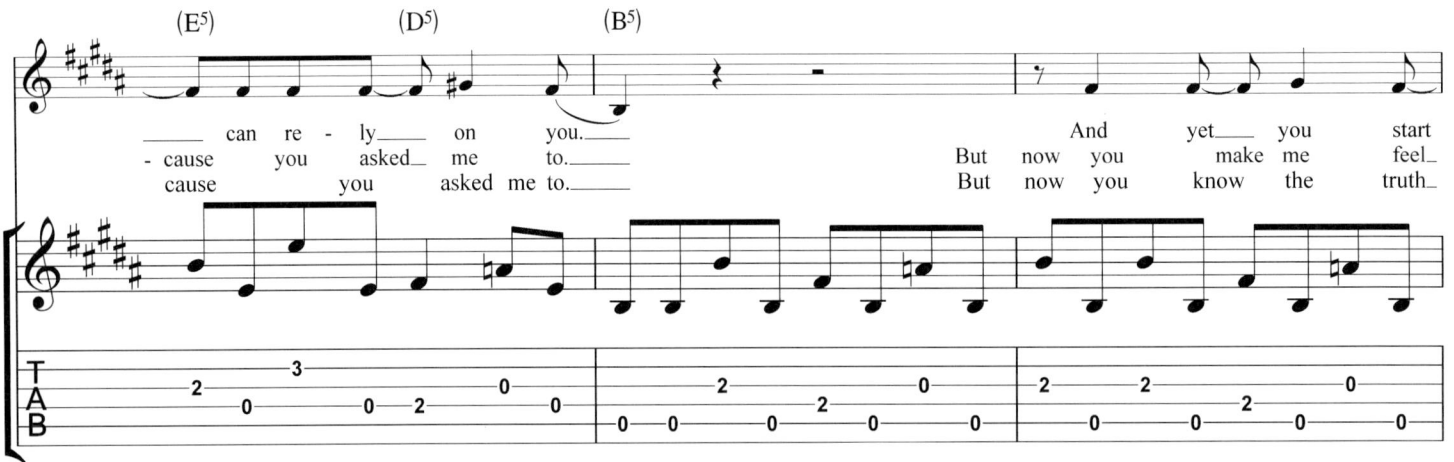
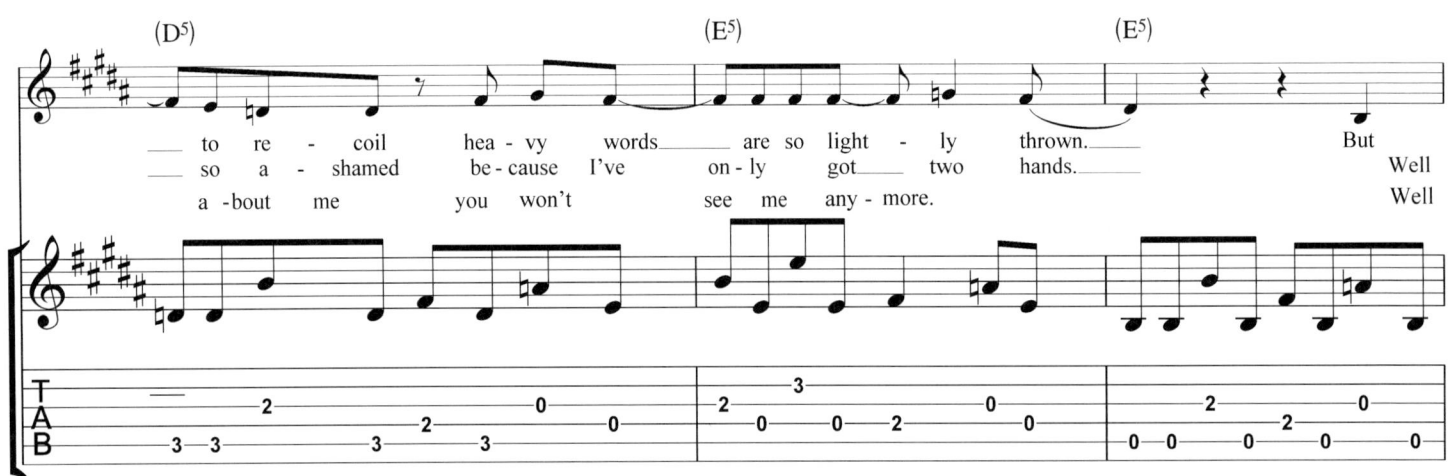
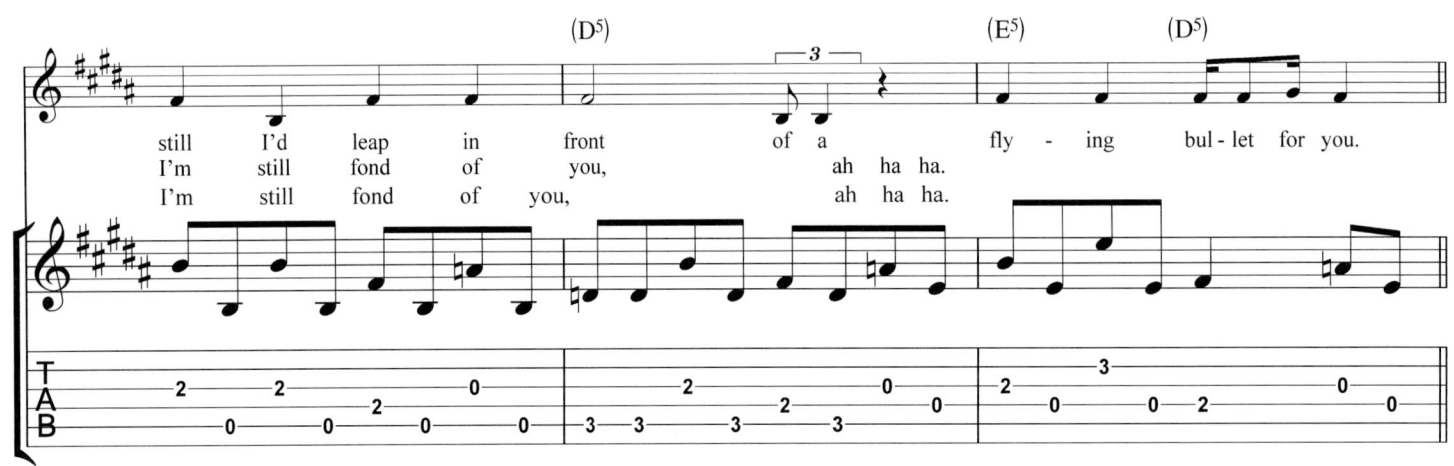

William, It Was Really Nothing

**Words & Music by
Morrissey & Johnny Marr**

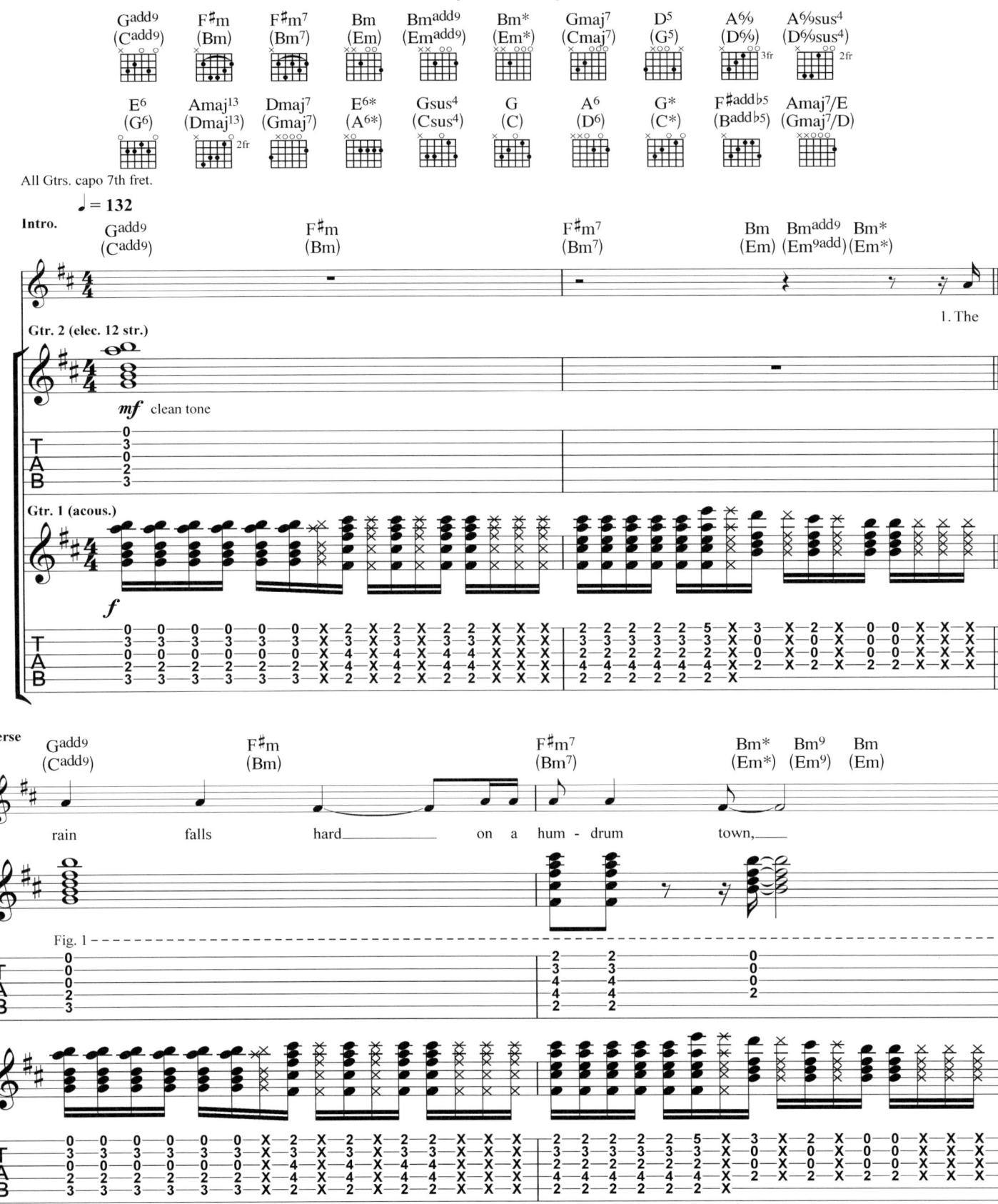

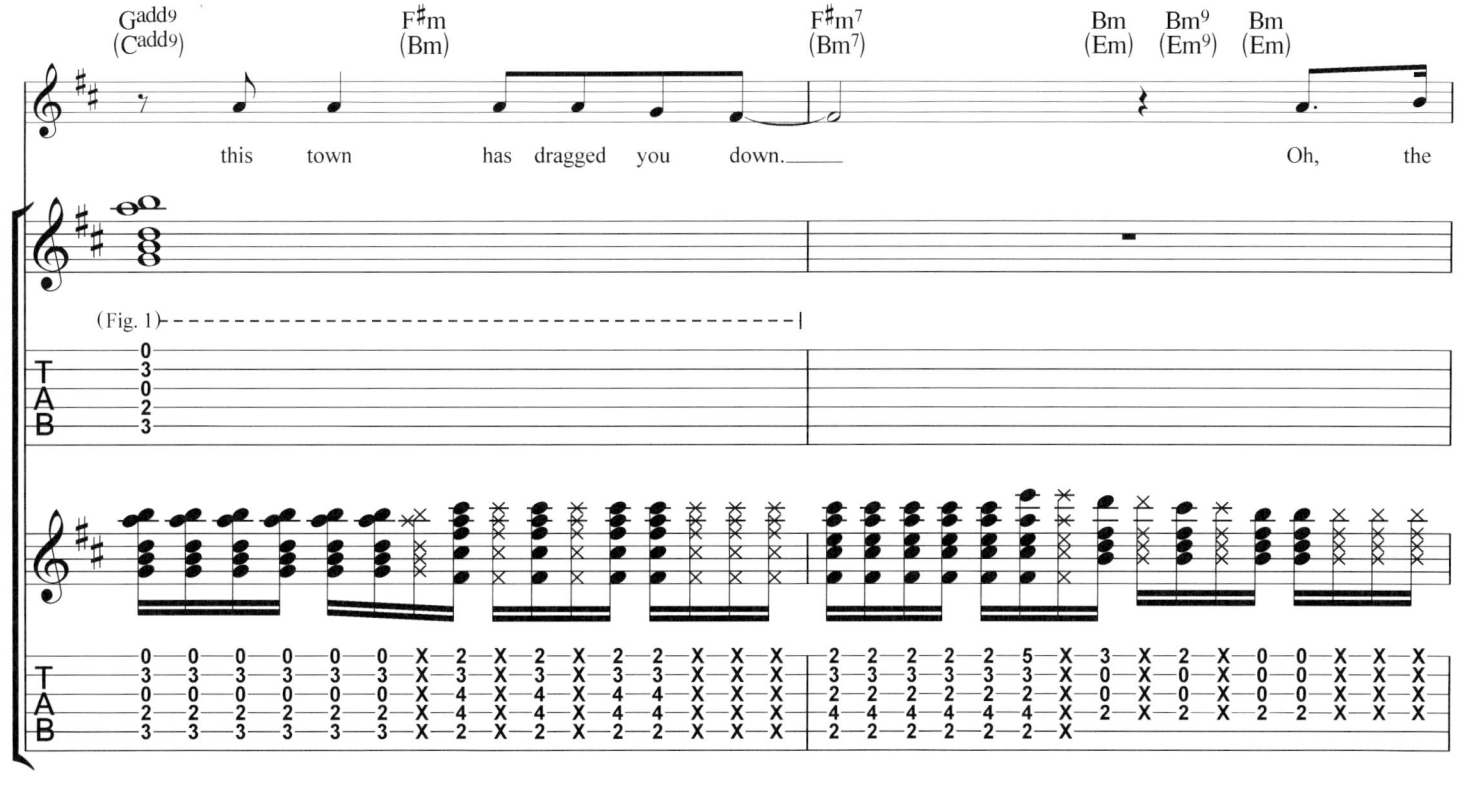
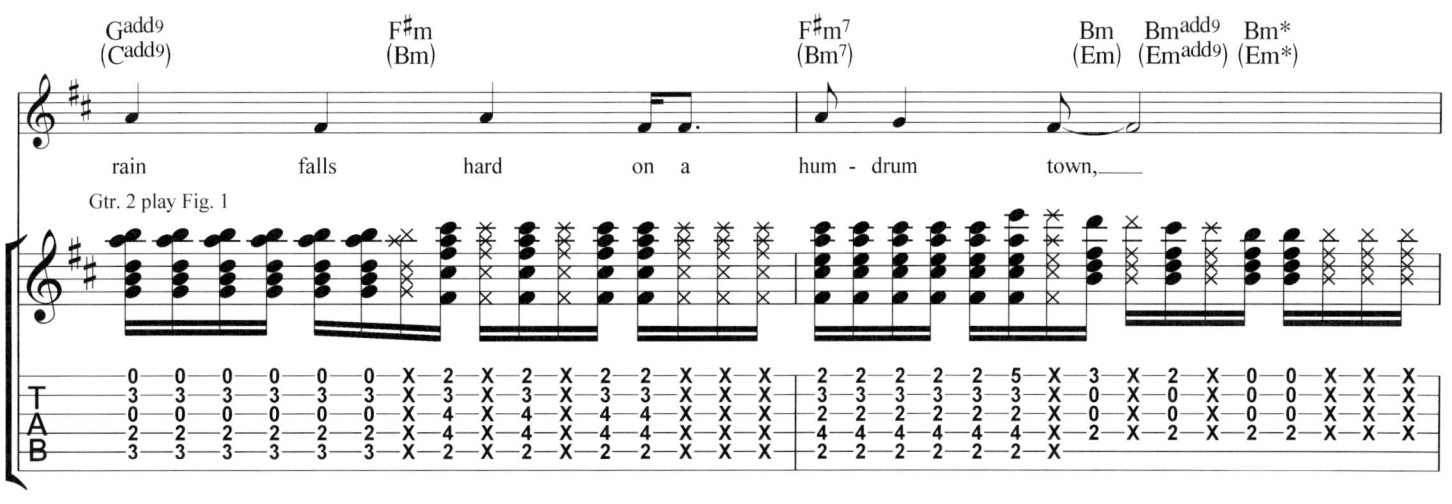
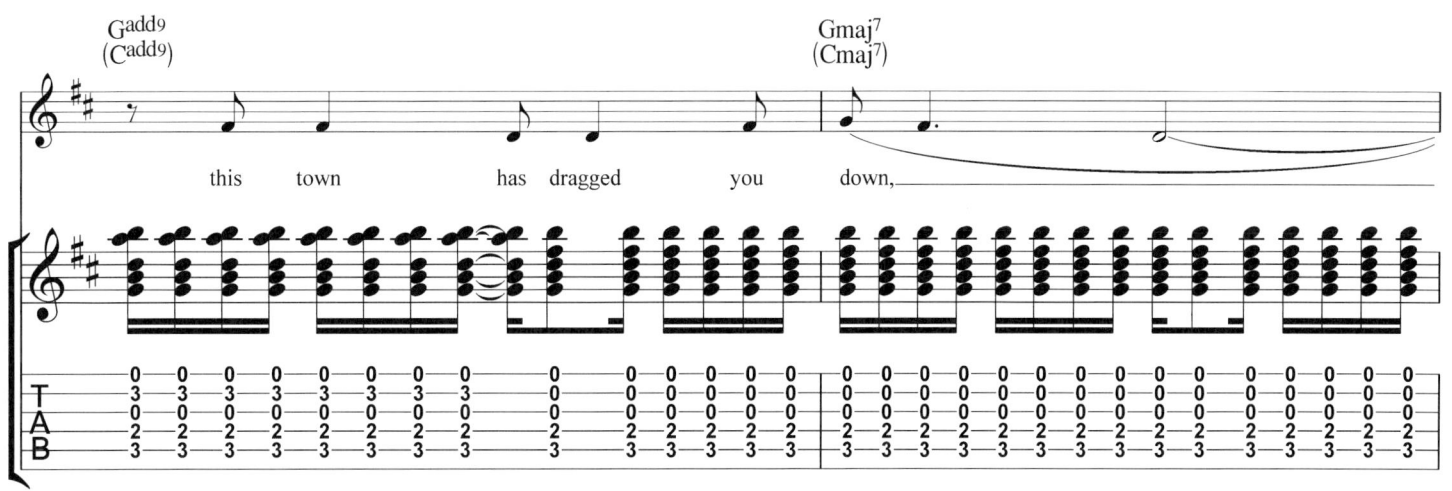

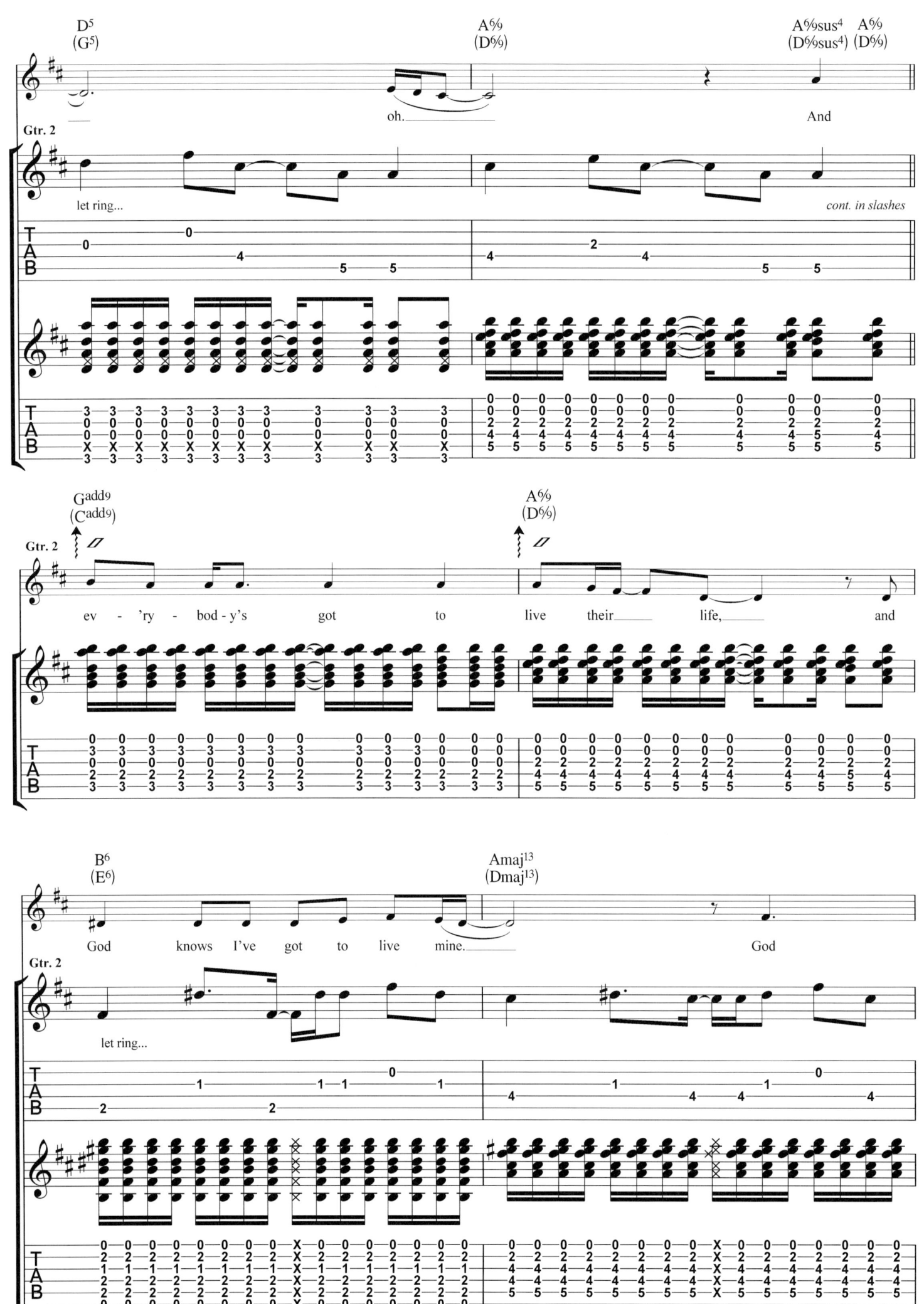

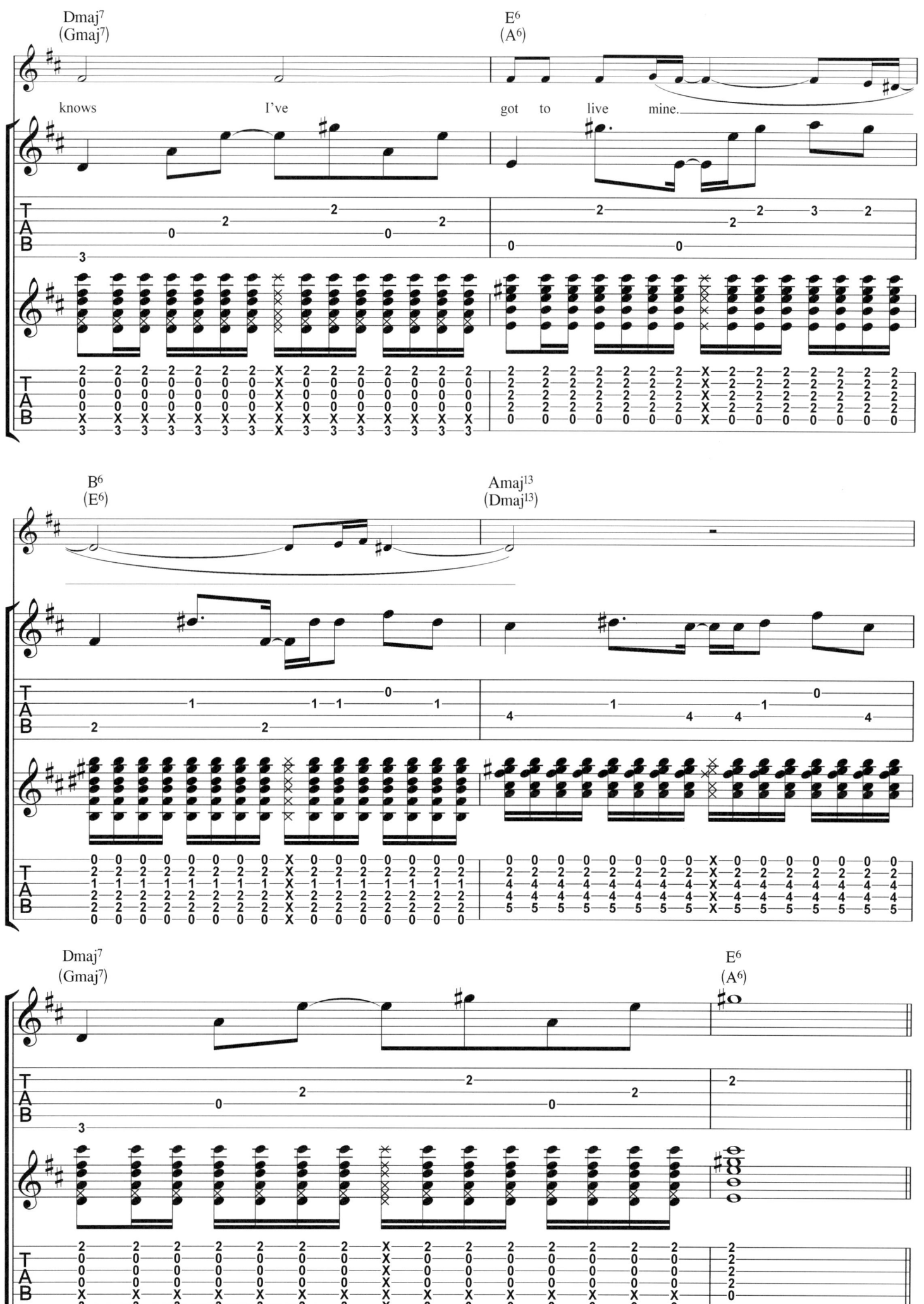

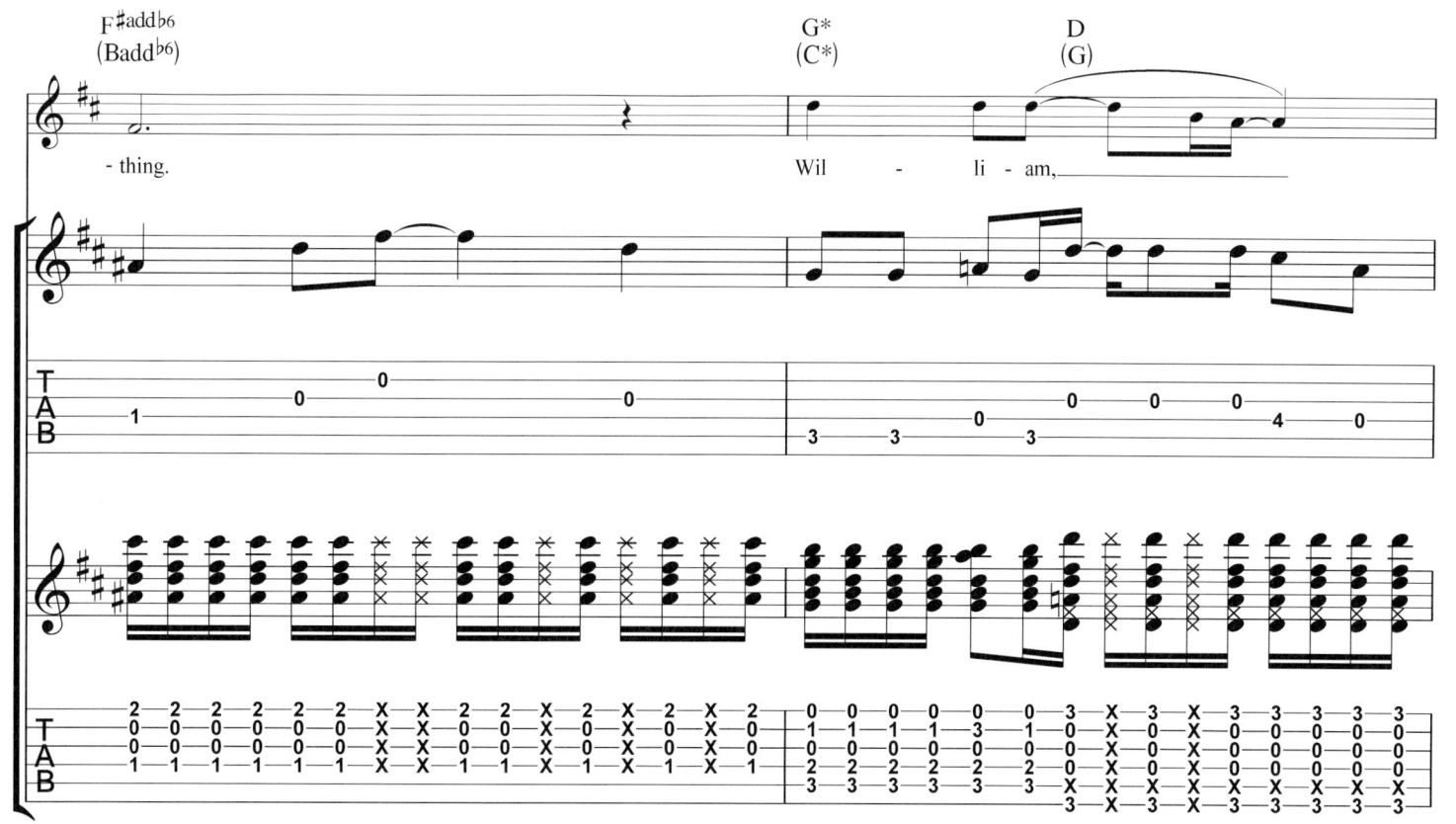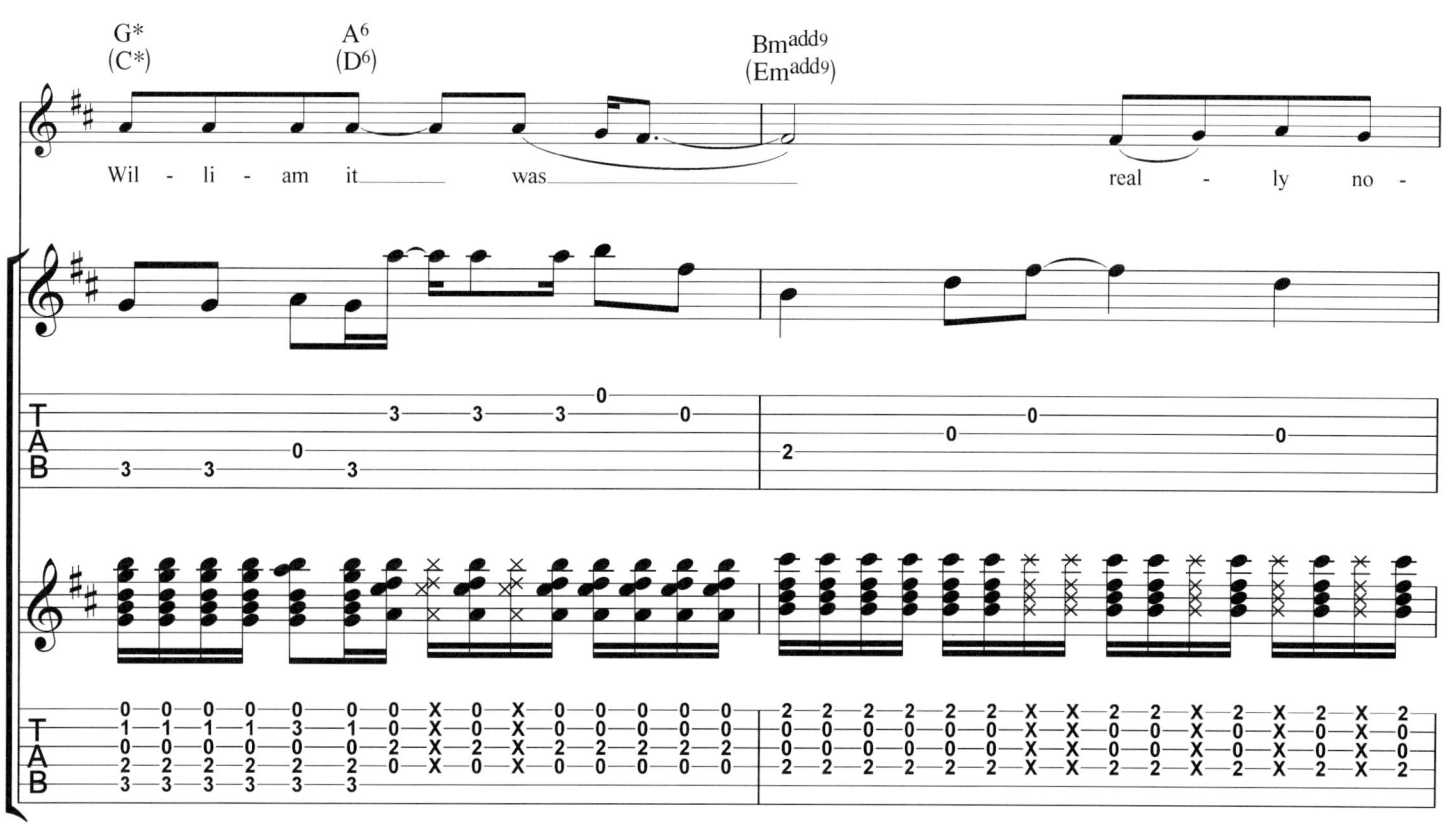

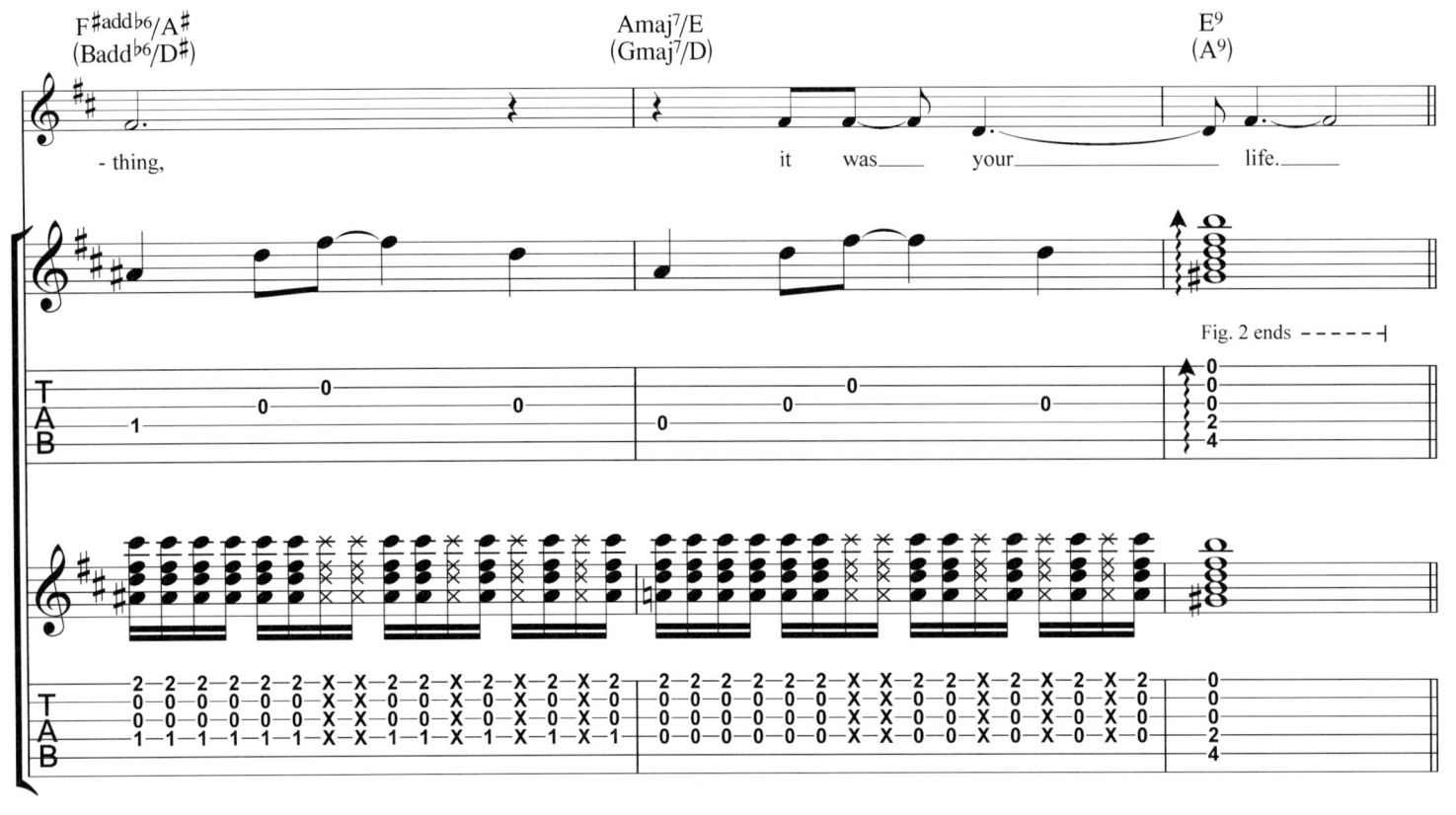
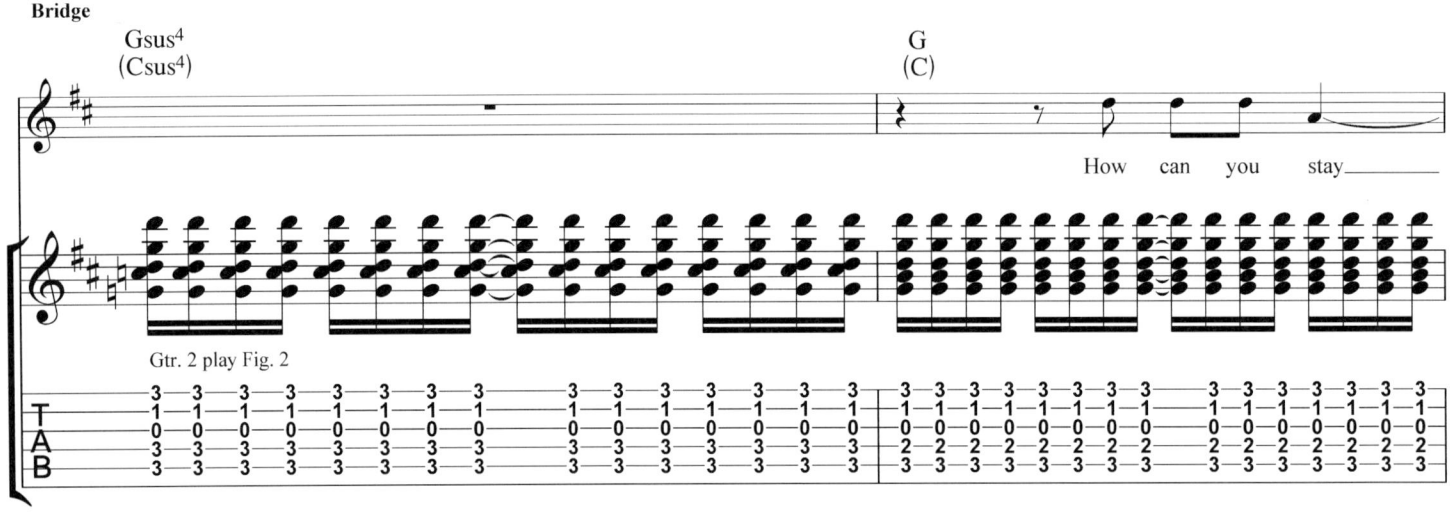
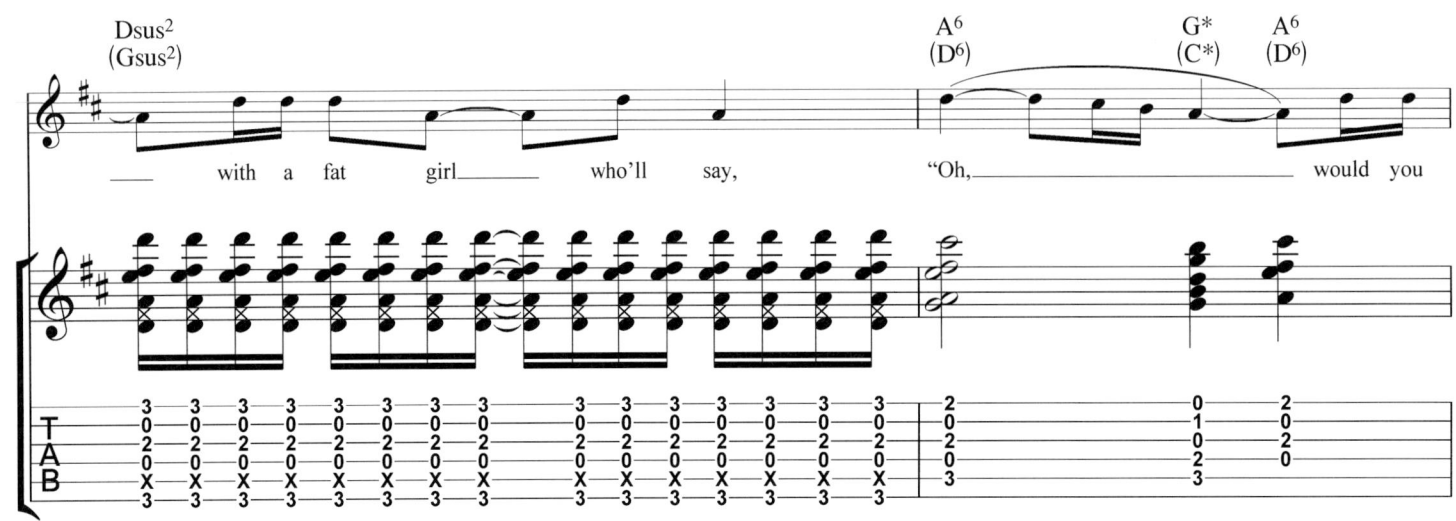

138

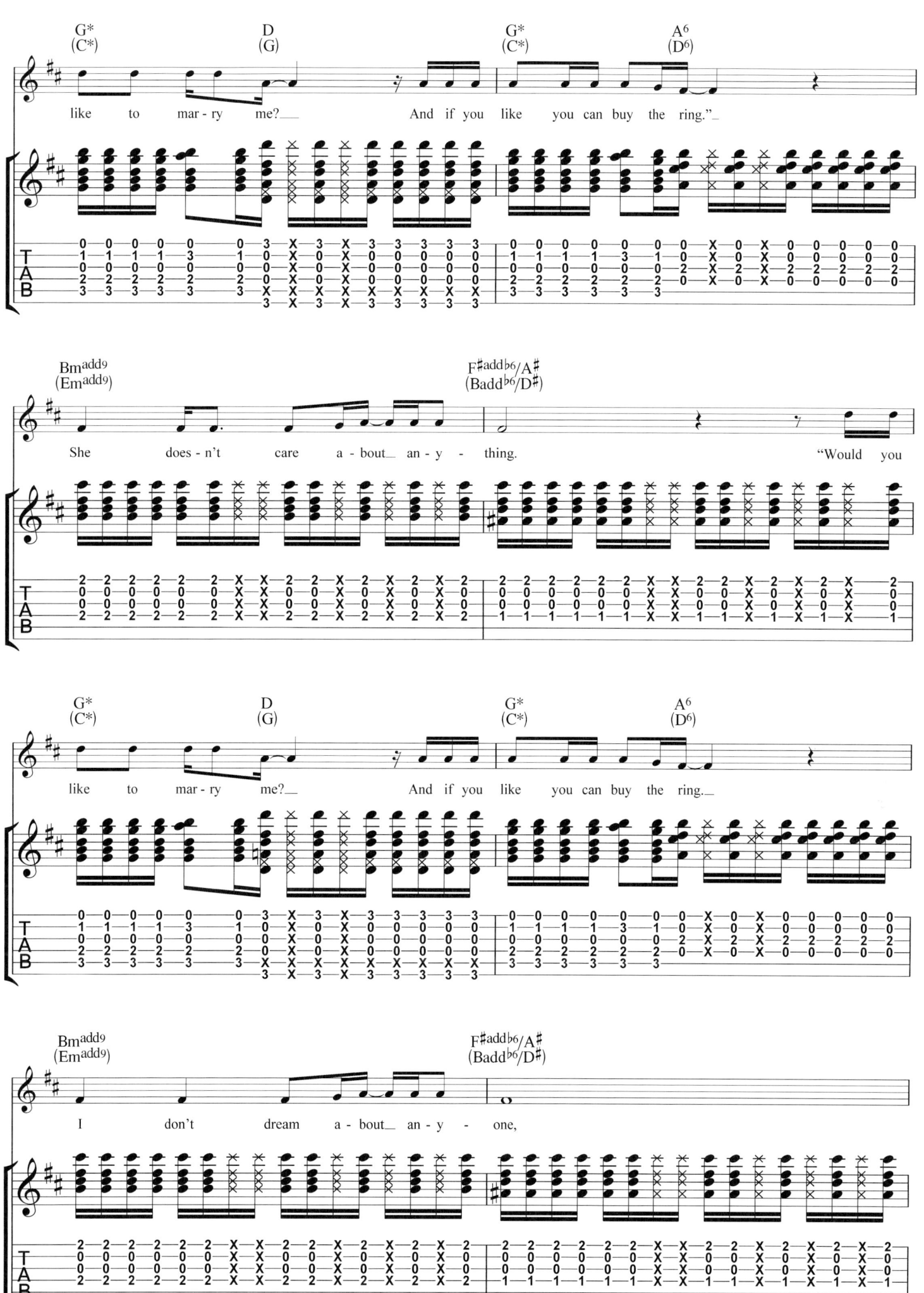

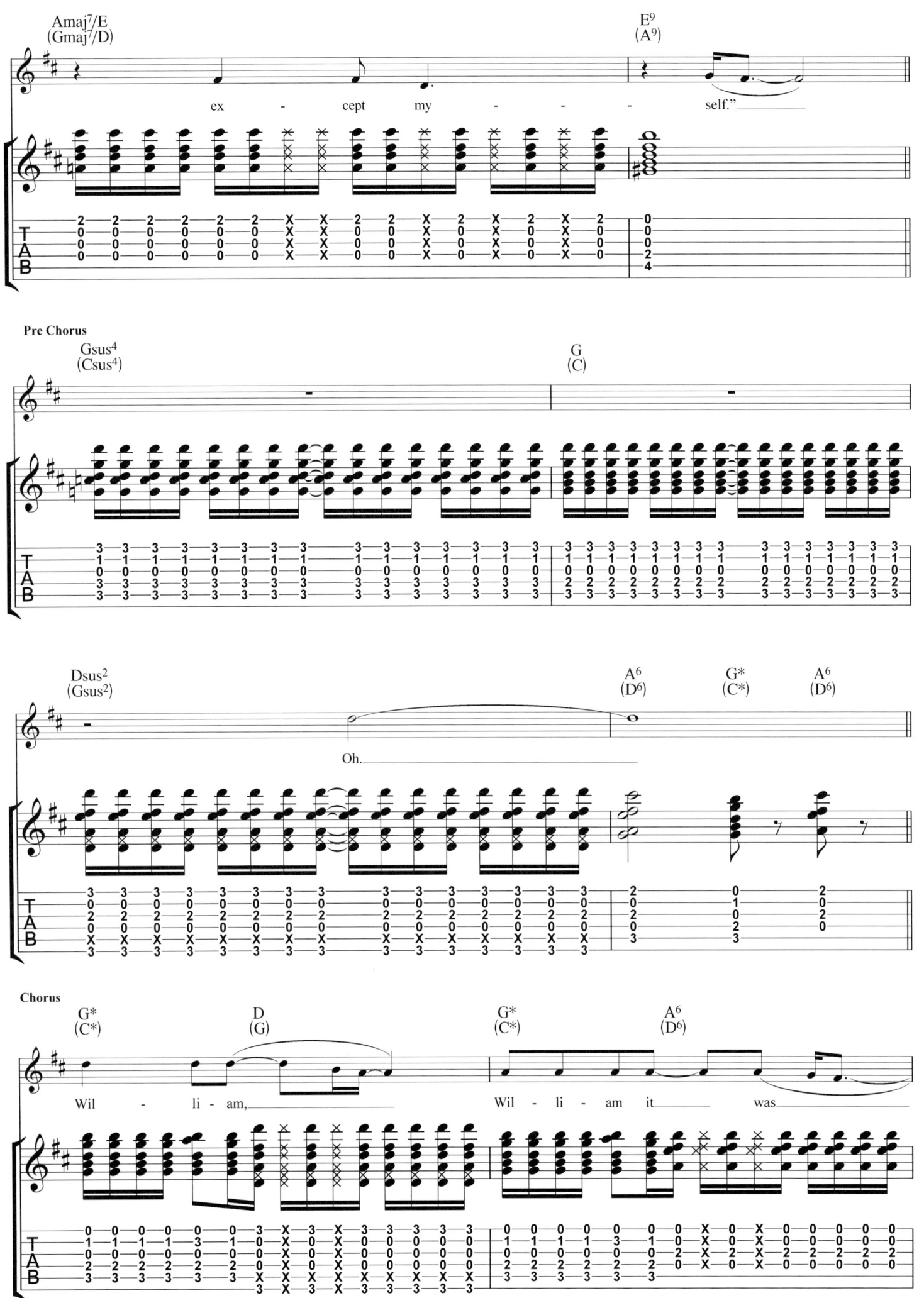

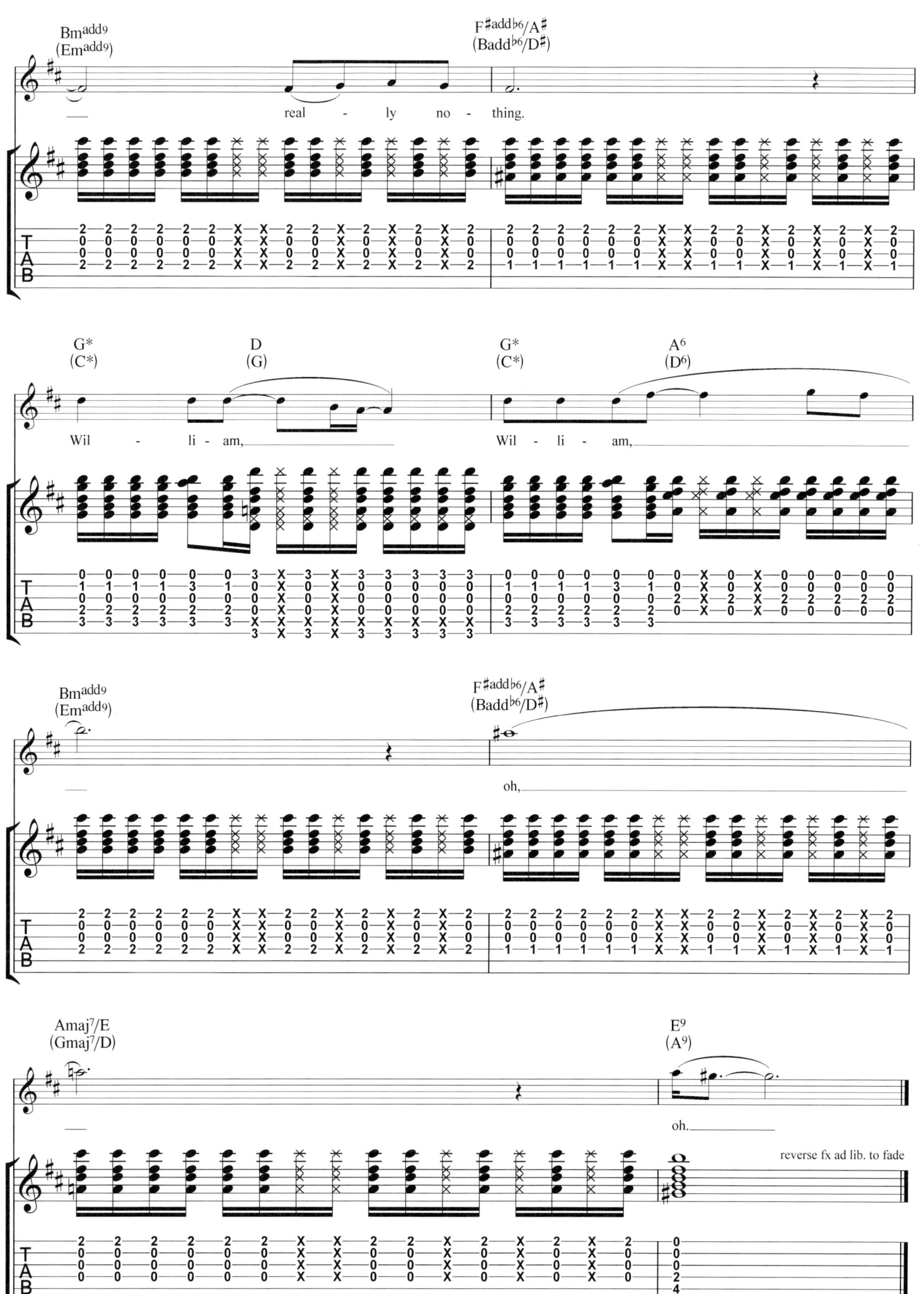

Guitar Tablature Explained

Guitar music can be notated in three different ways: on a musical stave, in tablature, and in rhythm slashes

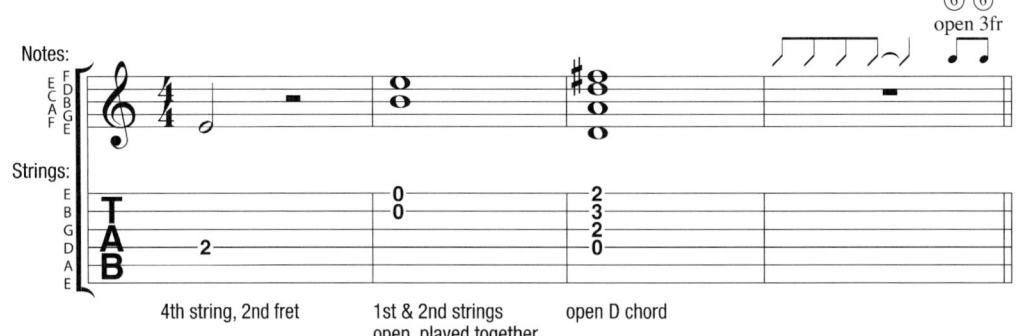

RHYTHM SLASHES are written above the stave. Strum chords in the rhythm indicated. Round noteheads indicate single notes.

THE MUSICAL STAVE shows pitches and rhythms and is divided by lines into bars. Pitches are named after the first seven letters of the alphabet.

TABLATURE graphically represents the guitar fingerboard. Each horizontal line represents a string, and each number represents a fret.

Definitions For Special Guitar Notation

SEMI-TONE BEND: Strike the note and bend up a semi-tone (1/2 step).

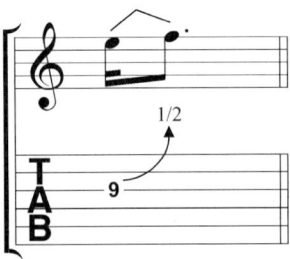

WHOLE-TONE BEND: Strike the note and bend up a whole-tone (whole step).

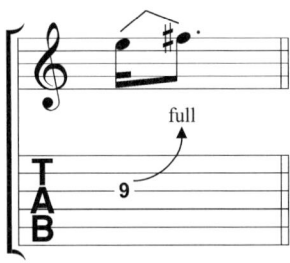

GRACE NOTE BEND: Strike the note and bend as indicated. Play the first note as quickly as possible.

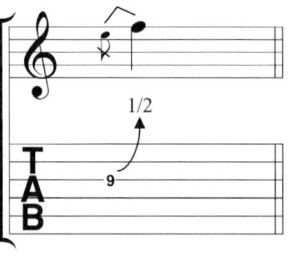

QUARTER-TONE BEND: Strike the note and bend up a 1/4 step.

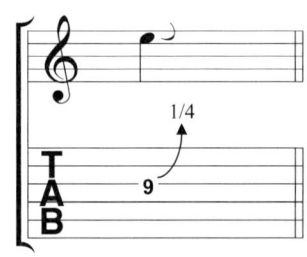

BEND & RELEASE: Strike the note and bend up as indicated, then release back to the original note.

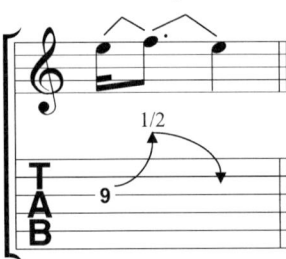

COMPOUND BEND & RELEASE: Strike the note and bend up and down in the rhythm indicated.

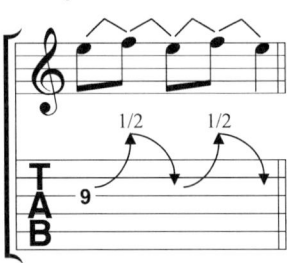

PRE-BEND: Bend the note as indicated, then strike it.

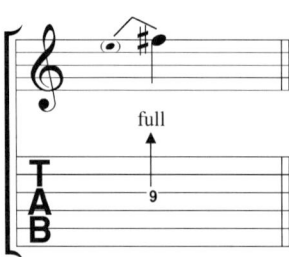

PRE-BEND & RELEASE: Bend the note as indicated. Strike it and release the note back to the original pitch.

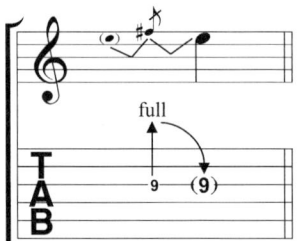

HAMMER-ON: Strike the first note with one finger, then sound the second note (on the same string) with another finger by fretting it without picking.

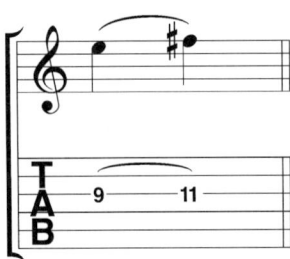

PULL-OFF: Place both fingers on the notes to be sounded, strike the first note and without picking, pull the finger off to sound the second note.

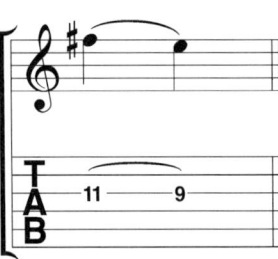

LEGATO SLIDE (GLISS): Strike the first note and then slide the same fret-hand finger up or down to the second note. The second note is not struck.

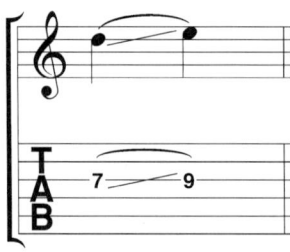

MUFFLED STRINGS: A percussive sound is produced by laying the fret hand across the string(s) without depressing, and striking them with the pick hand.

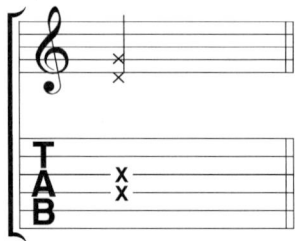

NATURAL HARMONIC: Strike the note while the fret-hand lightly touches the string directly over the fret indicated.

PICK SCRAPE: The edge of the pick is rubbed down (or up) the string, producing a scratchy sound.

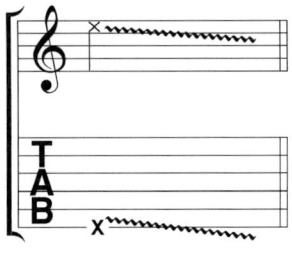

PALM MUTING: The note is partially muted by the pick hand lightly touching the string(s) just before the bridge.

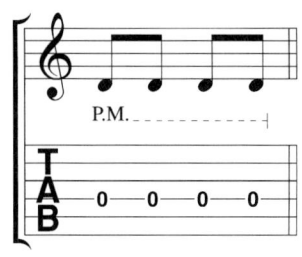

SHIFT SLIDE (GLISS & RESTRIKE): Same as legato slide, except the second note is struck.

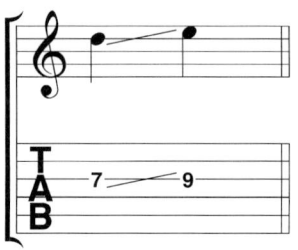

NOTE: The speed of any bend is indicated by the music notation and tempo.

SHIFT SLIDE (GLISS & RESTRIKE): Same as legato slide, except the second note is struck.

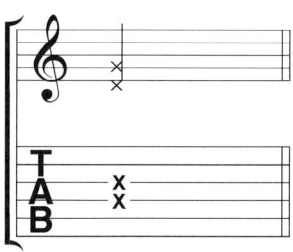

TRILL: Very rapidly alternate between the notes indicated by continuously hammering on and pulling off.

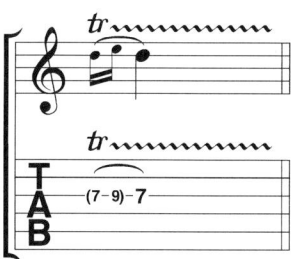

TAPPING: Hammer ("tap") the fret indicated with the pick-hand index or middle finger and pull off to the note fretted by the fret hand.

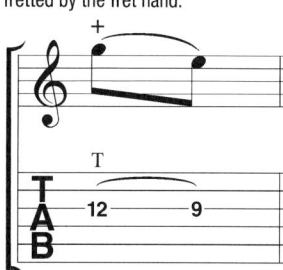

PICK SCRAPE: The edge of the pick is rubbed down (or up) the string, producing a scratchy sound.

MUFFLED STRINGS: A percussive sound is produced by laying the fret hand across the string(s) without depressing, and striking them with the pick hand.

NATURAL HARMONIC: Strike the note while the fret-hand lightly touches the string directly over the fret indicated.

PINCH HARMONIC: The note is fretted normally and a harmonic is produced by adding the edge of the thumb or the tip of the index finger of the pick hand to the normal pick attack.

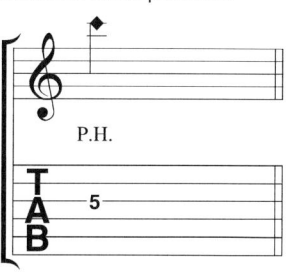

HARP HARMONIC: The note is fretted normally and a harmonic is produced by gently resting the pick hand's index finger directly above the indicated fret (in brackets) while plucking the appropriate string.

PALM MUTING: The note is partially muted by the pick hand lightly touching the string(s) just before the bridge.

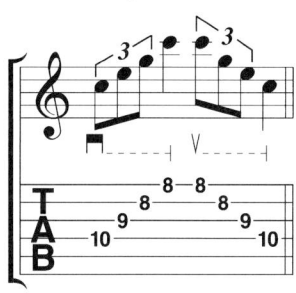

RAKE: Drag the pick across the strings indicated with a single motion.

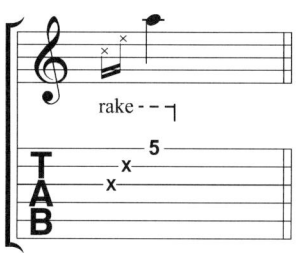

TREMOLO PICKING: The note is picked as rapidly and continuously as possible.

ARPEGGIATE: Play the notes of the chord indicated by quickly rolling them from bottom to top.

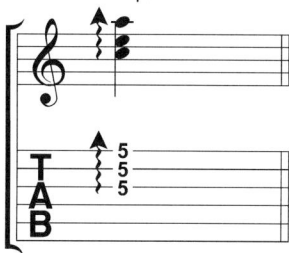

SWEEP PICKING: Rhythmic downstroke and/or upstroke motion across the strings.

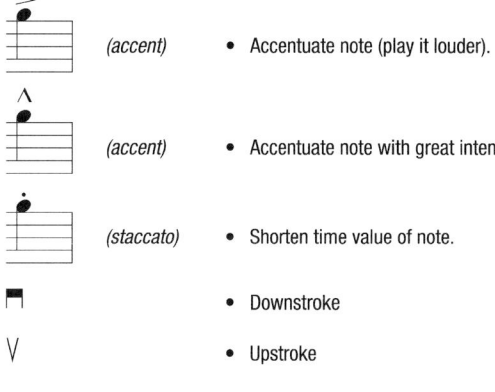

VIBRATO DIVE BAR AND RETURN: The pitch of the note or chord is dropped a specific number of steps (in rhythm) then returned to the original pitch.

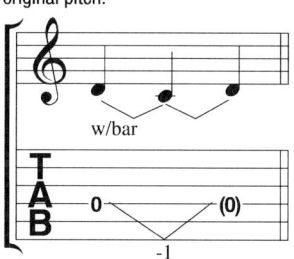

VIBRATO BAR SCOOP: Depress the bar just before striking the note, then quickly release the bar.

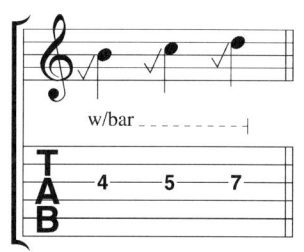

VIBRATO BAR DIP: Strike the note and then immediately drop a specific number of steps, then release back to the original pitch.

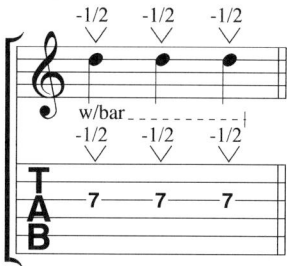

additional musical definitions

(accent)	• Accentuate note (play it louder).	
(accent)	• Accentuate note with great intensity.	
(staccato)	• Shorten time value of note.	
⊓	• Downstroke	
V	• Upstroke	

NOTE: Tablature numbers in brackets mean:
1. The note is sustained, but a new articulation (such as hammer on or slide) begins.
2. A note may be fretted but not necessarily played.

D.S. al Coda — Go back to the sign (𝄋), then play until the bar marked *To Coda* ✛ then skip to the section marked ✛ *Coda*.

D.C. al Fine — Go back to the beginning of the song and play until the bar marked *Fine*.

tacet — Instrument is silent (drops out).

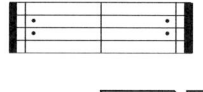 — Repeat bars between signs.

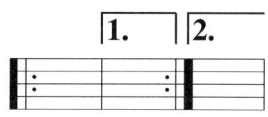 — When a repeated section has different endings, play the first ending only the first time and the second ending only the second time.